COMING OF AGE

CONTINUED PRAISE FOR COMING OF AGE

"Noor Sweid is telling a unique story about the Arab world, one that you will rarely find in other sources. A story of entrepreneurs, builders and change makers; a must-read."

FADI GHANDOUR

Executive Chairman of Wamda Group, Founder of Aramex

"Capturing MENA's entrepreneurial surge, this book demonstrates how the region's bold vision and innovative spirit are driving global economic influence."

DAVID FIALKOW

Co-founder and Managing Director of General Catalyst

"Noor Sweid provides a powerful testament to daring entrepreneurs who saw opportunities where others saw barriers – demonstrating the power of vision and relentless pursuit."

RANDY KOMISAR

Bestselling Author and General Partner at Kleiner Perkins

"*Coming of Age* brilliantly captures how innovation in MENA is reshaping traditional industries. It's a testament to the region's ability to adapt, innovate and lead on a global scale."

HENADI AL SALEH

Chairperson of Agility

"Noor Sweid encapsulates the history, challenges and future of innovation in the MENA region in this one important read. *Coming of Age* chronicles the powerful diversity of the region that has given rise to a new set of tech-forward entrepreneurs and their multibillion-dollar ideas."

MAHA IBRAHIM

General Partner at Canaan

"Well below the traditional headlines, there has been an unleashing of technological innovation and successful start-ups building a new Middle East. Few have been more dedicated and courageous on the journey – having lived it all and helped build it. Noor's book is a mind blow at each page and a play book for anyone interested in opportunity."

CHRISTOPHER M. SCHROEDER

Author of the bestselling *Startup Rising: The Entrepreneurial Revolution Remaking the Middle East*

"*Coming of Age* captures the transformative impact of MENA's entrepreneurial rise on the region's economic landscape – an essential read for understanding high-growth emerging markets."

ANNE GLOVER

CEO and Co-founder of Amadeus Capital Partners

"An incredible revelation of how MENA's pioneering founders transformed infrastructural challenges into a thriving entrepreneurial ecosystem, overcoming barriers with ingenuity and resilience."

BRENT HOBERMAN

Chairman and Co-founder of Founders Forum Group, Founders Factory and firstminute capital

"A compelling narrative that showcases MENA's entrepreneurial spirit and dynamic investment landscape, highlighting its emergence as a resilient and innovative economic powerhouse."

HERMANN HAUSER

Co-founder and Venture Partner at Amadeus Capital Partners

"*Coming of Age* eloquently captures the innovative and entrepreneurial passion, potential and promise of a region at an inflection point that will impact the economic and global marketplace for the next generation."

CHRIS VARELAS

Founding Partner of Riverwood Capital and Co-founder of Aspen Institute Finance Leaders Fellowship

"A powerful reflection of MENA's entrepreneurs turning cultural heritage into global brands – navigating challenges with vision and transforming ambition into successful ventures."

MONA KATTAN

Founder and CEO of Kayali, Co-founder of Huda Beauty and HB Investments

First published in 2025 by Motivate Media Group; second edition published in 2025 by
Noor Sweid, in partnership with Whitefox Publishing

www.wearewhitefox.com

Hardback ISBN 9781917523431
eBook ISBN 9781917523448
Audiobook ISBN 9781917523455

Originally designed and typeset by Motivate Media Group,
revised by Whitefox and Ketchup

Original cover design by Motivate Media Group, revised by Whitefox
Project management by Whitefox

COMING OF AGE

How Technology and
Entrepreneurship are
Changing the Face
of MENA

N O O R S W E I D

For Kinan, who teaches me patience in ways only he can.

For Jad, whose never-ending love of play reminds
me to find wonder in every moment.

For Karim, whose insatiable curiosity
inspires me to keep exploring.

CONTENTS

Foreword - 10

Introduction - 12

SECTION I - 16

CHAPTER 1 What is MENA? - 18

CHAPTER 2 Soaring Falcons - - - - - - - - - - - - - - - - - - - 34

CHAPTER 3 The Originals - 46

CHAPTER 4 Entrepreneurship Rising - - - - - - - - - - - - - 72

CHAPTER 5 The Adversity Advantage - - - - - - - - - - - - - 97

SECTION II - 102

CHAPTER 6 In the Absence of Finance - - - - - - - - - - - - 106

CHAPTER 7 Enabling Access to Care - - - - - - - - - - - - - 137

CHAPTER 8 Teaching the Young - - - - - - - - - - - - - - - - 169

CHAPTER 9 Feeding the Next Generation - - - - - - - - - - 196

CHAPTER 10 Reshaping the Global Supply Chain - - - - - - 222

SECTION III - 254

CHAPTER 11 Embracing Artificial Intelligence - - - - - - - 256

CHAPTER 12 Democratisation of Money - - - - - - - - - - - 271

CHAPTER 13 Fuel for Tomorrow - - - - - - - - - - - - - - - - 281

CHAPTER 14 Our Future - 293

Acknowledgements - 298

References - 302

FOREWORD
BY REID HOFFMAN

ENTREPRENEURIAL TALENT knows no boundaries. Instead, it arises wherever creativity, ambition and a drive to solve meaningful problems intersect. The MENA region, with its youthful population and hunger for technological innovation, is bursting with these characteristics. Every time I visit, I meet new founders who impress me with their grasp of what opportunities this particular technological moment presents – both in terms of solving pressing local challenges and also pursuing scalability that can resonate on a global stage.

What I recognise in these entrepreneurs are the same traits and aspirations that I've seen in founders in Silicon Valley, and also in emerging markets like Latin America and India. Granted, converting creativity, ambition, and strategic vision into a deeply rooted entrepreneurial ecosystem that's built for the long haul takes more than just talented founders. It also requires networks of investors, a skilled workforce, supportive regulatory frameworks, access to international markets, and a culture of mentorship and collaboration.

But as Noor documents in this book, that combination of forward-looking and resourceful founders and growing support for them is what makes this such a pivotal moment in the region's entrepreneurial journey to becoming a global hub of tech-driven innovation and prosperity.

Having been an active participant herself in the region's entrepreneurial ecosystem for nearly two decades, Noor writes with an authority that is driven by a profound understanding of the landscape and a clear vision of what's possible. As a founder, Noor led her start-up to a successful regional exit. As an executive, she took another company public globally. As the founding partner at Global Ventures and having initiated the Middle East Venture Capital Association, she's played an ongoing role in identifying, supporting and growing the region's entrepreneurial talent. As a former Director-in-Residence at INSEAD's Abu Dhabi campus, she taught corporate governance and other critical frameworks for navigating complex markets to a new generation of business leaders. As a current guest-lecturer at MIT, Stanford, and LBS, she inspires students to pursue their entrepreneurship goals and journeys.

All told, Noor's belief in the power of entrepreneurism as a force that can transform individual trajectories and economies alike is lived, practised, and earned. And now she shares her perspective with us in this book, as she documents a decade of entrepreneurial spirit, the rise of successful companies across various sectors, and the boundless opportunities that lie ahead.

For anyone seeking to understand the MENA region or catch a glimpse of the future of global innovation, *Coming of Age* is essential reading. But as much as this book is about specific founders confronting the challenges and opportunities that exist in a particular setting, it's also more broadly a book about hope, the power of ideas, and the courage to forge new paths by embracing risk and exhibiting creativity and adaptivity in the face of scepticism and status quo thinking. For any aspiring founder who has been told "it's not possible", these unflinchingly honest stories of triumphs, setbacks, and entrepreneurial resilience will strike a deeply resonant chord.

INTRODUCTION

THE AIRPLANE'S THUD jolted me awake. Followed by the second thud. Then the screeching of the tyres as we slowed down. And the crescendo of the deafening applause. In under a minute, every one of the 388 passengers on the 747 was furiously clapping. *"Alhamdullah al salameh!"* they excitedly repeated to each other. *Gratitude be to God for your safe arrival.* I would go on to hear that phrase incessantly over the coming two months. We had been transported back in time. Or so it felt every time I landed in Damascus as a child in the 80s.

Born in Boston, growing up in London and 'returning' to Syria for the summer and winter months each year, I was often confused when I was asked where I was from, unsure whether that meant the country I was born in, where I lived, or where my 'roots' were. Unclear what to answer, my response would often depend on who was asking and why. This was the way I could simplify life. Back then, hyphenated ethnicities had not yet been 'invented'. Neither had the term 'third-culture', which I later learned to identify as.

Damascus was a place where time stood still, and I stood out. With broken Arabic in a country and time where nobody spoke English, and where the number of cousins I had seemed to exceed the number of my classmates in London, I often felt out of place.

As the years passed and our annual pilgrimage continued, the differences I would observe between my home in London and my 'home' in Syria would only seem to increase in quantum and acuteness. Laughing with my siblings and cousins, I would often say that visits might last two months but felt like two days – that Syria was a place where 'time stood still', both in the feeling of the duration being spent there, as well as the advancement of the country at the time.

The relationship with time, and the expectations of what one could do with one's time, would have to be adjusted upon arrival, where the events of a day would often revolve around a family lunch, including all forty-two cousins, aunts and uncles. That would be the day, resembling a stark difference to what a day could 'achieve' back in London. The acceptance of the fluidity of time was a frustrating experience as a young girl who was always keen to get going and was accustomed to the punctuality of a British school-system and upbringing. Yet, once adjusted, the tyranny of the timepiece left back home in London, I quickly discovered that the fluidity of time allowed the building of deep relationships and community; of long, never-ending lunches where conversations flowed for hours and people cared for each other; of a community so strong, that even if we had very little in common, and saw each other infrequently, it was as if we were together only yesterday.

The only punctuality in time I could observe was the time which the electricity would cut every day. I could set my watch by the preciseness of the three o'clock power cut. The adults in the house would promptly and contentedly retire to their afternoon naps, rising just before the power returned, often at five but sometimes at six. As children, we were told to stay quiet to ensure the naps were restful, and to find ways to entertain ourselves – but to make sure we never opened the fridge since the cool air would escape and the lack of power meant the food would spoil. It was impossible to explain back 'home' in London to my friends that the electricity would turn off for two hours every day. It was impossible to explain most things, even as I grew up – the size of family and who we included in its definition, how we ordered too much food because that was the 'right' thing to do, and why, despite being such a war-torn part of the world, we were eternal optimists.

My tribe has always been global. The many friends and colleagues I have been blessed to encounter and learn from on my journey have not only enabled me to find my identity in between cultures and countries, but to share fond memories and stories about one 'home' while in another. I discovered that I was not from one place or another, but rather from all of them at the same time.

Moving to Dubai in 1995 with my family, I found a new place to call 'home'. A recently born 'city', Dubai was a place that matched my optimism in life, and although small, had huge ambitions and was a city in a hurry. It also, however, had to be 'explained' to my new classmates in college when, in 1998 I went to Boston to study – no, we didn't go to school on camels, we didn't sleep in tents, and yes, we had an airport and airline, Emirates, the rise of which is an emblem of the rise of the city, country, and region until today.

'Returning' to Dubai in 2005 after studying and working in the US, I was fortunate to be part of a growing generation that had the privilege of going abroad to study and work, and were coming back to the region, and in my case, Dubai, to build careers and ultimately, cities. The last thirty years of calling Dubai 'home' has given me the opportunity to witness first-hand the building and rise of the city. I have been fortunate to have been an entrepreneur, founding and exiting a company; an operator, scaling and listing another company; and to have had the privilege to work in government, and ultimately become an investor, working with the incredible founders building the entrepreneurial and technology ecosystems that are changing the face of MENA.

Observing the region's evolution from memories as a child in Damascus to where it is today, attracting the world's best talent to build the tallest buildings, most incredible technologies and some of the leading companies in the world has been an experience that has inspired me like nothing else. Being able to observe from a front-row seat, and participate, in a small way, in this growth has been nothing short of an incredible privilege.

I am immensely grateful and fortunate to be part of this growing ecosystem and infinitely humbled to have the honour to share, in the coming pages, a little about our culture, history, and our part of the world; and the incredible journeys of the many who are building it – the stories which lie behind MENA's *Coming of Age*.

SECTION I

IN MANY WAYS, the story of MENA's entrepreneurial rise is a mirror of the story of the region itself – a blend of ancient legacies and modern ambitions, where tradition and innovation meet in ways that are both unexpected and deeply intertwined. From the bustling souks to the gleaming towers of Dubai and Riyadh, this is a region shaped by contrasts, resilience, and vision. For centuries, MENA has been a bridge between worlds, a crossroads of commerce and culture, where influences from East and West merge and transform. Now, as it steps onto the global stage, this region is harnessing that same dynamism to forge a new path in entrepreneurship.

The journey to this moment didn't begin in boardrooms or co-working spaces; it began with a handful of daring pioneers who saw potential where others saw only barriers. These early founders laid the first stones in what has become an evolving ecosystem, building against a backdrop of complex histories, political shifts, and cultural nuances that have both challenged and fuelled their ambitions. Today, a new generation of entrepreneurs is rising, drawing on this legacy but pushing toward something wholly their own. They are reshaping industries, defying expectations, and proving that innovation here is not just possible – it's inevitable.

Yet, for all its promise, MENA's path is not without its unique trials and tribulations. With limited resources, a different cultural lens on failure, and a scarcity of traditional financing, the rules of the game here require a kind of resilience and ingenuity that goes beyond typical start-up grit. What emerges from this adversity is a region that does not merely imitate global trends but is forging its own blueprint for success. This is the story of MENA's coming of age, a story of visionaries who see possibility in their own backyards and of a region that, like its entrepreneurs, is ready to redefine what it means to be a player on the world stage.

But before sharing the stories, and in order to understand them deeply, it is fundamentally important to take a step back, and ask *What is MENA?*

CHAPTER 1

WHAT IS MENA?

الجنة بدون ناس ما تنداس

A paradise without people is not

worth stepping foot in.

– ARABIC PROVERB

THE ELUSIVE DEFINITION of *inshallah*, often combined with the fluidity of time, confuses and at times infuriates outsiders. Unlike Western society, which has often become used to what one could facetiously argue as the 'tyranny of the timepiece', the Arab culture is defined by a genuine hospitality and grace, a shared common understanding of values evolved over a long and culturally rich history of the region.

From the Sumerians, living more than five thousand years ago in what is now Iraq, who invented a data processing system better known as writing, to the glories of Egypt and the only Wonder of the World still extant – the pyramids – MENA has arguably the strongest claim to be the very cradle of civilisation.

To appreciate what has shaped MENA into what it is today, and what differentiates it from other emerging markets, it is important to fully grasp its inherent characteristics. What are the distinctive traits that define this region? How can its essence and potential best be unlocked? What is the cultural context that both local and international founders, investors and stakeholders operate in – as the culture and history seem both complex and at times even paradoxical.

DEFINING MENA

The 450 million people inhabiting MENA must include the many elements used to categorise any region, including geographical proximity, economic similarities, and intertwined histories, while accounting for a wider range of country-level particularities. However, just as it would be absurd to impose one European Union (EU) reality on all twenty-seven member states, the same applies to the MENA region. To take one example, the EU's average GDP per capita is $37,433, but varies from Bulgaria's $15,997 to Norway's $87,961.[1] Similarly, the MENA region exhibits a broad spectrum of GDP per capita, ranging from Qatar's $87,480 to Egypt's $3,512.

The idea of a MENA region – as a defined geographic and cultural area – is a relatively modern construct. Spanning an area composed of dozens of nation-states, each of which is demographically, ethnically, economically, socially, politically and topographically unique, its delineation, let alone definition, is highly contested. MENA encompasses Mesopotamia in modern-day Iraq, to the descendants of Pharaonic Egypt and the nation states of the Gulf, including the UAE, which has only existed as a country since 1971.

Even global authorities are unable to agree on the boundaries of what is called MENA. The World Bank considers it to be comprised of nineteen countries.[2] The Office of the United States Trade Representative counts fourteen.[3] UNICEF includes twenty countries under its regional umbrella.[4] Some define the region as constituting the twenty-one members of the Arab League, while others add Israel, Iran and Turkey to the list. Whereas MENA is considered a single region, taking in the colonial borders formed by the British and French in the early twentieth century, the regional bloc does not imply homogeneity. The purpose of clarification is simply to acknowledge those common factors which bind the countries together.

The complementarity and interconnections between these markets allow us to envision a single economic market, which flows across borders and is no longer as constrained as it used to be by geopolitics. It is the shared understanding that enables an Egyptian or Jordanian to understand a Bahraini or Emirati more easily than a European person might.

UNITING MENA
SHARED LANGUAGE

An estimated 310 million people speak Arabic as their first language across approximately twenty-two countries in the Arab world.[5] To a non-Arabic speaker, they may all sound the same: heavy on the throat, with lots of strange letters such as ق, ح, and ط. However, there are over thirty variations of the language. Just as French sounds different whenever it is spoken across cities and regions of France or Canada, Arabic dialects differ from one country to the next. Nonetheless, there remains a standard baseline Arabic, known as Modern Standard Arabic or Classical Arabic. It is used and understood by almost every Arab speaker in the region and around the world. It is also the version used in official documents, media, and law, as well as the collective language of business and is the only Arabic taught at all levels of education. And it is almost impossible to learn. It is as if one were to study English from 1,400 years ago (a thousand years before Shakespeare) and attempt to conduct business and legal matters in such a language today.

Written Arabic has not changed, leading to the many dialects that have evolved from the same root allowing for modernity in the spoken tongue but keeping the classical Arabic as written. Until instant messaging and social media came along. Suddenly, Arabs began writing the way they spoke, sparking a cultural and inter-generational uproar. A new dialect emerged, commonly known as Arabizi or Arabish. This was a blend of Arabic and English, where Arabic words were transliterated using Latin characters and numbers to stand in for Arabic sounds without an English equivalent. For instance, the number "7" represented the Arabic letter ح, so phrases like "*Kif 7alak?*" – meaning "How are you?" – became popular in this new digital language.

That pitted generations and ideologies against each other. On one side were those determined to preserve Arabic as it had been for millennia; while on the other were those eager to bring the language closer to the modern world, adopting a more globalised form. As digitally native generations emerged, Arabizi gained traction, bridging the gap, gradually bringing an increasing number of people on board and becoming a bridge for generations.

At the same time, English is the language of global business, used by many multinationals to facilitate communication and performance across geographically diverse functions and business endeavours. Similarly, Modern Standard Arabic is used across the entire region, enabling cross-border collaboration and expansion at a regional level. On a global level, Arabic is the sixth most spoken language after English, Mandarin, Hindi, Spanish and French. Today, it is the fourth most used on the internet, an indication of how deep the well is for MENA tech potential.[6] The majority of Arabic-speaking countries are located between the Arabian Peninsula (Bahrain, Kuwait, Oman, Qatar, Saudi Arabia, the UAE, and Yemen), North Africa (Algeria, Egypt, Libya, Mauritania, Morocco, and Tunisia), and the Levant (Lebanon, Syria, Jordan, and Palestine). However, more than thirty countries globally consider Arabic an official, co-official or minority language.[7]

The reach of the Arabic language extends beyond regional borders. US Census Data shows that it is the seventh most common non-English language spoken in American homes, and its growth outpaces that of other languages, including Persian/Farsi, Hebrew, and Turkish. The number of people who speak Arabic at home in the US grew nearly sixfold in the last forty years, from 215,000 in 1980 to 1.4 million in 2021.[8] When we consider the size of the Arabic diaspora, which, for some nations, is larger than the in-country population (Lebanon and Palestine), the language's range is even larger.

This shared language lays the foundation for regional expansion, allowing businesses to scale seamlessly across borders within MENA and beyond. It means the technology developed here can address a vast, interconnected market, enriching communities with solutions tailored to their shared cultural and linguistic context. Such reach and cultural alignment offer start-ups a rare advantage in leveraging the potential of MENA, illustrating just how much potential there is for tech-driven growth in this region and far beyond.

Although Arabic is the common connector, most people in the region speak a second language, in large part due to the legacies of British and French imperialism (and the difficulties of the Arabic language in its authentic and written form). A sizable portion of the MENA region's population is bi or trilingual, including the Lebanese, many of whom switch effortlessly between Arabic, French, and English – both in language and culture, driving forward the definition of a 'third-culture' generation. The importance of speaking these languages and being 'third-culture' cannot be underestimated as a facilitator of hospitality, cultural understanding, and building a part of the world where everybody feels welcome.

The other big driver is a rapidly changing demographic composition, especially within the Arabian Gulf. Arabic is the UAE's official language, but English is its lingua franca. Eighty-five per cent of the population is made up of foreign expatriates. Overall, an estimated 30 to 50 per cent of the region's population speaks the global language of business – English.

SHARED CULTURE

The second common denominator is a mix of shared culture and values that define and dictate business-building, making, and scaling. While each country has its own distinct differences, there are common underlying themes that create a symbolic sense of 'shared' culture. Aspects of this shared culture don't lend themselves to World Bank statistics and graphs and can only be fully understood and appreciated when experienced first-hand.

FOOD AND HOSPITALITY

If there isn't food left on the table when everybody has finished eating, then there was too little to start with. The Middle Eastern relationship with food is in stark contrast to most cultures where ordering only what is needed is often the norm. The insistence on feeding people is a sign of love and friendship. At home, a host must keep piling food onto each guest's plate until they are completely full, and guests must keep up. In many families, an 'auntie' passing around a box of chocolates to every visitor is a ritual not to be refused. Declining, or worse, hesitating to select one, is seen as a slight. She will insist – until hands reach in and chocolates are eaten, even if it means just one more piece. To say no to such a gesture is to risk offending the host, a faux pas understood universally across the region. There is pride in over-ordering, fighting over the bill and over-feeding people. It means we have done our job well. The cultural elements that make us order too much food are steeped in history. The roots of this hospitality date back to tribal times, particularly in the Arabian Gulf and parts of the Levant. A key pillar of the Bedouin ethos, hospitality was less about kindness, and more about safety and security. Bedouins welcomed strangers to their homes with the mutual understanding that the favour would one day be returned in the unforgiving environment of the desert.

The hospitality culture includes everything from food to music, dance, religion, and the arts. Arab hospitality fosters a welcoming environment for visitors and plays a crucial role in business interactions and relationship-building. In such an environment, hospitality transcends mere politeness. It embodies a genuine spirit of generosity and a deep-seated respect for others and is a key pillar of the culture.

That same generosity applies to the modus operandi of the region's business entrepreneurial ecosystem: in how regional funders collaborate with each other and welcome foreign investors; in the outward focus on knowledge-sharing; in the close association of ecosystem players, as well as the reach, scale, and frequency of ecosystem events.

THE FLUIDITY OF TIME
Another of these shared values is a general sense of fluidity when it comes to space and time. Most in the MENA region are infamous for

a lack of punctuality. Meeting times are often viewed as suggestions rather than strict appointments. If someone arrives five, ten, even fifteen minutes late, it's hardly given a second thought – it's just part of the acceptable norm. Arriving at a dinner invite scheduled for eight usually means you'll be waiting alone at the restaurant for at least thirty minutes before the other guests appear. There's an unspoken understanding: an "eight o'clock dinner" often really means leaving the house or starting to get ready at that time. This is not meant to be disrespectful but rather reflects a different approach to time, and its other side, the importance of long-term relationships.

This fluidity extends into the manner in which relationships are built. In other parts of the world, a meeting is considered successful when it leads to a quick outcome or a decision. In this part of the world, it takes much more than that – and a successful meeting often means a series of follow-up meetings will ensue. The malleability of time means that there is no such thing as a bad meeting, but rather a prerequisite series of meetings with the aim of building a long-term relationship based on mutual respect and trust. While it takes longer to close a transaction or conclude a deal, the equation is rooted in success through long-term partnership.

In the context of business-building, this fluidity translates to a longer-term view of performance and success compared with counterparts in more fast-paced markets. The relative nascency and scarcity of financial and non-financial resources means that regional entrepreneurs are hardwired for endurance. Their metric for success is not measured solely by big funding rounds, rapid scaling, and quick exits, but healthy unit economics at the onset, multiple product iterations, and a resilient business model that stands the test of volatile markets and eventually naturally leads into these global perceptions of success.

"INSHALLAH"

One of the most commonly spoken words, from Morocco to Oman, *inshallah* combines the concepts of fate and fluidity of time, culminating in a word that simultaneously terrifies people looking to 'get things done' and calms those who are concerned about the ultimate outcome.

To a child, inshallah is the word parents say to avoid giving an answer. For some children, this is heard as a no, for others as a yes – depending on the level of hope they harbour and their past experiences. Inshallah is every Arab parent's cop-out of giving an answer to remove the weight of promises on themselves. God willing.

For adults, similarly, hearing the word, inshallah, could either mean that the person facing them has a very strong faith and will proceed with the best possible intentions, but leave the ultimate result to God; or it is simply a way to avoid answering the question with a clear answer. It is important not to mistake this for a lack of commitment. Its roots lie in faith, optimism, and a humble acknowledgment of the unpredictable nature of life. In the same vein, the people of the MENA region share an entrenched realism, gratitude, and humility born out of the hardships of the desert which their ancestors survived only two generations ago.

Similarly, entrepreneurs and business leaders typically exude a sense of realism because they know that capital is difficult to come by; volatility is an inherent part of doing business and risk is always looming.

BEYOND BLOOD TIES; THE DEFINITION OF FAMILY

If there is one other value characteristic which helps define the culture, it is a deep sense of community and collectivity. This is evident in how the region defines family. Whereas many in the West consider family to be their immediate relatives, we include the extended family, as well as the intricate web of obligations and connections that bind its members. In the richness of the Arabic language, where a single written word has, on average, three meanings, seven pronunciations, and twelve interpretations, there are three words for family: ahl, 'a'ila and usra.

The first – ahl – refers to the shared living space among family members. The second – 'a'ila – goes a step further, highlighting the mutual service and fulfilment of each other's needs within the family unit. The term – *usra* – meanwhile, originally referred to male relatives tasked with protecting the family.

Beyond blood ties, we extend the titles of 'uncle' and 'aunt' to our friends' parents and even our neighbours. As a child, bringing a friend home meant one thing: your grandmother would immediately set out to unravel their entire family tree, starting with their surname, their mother's maiden name, where in the country they come from, determined to find a shared connection or a distant relative in common. And without a doubt, they will succeed in finding a common thread. No one is truly a stranger – just family waiting to be discovered or reconnected with.

The closeness of those relationships is precisely what builds the foundational entrepreneurial ecosystems in the region. As a founder, one knows that when extending a hand to help another – offering advice or making introductions – they are working with family, and are likely to return the favour. They are building the web that becomes the ecosystem. It is not transactional in nature. It is about nurturing a culture of mutual support, where collaboration and trust are woven into the fabric of the entrepreneurial journey. This is what gives the region its unique, enduring strength, creating a cycle of giving and receiving that drives us all forward.

In contrast to the emphasis on individualism in countries such as the US, the MENA region thinks 'we' and rarely 'I'. Research clearly demonstrates that entrepreneurship creates an economic multiplier effect in emerging markets. Why? Because a single job indirectly benefits a wider group of people beyond the individual who has been directly employed. Both men and women in the MENA region often bear financial responsibilities not only for themselves but for extended family members, including cousins, nieces, nephews, or even neighbours. The multiplier effect of one job is very real in every way.

DOCTOR, ENGINEER, LAWYER

As with many rising cultures and emerging markets, until recently, the definition of a child's success is their graduation and subsequent employment as a doctor, lawyer, or engineer. The pride a parent feels in saying, "My daughter is a doctor" or "My son is an engineer", is almost immeasurable. Pursuing a career in finance, marketing, or the broader business world was often seen as a fallback – a sign that the child either hadn't lived up to expectations or was still searching for direction in life. Only very recently has the shift in mindset allowed entrepreneurship to be considered a 'prized' outcome or success metric.

Within these family groups, education is highly prized. There is continuous emphasis on learning, and a tendency for parents to enrol their children in tertiary institutions outside the region, enabling them to pursue higher quality learning and employment opportunities abroad. In 2020, a total of 115,000 students from Saudi Arabia were studying business and management, engineering, and medical sciences abroad, primarily in the US.[9] In 2018, the UK was the second top destination for Saudi sponsorship student holders, with over 9,000 students following further and higher degree courses in the country.[10] Student inflow from the UAE to the US had also risen 11 per cent, while the number of students from Oman and Kuwait had increased by 12.8 per cent and 5.7 per cent respectively.[11]

These numbers continue to rise as international experience and higher education opportunities increase in importance. Yet, there is also an exponential increase in the number of universities in the region, particularly in the GCC, allowing an increasing number of students to study, and drastically increasing the amount of research and development opportunities.

PROFILING MENA

It's hard to overstate the radical changes in the MENA region's entrepreneurial landscape from when the first founders, referred to as "the Originals", were building their companies. Back then, those founders saw the potential of the MENA region to become a breeding ground for start-ups and technology, allowing them to scale and succeed in solving significant regional and global challenges.

There is tremendous potential to engage the region's predominantly young population in the region's economic development. The domestic market comprises around 450 million people, half of whom are under the age of 30 and who nearly all own a smartphone – or even two. It is a group underserved in virtually every sector, including financial services. However, it still manages to top the rest of the world when it comes to social media usage, with individuals spending an average of three hours per day on platforms – over thirty minutes more than global counterparts.

At the same time, they possess the skills, education and drive to be the disruptors generating new technological solutions to export to the world. This is just one of the unique and non-replicable assets in the MENA region, which, when combined, creates the perfect opportunity for a thriving and bustling entrepreneurial ecosystem.

THE MENA YOUTH BULGE

In contrast to the pessimism of many countries, including Japan, where birth rates are falling, the youth demographic in the MENA region is booming. And it is to this population that businesses are turning to ignite growth on a local, regional and eventually global scale. The majority of countries in the region share this population profile. In Egypt, one of the region's largest countries, 60 per cent of the population is under the age of 30.[12] Sixty-three per cent of Saudi Arabia's population is under 30. The same is true of Jordan.[13] By contrast, the average percentage of those under 30 in Organisation for Economic Cooperation and Development (OECD) markets is 36 per cent.[14]

Only a handful of other regions in the world have a similar demographic profile. Africa is one, with 60 per cent of the population under the age of 25.[15] India is another, at 40 per cent.[16] The percentage of Latin America's population aged between 15 and 24, meanwhile, stands at 16 per cent.[17] In his book, 2030, Dr Mauro Guillén – one of the world's foremost experts on global trends – highlights how the world's consumer demographics are on the verge of a dramatic shift. Declining birth rates in developed nations contrast sharply with the population boom in regions like Asia and Sub-Saharan Africa. This evolving dynamic, he suggests, will result in a middle class in Asia and Africa surpassing that of the U.S. and Europe by 2030, reshaping the global economy. He captures this transformation succinctly, "For every baby born nowadays in developed countries, more than nine are being born in the emerging markets and the developing world."

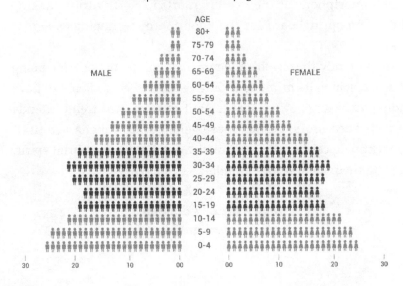

MENA Youth Bulge

Total Population in MENA by Age and Sex

Source: Financial Times (2020)

CONNECTED

It is no coincidence that MENA is one of the fastest-growing markets for digital adoption. The region's youth are embracing digital technology at an unprecedented rate, aligning their experiences with trends that have become standard in more developed parts of the world. Smartphones are ubiquitous, with a 79 per cent adoption rate overall and an impressive 91 per cent penetration rate specifically among the young. By 2030, there will be over 800 million smartphone connections in the MENA region.[18] That is more than the combined population of the US and the EU. In some parts of the region, such as Qatar, Bahrain, and the UAE, mobile cellular subscription rates are 144, 131 and 195 for every 100 people respectively, implying that many people have more than a single subscription.[19] For comparison, the world average is 108.[20]

Despite discrepancies in technological penetration across the region, the digital landscape has grown tremendously with the higher income countries of the Gulf leading the pack. Research has shown that consumers in the Gulf Cooperation Council (GCC) are six times more likely to own a laptop and twice as likely to own a smartphone as their counterparts in North Africa, making the Gulf a springboard for the adoption of technologies across the region.[21]

Importantly, the region's millennial generation, or Gen Y, is coming of age, reaching its prime spending years, and is predicted to have more purchasing power than its predecessors. This trend extends to their successors, Gen Z. These generations are characterised by technological fluency, adaptability, and entrepreneurial spirit, making them ideal future founders.

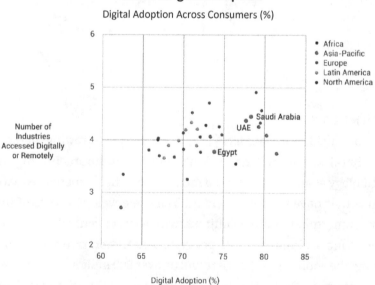

MENA Digital Adoption

Digital Adoption Across Consumers (%)

Source: McKinsey (2023)

The youngest populations in the world will be the fastest digital adopters and, by extension, digital creators. The result of these demographic trends is a young, hungry, eager, tech-savvy population that shares a common language and similar values.

It is not only the increased level of digital adoption that points to the potential the region has for growth in the digital domain, but also the standard of education. Today's youth is more educated than its predecessors. While 27 per cent of the region's adult population holds a university degree, 35.8 per cent of its youth do – and that number is only increasing over time.[22] This is largely explained by the region's history of migration, coupled with the ease of travel that now exists between the Middle East and the West.

The biggest challenge of the early 2000s, that has been addressed at a government level, is the brain drain that has left the region with a considerable talent gap. Today, this trend is shifting as an increasing number of young people are recognising the promise of building a career in the region and the opportunity to make a meaningful impact close to home. In the UAE, the government is actively working to attract top Arab talent through initiatives like the *Great Arab Minds* programme, which invites professionals from various fields to contribute to the nation's growing role as a regional, and global, innovation hub.

Similarly, Saudi Arabia has embraced a strategic focus on local talent retention within its *Vision 2030* framework, building a robust ecosystem for research, technology, and entrepreneurship. These initiatives reflect a shared understanding across the region: the key to a thriving future lies in nurturing and retaining home-grown talent.

Part of the solution lies in encouraging and safeguarding the growth of small and medium enterprises. They comprise 90 per cent of businesses in the MENA region and create seven out of every ten jobs in emerging markets. Fortunately, policymakers across the region are committed to making entrepreneurship a cornerstone of the regional economic landscape. In relatively centralised or semi-centralised market environments, the role of policymakers can make or break entrepreneurship and innovation. Across the

MENA region, the regulators have helped create the ecosystem. Over the past decade, they have been playing an enabling role in adding and strengthening the core components necessary to build an environment conducive to the creation of start-ups.

* * * * *

Unlike Silicon Valley or Europe, entrepreneurship is not simply an investment vehicle with a lucrative risk-return profile that produces incremental improvements to daily life. In the MENA region – and emerging markets more broadly – it is an attractive investment opportunity that also creates widespread socio-economic impact at the level of the individual, the economy, and the nation in its entirety.

Over the last decade, governments have actively championed entrepreneurship-driven innovation because of its ability to uplift national economies and communities. In the region's most active entrepreneurial markets, including Saudi Arabia, the UAE and Egypt,[23] the transition to knowledge-based economic models is about building sustainable, long-term growth – and regulators understand that doing that is a matter of leaning into entrepreneurship.

Over the years, regulators in the MENA region have crafted a start-up-enabling ecosystem, working alongside founders as they brought new innovation into the region. This transformative environment is supported by progressive initiatives that anchor innovation to regional priorities. In 2019, the Dubai Health Authority (DHA) launched a health innovation lab, enabling healthtech start-ups to pilot solutions such as telemedicine while operating under stringent regulatory guidance to ensure safety and efficacy.

The Dubai International Financial Centre Innovation Hub has helped launch more than 1,000 innovation and tech firms. Abu Dhabi had a similar groundbreaking moment in 2006, when it introduced Masdar, the Abu Dhabi Future Energy Company, along with plans for Masdar City – a visionary carbon-neutral, zero-waste community. Most recently, in 2023, The Catalyst, the region's first start-up accelerator focused on sustainability and clean technology, launched with a $5 million investment in partnership with BP. The Catalyst aims to foster innovation, entrepreneurship, and the development of a robust cleantech ecosystem across the region.

National governments have also made strides in fintech by creating regulatory sandboxes that allow start-ups to test their ideas in a more flexible environment. Meanwhile, Open Banking frameworks have been implemented across key markets like Saudi Arabia, the UAE, and Bahrain, signalling a commitment to modernisation and a thriving entrepreneurial landscape.

The combination of the culture, the connected youth, and the forward-thinking, technology-led leadership has enabled MENA to redefine itself over the last decade into what we see today. Understanding the culture, the people, and the population's desire to participate in its own economic growth and prosperity on its own terms is key to unlocking the future.

CHAPTER 2

SOARING FALCONS

المختصر المفيد

The abridged and useful.

– ARABIC PROVERB

ALTHOUGH IT IS IMPOSSIBLE to capture the full history of MENA in any book, and while there are many countries that comprise MENA, the purpose of this book is to focus on those that are emerging economies where entrepreneurship has taken a lead in driving growth and ecosystems, propelling the youth forward into the future. Accordingly, and to contextualise the stories that will unfold in subsequent pages, the main focus is on four key countries that exemplify this transformation: the UAE, Saudi Arabia, Egypt, and Jordan – the 'Rising Falcons'.

Each of these nations has demonstrated unique strengths and distinct paths to fostering entrepreneurship and innovation. The UAE stands out as a global hub for business and technology, with a robust infrastructure supporting start-ups and scale-ups alike. Saudi Arabia has made remarkable strides in transforming its economy, moving away from oil dependency through Vision 2030, and making significant investments in technology, innovation, and entertainment. Egypt has positioned itself as a regional economic powerhouse, focusing on infrastructure development, industrialisation, and a burgeoning tech ecosystem. Meanwhile, Jordan has showcased resilience, fostered a vibrant tech-driven economy and become a leader in talent development and entrepreneurship despite limited natural resources. With its young, dynamic population, Jordan continues to drive innovation and create opportunities for the next generation. Together, these four nations are laying the groundwork for a dynamic entrepreneurial landscape, interconnected and supportive of one another. The Rising Falcons exemplify how MENA's youth, talent, and ambition are unlocking opportunities and positioning the region as a hub for innovation and growth on the global stage.

Additionally, it is important to acknowledge the other countries that have also made significant strides in the growth of their knowledge economies and entrepreneurial ecosystems, including but not limited to, Bahrain, Qatar, and Oman, some of whose founders will appear in later stories.

THE UAE AND SAUDI ARABIA

It is impossible to separate the Gulf's meteoric rise from the discovery of oil and gas. Millennia ago, large quantities of organic matter rested deep beneath the undulating sands of the Arabian Peninsula, gradually transforming into pools of hydrocarbons. The discovery of oil in commercial quantities in the Eastern Province of Saudi Arabia in 1938 changed everything. Oil brought an immense increase in national wealth and an improvement in the welfare of the population as a whole. Prior to the discovery of oil, people had lived lives of considerable austerity, with very little in the way of healthcare or formal education. There were no paved roads, few professional jobs, and life continued much as it had done for the previous few centuries. The astonishing transformation, from desert to modern marvel, has all unfolded in just a few short decades since the 1970s – a testament to the region's remarkable evolution.

Historically, the emirates of the UAE were renowned for their pearl diving, which dictated the rhythm of life, shaped the country's identity, and provided the primary source of income for communities along the coast for centuries. That trade supported the local economy and was a considerable export, especially to India and parts of Europe prior to the discovery of oil. Coastal villages such as Al Jazirah Al Hamra in Ras Al Khaimah, known for their historical significance in pearl diving and seafaring, were active pearling centres up until the 1960s, although pearling had begun to lose its lustre following the introduction of the cultured pearl in the 1930s. Local tribes were also fishermen, making sea trade a vital economic activity, and the geographic position of the UAE along the Arabian Gulf facilitated far-reaching maritime trade with other parts of the world. It also played a crucial role in the region's economic and cultural exchanges.

From the 1950s onwards, as industrialised nations sought new sources of energy to fuel their economies, these hydrocarbons were brought to the surface in far greater quantities and assumed global significance. Oil from the Arabian Peninsula quickly became the linchpin of the global economy and the Gulf experienced material growth on a scale the world had never seen before. Abu Dhabi, one of the emirates of the Trucial States and now the capital of the UAE, paved its first road in 1968 to accommodate less than 100 cars.[24] By 2016, more than 1 million vehicles were using its highways.[25]

In the early 1970s, Dubai's fledgling Sheikh Zayed Road had a sprinkling of buildings alongside it, including the Nasser Rashid Lootah Building (also known as the Toyota Building). The rest was desert. Today, the highway runs for 558 kilometres from the border of Abu Dhabi to the rugged mountain landscape of Ras Al Khaimah, with over half a million cars, cruising along daily. With a population of 11 million today, predominantly expatriates, the UAE has achieved a GDP per capita approaching $50,000.

In Saudi Arabia, before oil was discovered in 1938, and in the late 1950s in the Trucial States (the forerunner to the UAE), both countries were tribal societies, living and working in the unforgiving deserts of the Arabian Peninsula. Saudi tribes were either nomadic or semi-nomadic pastoralists who herded livestock such as camels, sheep, and goats, or subsistence farmers who worked the very little amount of fertile land available to them. They were also weavers and potters, as well as fishermen and pearl divers, particularly on the coastline of the Arabian Gulf. The fruits of their labour were often utilised to craft jewellery, weapons, and tools, which were then traded with neighbouring communities and across Asia.

Saudis were astute traders, leveraging the land's millennia-old trading routes to exchange spices, perfumes, and textiles between the Arabian interior, the Levant, and North Africa. Its coastal ports, especially Jeddah on the Red Sea, connected traders to a wider network that extended as far afield as Asia, Africa, and Europe. These merchant traditions stretched back millennia. The ancient kingdoms of Dadan and Lihyan, in what is now north-west Saudi Arabia, thrived off the lucrative trade in frankincense and myrrh, and in the first century BCE the mercantile Nabataeans built the city of Hegra (the sister city of Petra in Jordan) on a desert plain just north of Wadi Al-Qura.

Many of the peninsula's villages, towns, and cities also lay on the pilgrimage routes to Makkah and Medina, two of the holiest cities in Islam. The Hajj – the annual pilgrimage undertaken by Muslims to Makkah – is the fifth pillar of Islam and every adult Muslim across the globe is required to undertake it at least once in their lifetime, provided they are physically and financially able. Of profound spiritual significance, the Hajj is also a major contributor to the economy of Saudi Arabia. Once a daunting and sometimes harrowing undertaking that could take months to perform on foot, the Hajj attracted over a million pilgrims in 2024, the vast majority of whom were international worshippers.[26] The current demographic composition of Jeddah, one of Saudi Arabia's main cities, is reflective of the historical flow of people, thousands of whom descended on the city every year following the emergence of Islam in the seventh century. Today, Saudi Arabia has a population of more than 33 million with a GDP per capita of almost $33,000.

In two short generations, oil changed the fate of the Gulf nations forever. It was, and is, responsible for much of the exponential development, wealth creation, and socio-economic betterment that has taken place over the past seventy years. In Saudi Arabia, the country's leaders began to modernise the country's economy and infrastructure from the 1950s onwards, paving the way for the nation's future prosperity. The Directorate of Oil and Mineral Affairs was established in 1954 and oversaw the exploration and development of Saudi Arabia's oil reserves. It would later become the Ministry of Industry and Mineral Resources. The seeds of change were being sown. Oil would drive successive economic booms in the country and transform Saudi Arabia into a global economic powerhouse.

Although buoyed by the wealth generated by oil and gas, the nations of the GCC are acutely aware of the dangers associated with their dependency on hydrocarbons. As such, they have enacted some of the most ambitious economic diversification agendas in the world. Saudi Arabia launched industrial initiatives for the by-products of oil as far back as the 1970s and has set ambitious goals through its Vision 2030 plan. Similarly, across the GCC, policies implemented over the last decade have placed diversification at the forefront of national agendas.

Initiatives are already underway throughout the region with the goal of moving gradually to a knowledge-based economy. If entrepreneurship is understood as the process of leveraging intellectual capital to create value in the form of products, services and processes, then its role in these diversification agendas is central.

MENA VC FUNDING

Venture Capital Funding Evolution in MENA

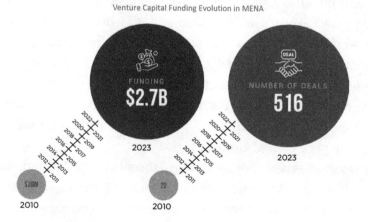

Source: MAGNiTT (2024)

What this brief exploration of these nations' economic history teaches us is that there are common denominators that rationalise these governments' focus on business and entrepreneurship. The fact that they are legacy trading hubs embodying a unique spirit of exchange, especially the port cities of Dubai and Jeddah, illuminates the recent national efforts to integrate their respective historical strengths with contemporary economic practices.

Both Saudi Arabia and the UAE are leveraging their geographical positions at the crossroads of key international trade routes to re-establish themselves as global logistics and trade hubs. Saudi's Vision 2030 and the UAE's Vision 2021 have strong emphases on logistics: enhancing ports, improving logistical infrastructure, and utilising technology to streamline customs and border processes to make them competitive in the global market. Both are heavily investing in tourism and cultural initiatives: Saudi Arabia with the likes of The Red Sea and NEOM, and the UAE with its world-renowned hospitality sector and success of DP World, one of the world's largest port operators.

These countries are embracing and leveraging their original roles as connectors – spaces where East meets West, North meets South, and modernity meets tradition. In the drive toward economic diversification, they are not reinventing the wheel per se, but finding their way back to, and leaning into, the comparative advantages that they have held for centuries. Leading technology conferences, such as Dubai's Gitex and Saudi Arabia's Future Investment Initiative and the LEAP event, draw industry players from across the globe to the GCC, transforming the region into a vibrant nexus of innovation. As these events unfold, they don't just showcase cutting-edge advancements; they also illustrate the region's expanding influence on the global technology stage.

When we examine the non-oil contributors to both countries' national GDPs today, we find real estate, tourism, logistics, mining, manufacturing, and seafood remain significant engines of economic activity, or that there is a national push towards increasing their contribution to national GDP.

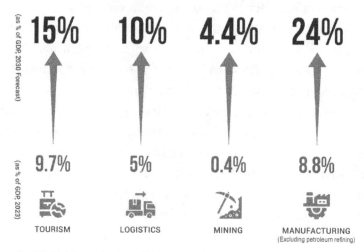

SECTOR CONTRIBUTION TO GDP
Key Sectors Contribution to GDP in KSA

(as % of GDP, 2030 Forecast)

	TOURISM	LOGISTICS	MINING	MANUFACTURING (Excluding petroleum refining)
2030 Forecast	15%	10%	4.4%	24%
2023	9.7%	5%	0.4%	8.8%

Source: Saudi Arabia's General Authority for Statistics (2023)

SECTOR CONTRIBUTION TO GDP
Key Sectors Contribution to GDP in the UAE

	TOURISM	LOGISTICS	MINING	MANUFACTURING (Excluding petroleum refining)
2030 Forecast	15%	14%	3.5%	25%
2022	9%	7.7%	<1%	11%

Source: UAE Embassy, Invest UAE and UAE MOCCAE (2022)

Propelling the economic transition is visionary leadership with truly remarkable foresight. The UAE appointed the world's first Minister of Artificial Intelligence back in 2017, years before ChatGPT mainstreamed conversations around a technology that had been around for decades. His Excellency Omar Sultan Al Olama, born in 1990, and the UAE's Minister of State for Artificial Intelligence, Digital Economy, and Remote Work Applications, opened an article for *Time* by recounting a remark he had heard from a foreign government official about his appointment: "A Minister of Artificial Intelligence who is the age of my son, appointed to regulate a hypothetical technology, proves to me that your government has too much time and resources on its hands."[27] In 2024, His Highness Sheikh Hamdan bin Mohammed bin Rashid Al Maktoum, appointed twenty-two Chief AI officers to spearhead AI strategies and implementation across various governmental entities.

He addresses the remark in his article, stating: "I distinctly recall feeling a pang of indignation by their equating youth with incompetence, but even more so by their clear disregard and trivialisation of AI."[28] A young leadership bloc is one that understands and can closely address the needs of its predominantly youthful population. It is a common and intentional trait in both the UAE and Saudi Arabia. In 2016, the average age of the UAE's cabinet was 38 and its youngest member was 22.[29] Mohammed Bin Salman was 27 years old when he was appointed defence minister, and 34 when he became the prime minister of Saudi Arabia.

The youngest leadership in the world – they are the ones building the future. They are accountable for their decisions well into the future and will live to see the outcomes – this creates a very different mindset and shift to leaders and governments that are focused on shorter time-frames, election cycles, and their individual legacies. Countries that publicise their ten-year plans, and where leaders set out to execute them largely in collaboration with the private sector are ones that are focused on building for the long-term, hand-in-hand with the people.

EGYPT

And then there's Egypt. Birthplace of the Pharaohs, home to the wonders of Luxor, and the Arab world's beating cultural heart. In the eyes of its people, and many across the region, Egypt is 'Om El Donya' – Earth's mother.

Entrepreneurship has always been a significant part of the country's DNA. An entrepreneurial affinity can be traced back to the ancient Egyptians, whose architectural and engineering prowess led to the creation of the Great Pyramid of Giza and other monumental structures that required innovative solutions and complex project management. They built sturdy ships for long-distance travel, competed fiercely for dominance of the Red Sea with the Greeks, Nabataeans, and Lihyanites, and gave birth to the Mamluks, a military and political order known for its strategic acumen. They also created sophisticated irrigation systems capable of nourishing the lands around the Nile and gave us twentieth century singers such as Umm Kulthum and Abdel Halim Hafez.

The early 2000s saw the establishment of the Information Technology Industry Development Agency and the construction of Smart Village Egypt, a hub for start-ups in Cairo, replete with state-of-the-art facilities and infrastructure aimed at attracting local and global businesses. By 2004, the government had launched its e-government initiative to transition public services into the digital realm, and by 2009 the wider MENA region had begun to witness its early successes, including Maktoob, which was acquired by Yahoo! for an estimated $85 million.[30]

Fawry, the payments giant, is another remarkable success story from the region, rooted in the Egyptian market back in 2008. What began as a local solution quickly gained traction, with over 400,000 customers adopting its services within six months of launch.[31] By 2015, Fawry's success attracted a consortium of international financial investors, who acquired a majority stake in a deal valued at $100 million.[32] The company's most groundbreaking moment came in 2019, when it became the region's first tech IPO, listing on the Egyptian Stock Exchange – a historic achievement that propelled it to unicorn status just a year later in 2020, solidifying its legacy as a pioneer in MENA's entrepreneurial ecosystem.

How much of a catalysing effect the 2011 Egyptian Revolution had on the nation's young is open to debate, but it renewed many Egyptians' belief in a better future for their country. They were emboldened by a vision of better healthcare, education, agriculture, and financial services – and believed they were the vehicle through which that vision could come to life. Not long after the seismic events of the wider Arab Spring, a series of enabling stakeholders emerged, from investors to accelerators, including a state-owned incubator called the Technology Innovation and Entrepreneurship Centre.

Others followed, among them Flat6Labs, which supported early-stage start-ups, the Cairo Angels, The GrEEK Campus, Sawari Ventures, Algebra Ventures, and the American University of Cairo's Venture Lab. Key corporations, including Vodafone, Etisalat, and EFG Hermes, joined in the action, building out venture arms and dedicating pools of financial capital to invest in the country's burgeoning start-up scene.

Egypt is the most populated country in MENA with more than 100 million individuals and a GDP per capita of around $3,500.

JORDAN

Nestled at the crossroads of ancient trade routes, Jordan's history is steeped in a legacy of ingenuity and resilience. From the rose-red city of Petra to its strategic role in the development of the Arabic script, the country has long been a bridge between civilisations. Today, this legacy manifests in its people – one in every forty Jordanians is an engineer, earning Jordan the distinction of having the highest number of engineers per capita globally. For a country of 11 million people, this density of expertise underscores Jordan's status as a hotbed of knowledge economy talent.

Entrepreneurial spirit flows deeply in Jordan's veins. Around 27 per cent of all technology entrepreneurs in the MENA region are Jordanian, despite the country accounting for just three per cent of the region's population.[33] This talent pool has produced regional titans like Aramex, which began as a modest logistics operation and grew into an international courier powerhouse, and Zain, a local telecommunications provider that emerged as a regional leader.

Jordan has also made its mark in the tech start-up scene, giving birth to companies like Maktoob, the region's first Arabic-English email service provider, and Jawaker, a leading platform for card and board games. These success stories have helped position Jordan as a launchpad for innovative start-ups, inspiring both investors and policymakers to take notice.

Jordan's entrepreneurial ecosystem has been shaped by a dynamic network of organisations and initiatives working to support and scale innovation. The Queen Rania Centre for Entrepreneurship (QRCE) has been a key player, fostering a culture of entrepreneurship by offering mentorship, training, and resources to help start-ups take their first steps. Building on this foundation, Oasis500 emerged as one of the region's earliest accelerators, providing funding and hands-on guidance to early-stage start-ups in technology and the creative industries. Endeavour Jordan has further strengthened the ecosystem by focusing on high-impact entrepreneurs, helping them scale their ventures through access to global networks of mentors, investors, and market opportunities. This network of support has been shaped by key infrastructure projects like the King Hussein Business Park, which has become a hub for innovation and collaboration, attracting global players and providing a vibrant base for start-ups and corporates alike.

Beyond its economic contributions, Jordan stands as a beacon of stability and education in the region. Its universities are renowned for producing highly qualified graduates, many of whom lead technological innovation across MENA and beyond. With a GDP per capita of $4,600, Jordan is steadily building a narrative that combines talent, resourcefulness, and ambition, setting the stage for its continued transformation into a regional entrepreneurial powerhouse.

* * * * *

Combined, the 'Rising Falcons' have all the components to drive growth and innovation forward. From history to education and from regulation to market size, these four nations, underpinned by a shared culture, language, and history, illustrate the makings of a rising tide and new economy.

Their strategic position at the crossroads of Africa, Asia, and Europe, makes these markets tactical hubs for start-ups to be born and scale globally. The collaborative efforts of a diverse array of stakeholders – including corporate venture capitalists, incubators, universities, and venture capital investors – create a rich and diverse ecosystem, one that is full of potential.

Saudi Arabia continues to stand out as one of the region's largest and most rapidly evolving markets with a population exceeding 32 million – the remarkable pace of transformation has caught many by surprise.[34] As Chris Schroeder says: "The level and speed of change and innovation in Saudi Arabia seemed almost beyond anyone's imagination a decade ago, and its multiplier impact on the region."

The UAE, although a smaller market, provides strong regulatory infrastructure and is the preferred base for multinationals. It therefore has an attractive roster of prospective clients for regional start-ups and has long been a magnet for international talent, many of whom are now building global companies, based in Dubai and Abu Dhabi.

Egypt combines its significant market size, educated workforce, and robust infrastructure to establish itself as a prominent player in the innovation arena. With a population eager to embrace technology and entrepreneurship, Egypt has become a key driver in the regional start-up ecosystem.

Jordan, with its young, dynamic population, resilient economy, and emphasis on tech talent development, has emerged as a vibrant entrepreneurial hub. Despite limited natural resources, the country is leveraging its strengths to drive innovation and support start-ups that are solving regional challenges.

These nations are interconnected, feeding off and supporting each other to create a cohesive network of entrepreneurial hubs. Deploying technology to leapfrog stages of development, they are tackling regional challenges while navigating cultural, economic, and social complexities.

The youth of the Rising Falcons – dynamic, connected, and ambitious – are the driving force behind this transformation. They are unlocking new opportunities, placing the region firmly on the global innovation map, and solidifying their positions as leaders in the future of the tech world.

CHAPTER 3

THE ORIGINALS

لن تكون قادراً على قطع المحيط إذا لم يكن

لديك الشجاعة أن تخسر مرآى الشاطئ'

You can never cross the ocean unless you

have the courage to lose sight of the shore.

– ARABIC PROVERB

EVERY INDUSTRY HAS its beginnings with a handful of original thinkers, original shapers. The Hedge Fund industry had Julian Robertson, Alfred Jones and Jim Simons, Private Equity had Henry Kravis, Ronald Cohen and Steve Schwarzman, and Venture Capital had Dave Packard, Don Valentine and Tom Perkins.

Silicon Valley's Google alumni and PayPal mafia were founders who became the architects of what we now know as our current digital reality. They all share some impactful attributes and circumstances: stubborn, tenacious, and visionary. They left high-paying careers to pursue a conviction, a purpose, and to drive impact within an ecosystem that had not yet fully formed – building the plane while in mid-air.

For MENA, this is the group we call 'the Originals'. Their circumstances were such that none should have had any chance to succeed, yet they ended up shaping the current MENA ecosystem.

When the Originals began their business journeys near the start of this century, the outlook was far from promising. In 2005 the launch of the Apple iPhone was still two years away and even the United States was only just seeing the beginnings of its e-commerce revolution with a mere 2.5 per cent of sales in the USA online at that time.

This is why the founders who feature in this chapter are some of the real heroes of economic development in the MENA region. As individuals, they are each very different. What links them is that they each saw a gap in the market and were driven by the knowledge they had to fill it, build something, and make it work. At the same time, as they identified each insurmountable obstacle, they were prepared to change direction where necessary and pursue a new path, adapting to the ever-changing world around them.

If we take a trip back to 2005, the technological landscape in the MENA region was even less developed. Internet penetration rates averaged a meagre 10 to 15 per cent, and online payments were virtually non-existent,[35] with only 1 or 2 per cent of transactions happening digitally. The region was notably fragmented, with each country having its own set of regulations, banking systems, and logistical infrastructure.

The region, however, did have one promising ingredient, setting it apart from other geographies. Approximately 60 per cent of MENA's population was under the age of 30.[36] This compares to 37 per cent in the US[37] and 32 per cent in Europe[38] where the Baby Boomer generation was retiring free of mortgages and on comfortable pensions.

However, let's go back twenty years to 2005, when only a few people – other than the Originals – could see the potential for MENA to be a hive of technological growth. From the large reservoir of those under 30 emerged a small group of entrepreneurs: unconnected, working alone or in small teams across a region spanning thousands of miles. They came from diverse backgrounds and had one thing in common – a thirst for innovation. Starting with limited resources, no funding ecosystem, and no mentors, most of the Originals had to pivot at speed when their initial ideas were met by deafening silence. Yet the results they achieved were remarkable.

This is the story of Samih, Ronnie, Mudassir and Magnus, Rabea, Mona, Michael, and Hosam. Each unique; each a true Original.

AMMAN, JORDAN
SAMIH TOUKAN

"I walked into the small internet café and typed 'Jordan' – my home country – into Yahoo!, and I was blown away," Samih Toukan recalls, eyes lighting up with the memory from 1994. In that moment, Samih knew they had to bring this technology to the Arab world. The only problem was the Middle East was far from internet-ready. Local internet providers didn't exist; to connect, users had to dial into European servers and be charged long-distant fees for each minute, which led to exorbitant international phone bills.

At the time, Samih had already taken a leap of faith leaving his secure consulting job and teaming up with Hussam Khoury to start a management consulting firm in Jordan. At the time, the concept of consulting was still foreign in the Middle East. "Back then, consulting was an unknown concept in our region," Samih reflected. Their first client, Fadi Ghandour at Aramex, was drawn to their innovative approach to reengineering processes and optimising systems, which quickly garnered them credibility and validation. Samih never imagined that his journey with this company would become the foundation for one of the Arab world's first tech giants.

As the internet gradually found its way into the region, Samih and Hussam began to realise the limitations of their consulting work. "Consulting wasn't scalable; we were selling our hours," Samih explained. They began experimenting with building websites and found an immense language barrier, but the lack of infrastructure and resources didn't deter the team; if anything, it galvanised them to create something meaningful for the region. "If the internet was going to spread in the Arab world, the Arabic language would be essential," he noted. From this insight, the idea for Maktoob – a name that means "letter" in Arabic – was born. They envisioned an Arabic-language email service, a culturally resonant alternative to Hotmail, that would connect Arabic-speaking users to the digital world.

Maktoob's success was far from instant. Bootstrapped from the beginning, they frequently encountered competitors who had significantly more funding. "Arabia Online had $22 million in backing while we flew economy class," Samih chuckles, recalling the humble circumstances of their early days. Despite financial constraints, the team focused relentlessly on refining their email service, building an intuitive and accessible platform while educating users about the internet itself. The results spoke for themselves: users grew from 10,000 to 100,000, and eventually, millions of Arabic speakers were logging onto Maktoob.

As the platform gained momentum, Samih's vision continued to grow. Over the years, as they scaled Maktoob and introduced millions to the online world, they helped shift perceptions about the region's digital potential. By 2009, Maktoob had attracted a massive 16 million users, a feat that captured the attention of Yahoo!.

The region Samih and Hussam first set out to serve was vastly different from today's Middle East. As Samih reflected, "We had to digitally go to Europe to get access. We had to pay hefty phone bills just to learn about the internet, let alone build for it."

Samih's journey with Maktoob wasn't just a story of building a tech company – it was the beginning of a larger digital transformation across the Arab world.

ALEPPO, SYRIA
RONALDO MOUCHAWAR

Ronaldo Mouchawar refused to go inside. He knew it was dark and could hear his mother calling him in for dinner, but he just wanted a few more minutes to shoot a few more balls. With a focused aim, the ball sailed through the air, hitting its mark – a perfect shot. It was a sign of things to come: despite everybody telling him that he should follow a more traditional career, Ronnie was determined to play basketball, and the 14-year-old boy in Aleppo knew that whatever he set his mind to, he could achieve.

Years later, a professional basketball player for Syria's foremost basketball team, Jalaa SC Aleppo, Ronnie was also studying at

Northeastern University in Boston. He was determined to become a sports star; and his family was determined for him to study – so he did both. His dual passions for sports and learning gave him a unique perspective, but it was the rise of e-commerce in the late 90s that would change the course of his life. Inspired by what he saw, he realised that the internet was on the brink of global transformation – and it was time to transition away from basketball.

With that foresight, Ronnie came back to the region to join Samih at Maktoob, the region's pioneering Arabic-first web portal, established in 1999. Initially, he concentrated on finding ways to connect Maktoob's large user base with online shoppers; but having observed where some of the biggest players in the US had made mistakes, he quickly understood Maktoob's strength lay in its ability to share information, not drive sales. Working from his apartment, he learned by observing people's online behaviour that both sharing information and driving sales could not take place on a single platform. Since the business models were not synergistic, the only way was to create a subsidiary auction-site.

"Inspired by Alibaba, we launched Souq.com in 2005, initially as a mobile phone and laptop marketplace," recalls Ronnie. "People were familiar with these products, and they were price sensitive, making them ideal for an online market." By 2009, Souq had become an independent entity, handling over $1 million in auction transactions every month.

Ronnie and his colleagues were convinced that the region was going to leapfrog and that the young population who didn't use laptops for shopping were never going to use them – they were going to use the iPhone, which had just come out in 2007. As they observed the rise of Alibaba and smartphone penetration in China, the founders decided to look East for inspiration rather than West. "We began reaching out to consumers who had never used laptops, particularly in Saudi Arabia and Egypt. These were mobile-first customers focused on comparing prices, allowing them to choose between different vendors and prices." The region was beginning to leapfrog – forgetting what was current and going immediately to what was coming next.

Together with his business partners, Samih Toukan and Hussam Khoury, Ronaldo's new targets were the small businesses who wanted to sell more than phones. They also recognised that to truly add value and build retailer loyalty they needed to offer much more than access to customers – and had to venture into payments and logistics. The move from an auction site to an e-commerce player was immediately met with resistance from sellers, who would now face the challenge of leaving the freedom of the auction site and competing with thousands of sellers and millions of stock keeping unit (SKUs). They had not anticipated this reaction.

"We quickly realised that the two components required for e-commerce to work well were logistics and payments. Those were the big gaps in the region. The only delivery services were provided by third party players, and they were really geared to either documents, bank documents and document transports or large B2B transport across countries. There wasn't anything about last mile delivery and consumer capabilities. Obviously, Aramex was there; Fadi Ghandour was there. He was supporting us, but somehow also with cash on delivery habits, the lack of addresses, the lack of use of technology in delivery, we felt there was just the gap between where the cost of delivery needed to be and where it was. Somehow, managing payments and the speed of delivery were gaps, so we quickly started looking to raise funds to fix these problems. Naspers and Tiger Global came on board."

Their response – a key aspect of the way the Originals built their businesses – was to provide a solution that would not only enable payments, which were still largely cash, but streamline them. The challenge was to allow the Souq platform to interface with bank systems operating on different IT systems. Instead of attempting to tackle this complex software design challenge internally, they treated the payment product as a standalone project, leading to the creation of PayFort.

"Our goal was simple: we needed to manage the cash flow of our merchants without draining our own resources – we were already stretched thin trying to fuel our own growth. Funding the working capital of our merchants was simply out of the question. But we couldn't sit back. Instead, we focused on creating tools that would give us control over cash flow, tools that would change everything for our merchants. We started working with logistics companies, trying to quickly recover cash that was being tied up in their own operations. We kept telling ourselves, 'We need to make sure the merchant gets paid within three days,' because without that, everything else would fall apart. This mindset led to the creation of PayFort, which went on to become the leading online payment provider in the Middle East. Today, it's a pillar of the region's e-commerce ecosystem, but in its early days, it was a lifeline. Now, Souq's transactions make up less than half of its business – what we built evolved far beyond what we imagined."

Just as Souq had been spun off from Maktoob and gone on to become a success story of its own; PayFort went on to become one of the region's leading payment providers, independently of Souq, expanding its customer base to other businesses across the region.

In 2013, Souq had evolved but still resembled its 2005 origins. The principles of e-commerce were refined, and positioning between East and West gave the founders a unique perspective. Dubai, though not yet a global hub for travel, provided access to new ideas and capital. What had changed was consumer behaviour – phones became the primary means of interaction, while payment methods lagged behind. Cash-on-delivery (CoD) was dominant, with low credit card penetration, creating a significant burden for merchants.

In response, the Souq team built a multi-function digital system linking cash-paying customers to higher-priced products and enabled delivery agents to log payments instantly via an app. This streamlined process made a significant impact, reducing consumer hesitation around buying unseen products.

Payments sorted – now for logistics.

The sea of road networks was continually evolving as Dubai's growth was exploding. Roundabouts appeared overnight, and roads that were closed off suddenly became the only way to get to the nascent communities being built. Given the speed of growth, confusion was inevitable. Until recently, and even now, many countries in the MENA region do not have postal codes, or even road names, which complicates the process of locating delivery and drop-off points using methods that had been developed with road names and postal codes in mind. How could deliveries reach homes that were address-less? With the best directions possible being "Take the first right after the gas station, then first left by the grocery store, then it's the sixth house on the right-hand side." Only a home-grown solution was going to find the answer to this issue, not least because no one in Silicon Valley was having sleepless nights wondering how to do last-mile delivery of parcels to an area with no street names.

Google was overstretched in mapping the built world, let alone the parts still under construction. Mis-deliveries didn't just end up at the wrong doorstep, sometimes they would end up in the wrong country. To exacerbate the problem, third-party couriers were inefficient and unreliable. Souq saw all of this and decided to take matters into its own hands. Their delivery network began with a small fleet of in-house drivers, crucially with local knowledge, and quickly expanded. While mapping software was being built, they used phones with embedded geolocation and shared mapping software and built up a picture of their areas of delivery long before Google Maps arrived. By using the same devices customers used to make purchases on Souq, the company could efficiently handle last-mile delivery.

So Ronnie and his team applied the same logic of business development to a region still making up the rules of how technology and commerce were going to interact. Q Express was born, offering e-commerce distribution, including warehousing, ordering, inventory management and product packaging, and further validating the need for the Originals to build the requisite infrastructure in order to build their companies.

In 2017, Amazon acquired Souq for $580 million in what was celebrated as an incredible success story for the region – it was the first time that Amazon had made an acquisition as a geographical expansion, not a vertical integration. This was seen by many as an acknowledgment that Souq's unrivalled understanding and penetration of the region was not something even a behemoth like Amazon could compete with.

"From that day forward, I've seen the region's e-commerce landscape evolve dramatically – not just in terms of the quality and range of offerings, but also in the sheer convenience it provides. Today, many players in the Middle East deliver same-day or next-day, outperforming global benchmarks in several metrics and surpassing the efficiency of numerous markets worldwide," explains Ronnie as he reflects on the evolution of the e-commerce sector, comparing where it once was to where it stands today.

Today, if you type "Souq.com" into your search bar, you will be seamlessly redirected to Amazon.ae – a shift that marked a new chapter in e-commerce across the Middle East. Rapidly expanding its presence, Amazon established a robust logistics network in the UAE, including fulfilment centres and delivery stations that set new standards for speed and convenience, becoming a favourite among nearly half of online shoppers, capitalising on what Souq had built over the years. With the launch of Prime membership and home services, Amazon deepened its reach and appeal.

Souq, having enabled Amazon to come into the region, went beyond giving consumers access to e-commerce, but also provided financial and logistics solutions for e-commerce.

Through Amazon Web Services (AWS), Amazon continued to expand in the region, establishing cloud infrastructure first in Bahrain, then in the UAE and in Saudi Arabia, driving digital transformation and empowering other players in the digital market. "We're committed to helping sellers become successful, not only in the region, some of them are now becoming large enough to think 'we have a brand, how can we tap into other markets like Europe? How can we tap into the US?'" Ronaldo explained.

This strategic focus on both commerce and technology cemented Amazon's role as a regional innovator and digital leader. Ronaldo also highlights that 'Arabising' Alexa was one of the most exciting projects bringing Amazon into the region.

Thinking back to his basketball days, Ronnie reflects "Sometimes, you can see in my meetings where basketball comes up. I think the idea that you are a team, you have basketball, you play offence and defence. So, it's one of those unique sports where you have to have multiple skills, it's not one. It's a team sport, so even if you have stars, you don't win all the time. Actually, you miss more shots than you make in most of the games that you play."

DUBAI, UNITED ARAB EMIRATES
MUDASSIR SHEIKHA AND MAGNUS OLSSON

This brain aneurysm could have cost him his life. Magnus Olsson was terrified. It was 2011 and he was experiencing good health until he suddenly had to pause his life and focus on his health. In a big way. A Dubai-based McKinsey & Company consultant, he had not seen this moment coming.

"I realised I had to do something more purposeful with my life," says Magnus, in a disarmingly honest admission. His voice cracks slightly as he reflects on the gravity of that decision. "I had no idea what that purpose was going to be, but I was going to find it. I knew I wanted it to be about doing something for others. I also wanted to do something big. Because if I was going to do something meaningful, why do something small and meaningful? I might as well do something big and meaningful."

It was in a café in Dubai that a handful of friends, including Mudassir Sheikha, began to meet regularly to discuss potential ideas for investment and companies that could be big and meaningful. No idea was off the table. The simple premise of the gathering was to kick the tires on any ideas put forward to see whether they would stand up to scrutiny. They considered healthcare, education, and even fish farms. But it was a casual comment from an ex-colleague that sparked the idea which would change everything. The McKinsey team's frequent struggle to find reliable transportation across the region opened the door to something bigger – something no one had yet attempted in the Middle East.

"Twelve years ago, the ecosystem was not ready for start-ups. Everything was harder – starting with basic logistics," shares Mudassir, his voice laced with the memories of those early days. "Simple things, like accepting credit card payments, required $30,000 deposits and there were other roadblocks. Office spaces demanded upfront yearly payments, draining capital needed for business growth. The hurdles were immense. We had to constantly fight to just survive."

In the midst of these frustrations, a chance remark about McKinsey's Middle East-based employees struggling to find reliable transportation, sparked the kind of discussion that inspired a plan that can put a dent in the universe. Both agree: the idea came from nowhere, but by the time the group left the café, the idea was in place. It was decided on the spot that if Magnus and Mudassir chose to look at how to solve the problem of transportation for McKinsey, then the global management consultancy might become a customer.

It was an opportunity that was hard to resist, but Magnus was hesitant. "I'd been given a second chance in life and I'm going to build a car booking service for people in suits? That didn't feel like the most meaningful thing in the world. But the more we looked at it, the more we realised that there was an opportunity to have an impact." Magnus laughs as he remembers. There was a deep internal struggle, with a part of him wanting to do something larger than just solving the logistical inconvenience of the elite.

Yet, as the days passed, something shifted. They saw the potential impact on the lives of millions, including hard-working taxi drivers, not just the few. And so, despite the odds, they pushed forward – driven by a belief that this wasn't just about creating another service, but about creating something that would truly simplify life and unleash human potential. "For us, it wasn't just about building a company – it was about creating something that would stand the test of time, something that would serve the region in ways no one had anticipated." Mudassir continues.

In 2012, Mudassir and Magnus set out to build the first major ride-hailing company in the Middle East. Transitioning to entrepreneurship brought a significant shift in their perspectives. From the start, they agreed a large focus would be on drivers' well-being. "We had this notion that we could not only create job opportunities and provide a sustained income, but we could also upskill and train them and make sure they were treated with respect," explains Magnus.

Careem, after all, means generous in Arabic.

Careem launched on 22 July 2012 – the first day of Ramadan that year, and the founders were celebrating – they had managed to raise $100,000 – a huge achievement and an enormous figure at that time. They found and rented the most affordable office they could find – Shatha Tower in Dubai. Their office furniture was bought for 1,000 dirhams (approximately $300) from a bankrupt travel agent in Bur Dubai and both Mudassir and Magnus became masters of frugality. They caught the bus between Abu Dhabi and Dubai and had a clear-cut purpose on the most minimal of budgets: to simplify and improve the lives of people and to build an awesome organisation that inspires.

As Uber entered the region and the two companies competed neck and neck with each other to secure market share across the region, Mudassir and Magnus realised that they had to build differently and play to their local advantage. To begin with, the MENA region was still a cash-reliant economy and so they had to solve the challenge of drivers accepting cash as payment, and that payment being collected. Addressing and solving this challenge allowed them to gain market share and lead the regional ride-hailing opportunity. Solving other cultural differences such as advance booking and calling a call-centre further accelerated Careem's growth over Uber's. Understanding the cultural nuances and regional dynamics was a prerequisite for success.

As Careem grew in the UAE and Saudi Arabia, it also garnered traction in other markets around the region, working closely with regulators to ensure security and a streamlined approach to transportation. But it didn't stop there, Careem's growth also helped spur the growth of the wider start-up ecosystem.

In the years that followed, Careem raised some of the largest rounds of funding in MENA, becoming the region's first tech unicorn in 2016 and then being acquired by Uber in 2019, the largest acquisition of its kind in the region. The acquisition by Uber, though a monumental achievement, was not the end. It was the start of something bigger. Careem now operates in seventy cities across ten countries, from Morocco to Pakistan, creating earnings for over 2.5 million captains and serving more than 50 million customers.

"Our goal has always been and will always be simplifying people's lives." As they looked East, at the mobile revolution in Asia, they saw the rise of superapps and realised that the region would likely follow suit. Careem's transformation into a superapp, designed to simplify the lives of its customers, was inevitable. "We started as a ride-hailing service," Mudassir says, his voice filled with nostalgia and excitement. "But that was just the first chapter of our story. Now, we're an 'everything app,' your digital butler for everyday life." The app now allows customers to order food, schedule laundry pickups, book rental cars, pay bills, and even request house cleaning.

Reflecting on how far they've come, Magnus smiles. "Careem was born out of a problem," he says, his voice filled with emotion, "but it has evolved into a solution that has touched millions. What began as a simple idea over coffee in a café has become something much bigger. It's a story of transformation, of fighting through adversity, and of ultimately building something meaningful that serves not just a few, but an entire region."

RABEA ATAYA

The plane started its descent and Rabea Ataya was frustrated. He put away his tray-table as the seat-belt sign lit but wanted to continue writing. He had finally reached the point where he felt he had some great ideas! On his way home back to Dubai after what felt like another pointless business meeting, Rabea was trying figure out what he wanted to do next in life and had begun brainstorming some ideas in his notebook. When he had reached fifty ideas, he had started to narrow them down, and now he had to stop his process and prepare for landing. His thoughts continued though, and upon disembarking, he made the commitment to himself that it was time to choose one and relentlessly pursue it – and so, the seed for InfoFort, Rabea's records management platform was sown.

Though Rabea's idea was simple and powerful, this was just the beginning. The next challenge was to find the funding to make it happen. With no capital of his own, Rabea went to his natural financier – his father. When he requested money to start his new venture, his father asked, "How much money do you need?" to which Rabea threw out a random number. In response, his father asked, "where is your business plan". "I don't have one," Rabea admitted. His father then told him, "Go create a business plan and then we will talk."'

Rabea questioned what had made him move back to the Middle East in the first place. Having completed his master's at Stanford University and landed a high-powered investment banking job at Alex. Brown & Sons, on paper, he had been firmly on the path to success. He had a coveted dream job, one that he had worked so hard to land and that he had believed would allow him to ride the wave of Silicon Valley's dot-com boom. Yet, something hadn't sat right with him. "It was the classic path. Everything looks great on paper, but inside, I felt a pull, something that said, 'This isn't it. There is something else I'm meant to do," Rabea recalls. And that was it – Rabea quit his comfortable lifestyle in the US and came back to the region to focus on the opportunity he saw back home.

At first, he took the easy route – a secure job with his father in the construction business. Despite the stability the role offered, Rabea found construction to be a highly cyclical industry, having to deal many suppliers, hundreds of variables, bad payment cycles and different types of people. With each passing day, Rabea felt a growing sense of dissatisfaction – he needed something more. "I needed to go out and become an entrepreneur," he says.

Now, in 1997, Rabea found himself between balancing responsibilities and cranking out eighteen-hour workdays with his father in his construction business and struggling to find time to put together his plan – yet, with no other funding options. He remained steadfast in his goal. When the plan was finally ready, InfoFort was born. The early days were tough and he worried constantly about disappointing his father. As the months wore on, he was increasingly closer to running out of cash, and Rabea grew concerned about the lack of traction – nobody seemed to want his records management system.

Then, all of a sudden, securing their first client, a bank, marked a pivotal moment. "Suddenly, the floodgates opened, and all other customers were happy to sign on," Rabea recalls. Within two years, InfoFort was not just a profitable business; it had expanded across multiple cities, generating 50 per cent net margins and growing its revenue by over 100 per cent year on year.

But soon, Rabea was bored. He had been watching the internet boom in the late 1990s, and wanted to be a part of it. He was ready to jump onto the next challenge. 'I realised that while the records management business was very profitable and highly rewarding financially, it didn't satisfy a different need of mine, and that need was to contribute to the community." Reflecting on building InfoFort, Rabea realised that his biggest challenge in building the company had been access to talent. While he had faced the challenge himself, he also realised its impact on the region. With some of the highest levels of youth unemployment in the world being in MENA, and the highest proportion of migrant labour, Rabea saw an opportunity to leverage the power of the internet to connect talent to jobs. While job creation was one aspect, effectively connecting people to existing opportunities was hindered by a lack of technology and infrastructure – with internet penetration at less than 1 per cent at the time, most people had never used the internet for anything beyond email, and online job searching was almost unheard of. The need to address this gap presented a chance to build a business that could positively impact the community pushed Rabea to create Bayt.com in 2000 – an online platform that would change the way people in the Middle East found jobs.

"My co-founders and I dove in head first. Launching an internet business in the aftermath of the dot-com era, known then as the dot-bomb era, and with little to no capital available in the market seemed absolutely mad at the time. But we were committed to making it work." Rabea laughs, "We decided to raise just one round of financing, and decided that if we didn't become profitable within that round, we'd shut down." Their dedication paid off, and within eighteen months, Bayt.com was not only profitable by cash flow positive. "We never had to raise a second round of funding. What was more remarkable was that we were able to build a business that would endure and grow, becoming the longest-running internet business in the MENA region."

That said, the journey was never easy. There were moments of intense financial strain, where the future of the company seemed uncertain. "It's always scary, even now," Rabea admits. "But when you're young, you have so much less to lose, and that's what gives you the courage to take big risks." This sense of freedom and optimism was essential in a time when the future seemed uncertain. In the same vein, a valuable lesson that enabled Rabea and the team to help lay the foundation for generations to come was the importance of building sustainable businesses. "We were born of a different generation, where businesses were defined by their profitability, not by their valuations," Rabea recounts. "Our focus on long-term growth, free from the pressures of chasing perpetual rounds of funding, has allowed Bayt.com to thrive as a profitable, cash-flow positive business for over two decades, and it continues to grow."

Today, Bayt.com not only stands tall as one of the region's most successful businesses, but along the way, has also helped create other successful ventures, including the region's first e-commerce exit, GoNabit, which was built and sold to Living Social, and Mumzworld, which was incubated within Bayt's infrastructure. "We are exporting technology from the Middle East to North America, with Vfairs, one of the leading virtual event platforms globally." Rabea is focused on the future – continuing to invest in businesses that aim to bridge the digital divide and fuel innovation across the region. He reflects on his path with the belief that every risk and every leap of faith was worth it, and still, the best is yet to come.

MONA ATAYA

For Mona Ataya, a determined and articulate woman with a clear vision for the future, the opportunity to solve the talent puzzle in the Arab world led her back to Dubai in the early 2000s.

Mona has always been driven by curiosity and a strong work ethic. From a young age, she embraced learning in all areas of her life, whether in school, college, or her career. In college, she kept a journal, documenting her discoveries and observations, which reflected her keen awareness of her surroundings and dissatisfaction with the status quo. Her optimism, rooted in her Palestinian upbringing, reinforced her belief that anything was possible, with education seen as the key to success. Whether in academics or sports, she was self-motivated, driven by personal satisfaction rather than external validation.

This drive extended into her professional life. Undeterred by limitations, Mona pursued roles at Procter & Gamble as an undergraduate, even though the company typically only hired graduates. Her persistence secured her positions at P&G and Johnson & Johnson, eventually leading her to entrepreneurship.

At the time, she was living in Zurich, working for Johnson & Johnson, and enjoying what she called her "picture-perfect life". However, she began to question her future: "Do I want to keep climbing the corporate ladder, or be the master of my own destiny?" Driven by a desire to give back to her home region and her belief in entrepreneurship's power to create social impact, Mona embraced the risks. Despite knowing the challenges, like losing stability and income, her values and readiness to make a difference outweighed the negatives of the entrepreneurial route.

With a wealth of experience building winning global brands, she co-founded Bayt in 2000 with her brother, Rabea Ataya, who still leads Bayt.com to this date.

Bayt.com was founded to help solve the massive youth unemployment problem in the MENA region. The MENA region has the highest proportion of migrant labour in the world and the highest youth unemployment rates. Obstacles to the free flow of information prevented employers and jobseekers efficiently discovering each other. With the advent of the internet, Bayt was able to leverage the tools of open, internet communication to effectively match opportunity and talent.

In 2001, the Arabic version of Bayt.com was launched. Bayt.com opened offices in Kuwait and Bahrain to expand the region's employment market, and in May of the same year, the Jeddah office was opened. In October 2002, Rabea Ataya, CEO of Bayt.com, was awarded the 2002 Arabian Business "e-Entrepreneur of the Year" award and recognised by His Highness Sheikh Mohammed Bin Rashid Al Maktoum. In December 2006, Bayt.com received the Sheikh Hamdan Bin Rashid Al Maktoum Award for "Best Website in the UAE" at the 2006 UAE Web Awards. While other start-ups in the MENA region struggled in their first years, Bayt became profitable soon after its launch.

Today, Bayt is the longest running internet business in the MENA region. On the Bayt.com platform is over 53 million professionals who have built their profiles seeking better opportunities, growing at the rate of over 5 million new registered users annually. In most geographies Bayt operates, over half of the online labour population has their CV on the site. Bayt also serves tens of thousands of employers.

Over the years, Bayt has also used its considerable experience to build out other successful businesses in the world of tech. Examples include building the first group buying site, GoNabit, which was the first successful e-commerce exit in the region. Bayt also currently operates vFairs, a leading global event tech business, that derives 90 per cent of its revenue from North America; Talentera, the leading ATS SAAS provider in the MENA, serving most of the large banks, dozens of government entities, and hundreds of corporates; YallaMotor, the most comprehensive and leading autoclassified in the UAE; and more.

Bayt was then one of the earliest digital players to secure international venture capital funding.

A decade later, in the classic entrepreneurial spirit, Mona was called to another opportunity in the region. Drawing on her experience of the fragmented consumer market that she addressed with Bayt, along with her vibrant personality and determination, she turned to an issue that was much closer to home, both literally and metaphorically.

The mother-consumer had many unmet needs, including an inability to access the products she needed for her children at an affordable price," says Mona. Mona had always been attentive to the details that others missed. In Saudi Arabia, for example, mothers faced a unique dilemma; until 2018, women were not permitted to drive, which complicated their access to even the simplest necessities. Mona knew that empowering these women meant more than just providing products; it meant building an accessible, reliable platform tailored to their needs. And so, driven by a deep empathy for her fellow mothers, she set out to create Mumzworld, a dedicated online marketplace that would connect millions of women to an array of quality products for babies, children, and mothers – at the right price, delivered to their doorsteps. Her vision was to create a transactional and experiential platform for mothers through the widest product choice, convenience and the best everyday low prices and an engaged community to empower mothers to make the most informed decisions for their families.

But the road ahead wasn't straightforward. Mumzworld was entering a true 'blue ocean' market when e-commerce penetration in the Middle East was minimal, and no major player had tapped into the needs of mothers. As Mona described it, "E-commerce was a $1.6 trillion industry globally, but in the Middle East, it was still nascent."

Mona grappled with the challenge of navigating the vast array of non-homogeneous products housed on the Mumzworld platform, from nappies and cribs to branded baby clothes. Success in this vertical-specific e-commerce space hinged on maintaining an extensive, readily available inventory of stock keeping units (SKUs) while keeping prices competitive in a demanding market. Mumzworld's key advantage was its ability to achieve solid unit economics, ensuring the business could scale efficiently despite its complex product mix and supply chain. Additionally, Mumzworld's community features of content and deep entrenchment in the mother community set it apart from any other digital players at the time and created sticky features that kept mothers coming back to the platform again and again.

However, balancing regional specificity with a world-class operational model required constant adjustments. Expanding from Saudi Arabia to the broader GCC market introduced even more complexity, from navigating differing market dynamics and regulatory landscapes to meeting diverse customer expectations. As Mona reflects, "The fact that MENA is a fragmented market made matters worse and meant that tapping into the right products at the right time was difficult." Each country had its own rules and supply chains, and Mona found herself negotiating a patchwork of regulations, cultural expectations, and distribution bottlenecks. Where others saw insurmountable obstacles, Mona saw opportunities to innovate. Every country required its own strategy, and she became skilled at pivoting her approach to meet each market's unique demands.

The supply chain was a particular pain point – unreliable and inefficient, it often undermined her company's ability to optimise and scale quickly. "The immaturity of our supply chain meant we were frequently at the mercy of unpredictable systems," she explained. Suppliers struggled to keep up with demand, forcing Mona to continuously adapt and innovate. Even as her business displayed strong unit economics, these operational challenges slowed progress and demanded relentless problem-solving. "When margins across e-commerce were under 15 per cent, we operated with gross product margins over 40 per cent – a rarity at the time," Mona reflected, highlighting the strategic vision and discipline that drove her success.

As Mumzworld scaled, challenges persisted. Mona grappled with the realities of running a high-growth start-up. She had to make difficult decisions: managing supply chains, expanding logistics networks, and building a resilient team. Further still, securing funding was an ongoing challenge, particularly as women-led ventures secured less than 1 per cent of an already limited pool of venture funding. E-commerce too, was not a popular space for investors at the time, who viewed it as high-risk, capital intensive, and with a challenging road to profitability. Nevertheless, Mona and her team managed to raise six rounds of funding, making Mumzworld one of the most funded women-led e-commerce businesses in the region. This however, did limit the pace of scaling, as Mona was forced to balance her time between securing capital and managing the complex demands of the company's operations. In 2014, during Mumzworld's Series B round, Mona tapped into her creativity once again by opening a funding round exclusively for women. She believed that since women were Mumzworld's primary customers, it was only right that they be representative of the brand they were building. This unique round was highly successful, attracting women from across the region as early investors and weaving them into the broader ecosystem story.

Each challenge that Mona faced was met with her trademark persistence. Mumzworld's impact began to grow, catching the attention of the region's consumers and industry giants alike. Her platform didn't just sell products; it offered something revolutionary – a community. For the first time, mothers in the region could access reviews, compare prices, and make informed decisions, enabling them to feel confident in their choices for their families. By 2021, Mumzworld had reached an astounding tenfold growth, capturing the attention of Tamer Group, a leading Saudi retail conglomerate.

When Tamer Group extended a proposal, Mona was once again faced with a choice. Letting go of Mumzworld, her "fourth child", was not easy. But she recognised that the partnership could provide her beloved company with the resources, scale, and reach necessary for the next phase of its growth. "With Tamer Group's scale, size, reputation and regional know-how, our combined complementary entity will be transformative for the region," says Mona.

Today, Mumzworld services more than 3 million mothers across the region, offering an extensive range of products and creating a digital ecosystem that connects mothers, retailers, distributors, manufacturers, and brands.

MICHAEL LAHYANI

Michael looked at the number on the phone – his uncle never called him and he hadn't seen him in over a year. What could he want – was he okay? Michael answered hesitantly. "Where? Brunei? Oh, Dubai. I know nothing about Dubai." It was 2004 and the invitation to visit his uncle who had started a construction company and was building a palm-shaped island in Dubai was quite peculiar, especially for Michael, who was working in corporate finance in Geneva.

Born in Geneva to a Moroccan father and a French mother, Michael's life had been shaped by stability and tradition. His future seemed predetermined, with clear pathways toward careers in medicine, law, or engineering. After studying at the top Swiss business school, Hautes Etudes Commerciale (HEC) in Lausanne, Michael felt a desire to explore something slightly different, which eventually led him to spend a year at UCLA. In March 2004, Michael landed in Dubai for the first time, where his uncle introduced him to a city still largely made up of desert.

"My first time on the Palm," Michael reflects, "I was struck by two things: the sheer ambition of turning an ocean into a residential island with thousands of homes, and the speed with which Dubai's business environment moved. While the construction itself didn't excite me, I became captivated by what would happen after the homes were built. How would people know these properties existed? How would they be sold?"

That moment sparked something in Michael. It was clear there was an opportunity to create something that could change the landscape. By 2005, he launched Dubai's first property classifieds magazine, a simple but revolutionary move to help people find homes, with its website. It was distributed for free, and quickly became a trusted resource for agents and advertisers. Michael's innovative approach to organising the listings by location set him apart from the competition. It was a breakthrough and the momentum seemed unstoppable. Revenues were growing and he was on track to make large profits!

But as quickly as it came, that momentum came to a screeching halt. Half of Michael's clients cancelled contracts as another publication had signed them to exclusivity agreements which they decided to enforce. "I was in disbelief," shares Michael, "And out of business. Of course, none of my clients would continue to work with me if they would lose access to advertising in the classified section of the largest newspaper in the country."

"One day, I was invited to what I thought would be a usual meeting, but turned out to be one of the most important moments of my entrepreneurial journey – meeting the REA group." At that time, in 2007, Michael was feeling the weight of bootstrapping a business in Dubai, with little or no venture capital available in the region. Yet, as he sat across from executives of REA, he found himself captivated by their success story – a publicly listed company, backed by News Corp, generating $100 million in revenue with 45 per cent margins in exactly his business line. The numbers were staggering, especially for a business operating off a simple website. It was a pivotal moment for Michael. He realised the print-based model he had relied on wasn't sustainable, and focusing on the online portal was the only way forward.

Over the next nine months, Michael negotiated tirelessly with REA, ultimately convincing them to acquire 51 per cent of Property Finder, and the course of his business and his life was irrevocably altered. The partnership brought financial relief but also a new business model that would revolutionise the company's future. Michael learned the power of the subscription model, which offered consistent, recurring revenue without the constant need for new sales.

"For the first time, I was able to pay myself a salary. That was the real start of the journey and a turning point that transformed Property Finder. That's when I knew we were on the right track."

And just in time. One year after the investment, in 2008, the Global Financial Crisis affected the world and the region intensely. "Nobody wanted to buy real estate in Dubai. Or anywhere really. The real estate market crashed. I had to ask myself: do I even have a business anymore?" Michael says. "But my conviction in Dubai was unwavering. I knew I had to continue. I negotiated to buy out REA and kept going."

As the market recovered, so did Property Finder. With renewed determination, the company expanded across the region, growing into Bahrain, Egypt, Qatar, Saudi Arabia and Turkey, and attracted significant investment, including from General Atlantic. The team grew to 600 employees and today, Property Finder is valued at over $1 billion, reaching unicorn status and contributing to the wider property market in the region to provide intelligence into a sector that was once known as one of the key legacy sectors in MENA. And Michael strongly believes that what lies ahead is even more exciting:

"When you look at the TAM (total addressable market) that's ahead of us, you know, we're still getting started. Although it's been twenty years, there is a lot more growth ahead of us than there is behind us."

HOSAM ARAB

Working at Schlumberger after his electrical engineering degree, Hosam was bored. After moving to GE a few years earlier and gaining further engineering experience, he decided to switch paths and pursue his MBA at Harvard. There, he caught the entrepreneurship bug and started thinking about new ideas and businesses. Returning to the region after his MBA and starting a career in private equity, Hosam Arab couldn't shake the feeling that something was missing. He had a deep desire to create something of his own.

In 2011, Hosam decided to examine the region's e-commerce landscape more closely. Comparing it to more advanced markets like the US, he identified a glaring gap in fashion e-commerce. This realisation was the spark he had been waiting for. He knew he could fill this void. Hosam's drive, combined with his straightforward, no-nonsense approach, laid the foundation for Namshi. This had never been done before.

Hosam embarked on his entrepreneurial journey fully aware of the challenges and mysteries that lay ahead. He embraced it with determination and curiosity. As Namshi grew, he realised the need to strike a balance, constantly learning and optimising to propel the business forward.

At the outset, the challenge for Hosam and his co-founders was to persuade brands to trust Namshi and agree to sell their inventory through the platform given their strong convictions about regional consumer preferences around their scepticism towards digital platforms. They faced significant resistance until Nike came on board, which opened the doors to a wider range of brands and significantly increased their market credibility. Convincing Nike wasn't easy – it took persistent effort, countless meetings, and finding a key internal champion who believed in Namshi's vision. This individual had witnessed the success of e-commerce in other markets and saw potential in what Namshi was building in the region. After many discussions, he brought in Nike's team from Europe, and while the process wasn't quick, it ultimately paved the way for their breakthrough.

He and his co-founders, Faraz Khalid, Hisham Zarka, Hosam Arab, Louis Lebbos, and Muhammed Mekki, immersed themselves in every aspect of the company, from understanding consumer needs to building Namshi from the ground up, all while focusing on enhancing and refining and expanding operations. The cash-on-delivery culture meant setting up payment systems, until Payfort was built; and last-mile deliveries were very 'local' with few solutions. The Namshi founders did what they could and scaled the business bit by bit, using different parts of international and regional infrastructure to solve each pain-point along the way. Given the early quality of the region's existing infrastructure, they set about building e-commerce capabilities in-house, including their own logistics facility in Dubai, a delivery network, and a fleet of drivers – initially in the UAE and then later across other markets.

"The team continually tested new ideas, maintaining a lean approach of experimenting, refining, and optimising operations to boost customer retention," he reflected. "Our philosophy was to test widely, keep what worked, and accept that not everything would succeed." Though building supplier and consumer trust took time, under the leadership of Hosam, Namshi was transformed into a resounding success, demonstrating that Hosam's instinct to build and innovate was precisely what the region needed.

As Namshi grew into a regional retail leader, it initially attracted Rocket as one of its early investors, bringing with it a portfolio of leading retail players. Namshi's further growth caught Emaar's attention, sparking interest in how the platform could complement the conglomerate and help bring it further into the digital world. In

2017, Emaar acquired a majority stake in Namshi and completed its full acquisition two years later. Hosam felt great pride in that milestone at the time: "I felt like I was entrusting Namshi to capable hands, knowing that Emaar's leadership would open new doors for our team and elevate the business to greater heights."

Building on that success, Namshi was sold to Noon for over $335 million in 2022. Today, Namshi and Noon, continuing to operate within the realm of Faraz, one of the Namshi co-founders, alongside Amazon, stand as the top three retail platforms within the MENA region, shaping an e-commerce sector that barely existed twenty years ago.

Bringing it all together were the Originals who founded, created, and shaped it. With support of progressive regulators and governmental policies, they were part of a generation of start-up entrepreneurs who can be seen as the catalyst of what MENA has become. They laid the first bricks and broke many glass ceilings in the process. They helped turn the region into a magnet for other like-minded individuals, for international stakeholders and investors and helped shape what soon will become the centre for AI, Crypto and other advanced technology investments. The accelerated formation of this entrepreneurial ecosystem in turn led to the move towards the area becoming a global hub for industry focused on using AI to feed into everything from healthcare to farming, with the first Minister of Artificial Intelligence in the world announced in the UAE in 2017. Underscoring the entrepreneurial attractiveness of the region, with founders and government working in lockstep, and at the time already showing a first glimpse of the vast opportunity ahead over the many decades ahead.

CHAPTER 4

ENTREPRENEURSHIP RISING

من جد وجد

He who strives, triumphs.

– ARABIC PROVERB

WHEN VISUALISING A world where vast entrepreneurial expansion happens, we often think of a rapidly expanding city, of developments from agricultural roots to technology industries, of an influx of multi-cultural talent from across the world, of an influx of capital, of a rapidly developing infrastructure to support sustained business growth, of a progressive government support system, and of a culture of exploration and risk-taking, of a culture with purpose. Whereas this description aptly describes Dubai and Sheikh Zayed Road, it is an even stronger description of Silicon Valley in the 1970s.

Silicon Valley in the 1970s can best be described as a period of rapid technological innovation and entrepreneurial growth that laid the foundation for the region's future dominance. The period witnessed the founding of Atari, Apple and Oracle (1972, 1976 and 1977 respectively) on the operating side, as well as Kleiner Perkins and Sequoia Capital (both in 1972) on the venture capital side. At the time, the first fund of Kleiner Perkins was a mere $8 million and invested 16 per cent of that capital into a single deal (Tandem Computers). There were technological breakthroughs in the form of microprocessors by Dell and personal computing by Atari and Apple. The period also saw strong ties between Silicon Valley and the government to support NASA space programmes, laying the groundwork of the internet and creating strong ties with educational institutions like Berkley, University of California Los Angeles (UCLA), Caltech, all as strong talent feeders. It was the era when the region moved from agricultural roots to technology industry; where free-minded spirits and unconventional thinkers sought to redefine the world for the better, to pursue their purpose. In many ways, Silicon Valley in the 1970s exhibited strikingly similar elements to the MENA region today.

While these ecosystem elements are taken for granted today, they were often not available in many emerging markets at the time the Originals were building and shaping. Today's entrepreneurial ecosystems are vibrant networks that include start-ups, established firms, investors, and educational institutions, all of which contribute to an environment where innovative businesses can thrive. Many of these ecosystems are geographical centres of exploration – Silicon Valley being the most well-known. And the proximity that start-ups have to one another in these more mature markets is conducive to both formal information sharing, and job crossover as companies hire recruits from competitors. There is an informal osmosis of knowledge-sharing with many start-ups literally sharing physical workspace.

For us to assess the maturity and opportunity of the MENA entrepreneurial ecosystem, it is important to establish some form of framework to assess the various pillars that drive the growth of such network. Extensive academic and field research present various models and frameworks that illustrate how such complex systems foster and accelerate business creation and growth.

One of the most influential frameworks, which examined the drivers of innovation-driven entrepreneurship around the world, was produced by Professor Fiona Murray and Dr Phil Budden at the Massachusetts Institute of Technology (MIT) in 2017.[39] According to this framework, there are five essential components to build innovation capacity and entrepreneurship capacity, allowing the creation of entrepreneurial ecosystems:

1 **Human Capital:** defined as a mix of human talent, whether sourced locally or drawn from outside the region, equipped with the necessary education, training and experience;

2 **Funding:** understood as various forms of capital from both public and private sources that support innovation and entrepreneurial activities from inception to development, from idea to implementation or start-up to scale-up;

3 **Infrastructure:** described as the essential physical infrastructure needed at different stages of innovation and entrepreneurship, including space and equipment for research, production and managing supply chains;

4 **Demand (and Market):** including the specific level and type of demand for the products and services developed by innovation;

5 **Culture and Incentives:** defined as the influence of role models and celebrated figures, the cultural norms that dictate career choices and the incentives that drive individual and team behaviour.

In addition to these core five elements, the inclusion of governments and sovereign wealth funds as part of the market force and ecosystem enablers cannot be ignored, similar to the important influence of the government in establishing the original Silicon Valley. For the purpose of this chapter, this will be added as a sixth pillar.

This research has contributed significantly to understanding how ecosystems function, with MENA being no different. As the Originals faced their trials and tribulations on each of these while building their companies, the thoughts and reflections, and maturation of the ecosystem are astounding.

HUMAN CAPITAL

When each of the Originals decided to 'come back' to the region, or to leave their professional career to pursue a new path, there was nobody they could turn to for advice, mentorship, or who had started and completed this journey. They were not about to journey a path less travelled – they were embarking where nobody had gone and leaving a trail.

"It used to feel a bit lonely, and there was often a sense of uncertainty. We were lost. But now, there are so many peers, and a clear path on how to navigate things in the region. The precedents set over time give strength and hope to today's founders." Mudassir from Careem reflects how this was one of the hardest things about starting the company.

Dubai created 'Internet City' in 1999, but the infrastructure was not there to give individuals the freedom to work together and come up with new ideas. As a result, many individuals had to work on their projects in isolation, unable to tap into the core fundamentals that make these ecosystems function: creative energy and capital resources. The vision of the Middle East building cities for the future, out of nothing, in the middle of the desert became an apt metaphor for what these Originals had to face.

Creative isolation is a singular challenge and explains why so many of the Originals ended up completing at least a part of their formal education abroad. There, along with access to professors and teachers who had run their own businesses and could provide endless case studies of the rights and wrongs of how to build a start-up, these overseas educations gave the Originals access to a network of like-minded individuals who were better connected than they were.

In addition to finding it lonely, identifying and hiring talent, particularly luring people from top consulting firms, or finding engineers, was incredibly difficult.

Realising a vision as large as Careem's required a breadth of technical talent that simply did not exist in the region. Law, medicine, banking, and consulting were traditional career paths, not taking a risk on start-ups or entrepreneurship. "Back then, when you graduated, the aspiration was to work at a multinational," says Mudassir, who worked with Magnus at McKinsey & Company prior to the launch of Careem. "No one wanted to work at a start-up, let alone start their own company. The people we hired initially were paid AED 5,000 to 6,000 (approximately $1,500) a month. These were the only people we could attract and bring on board in our very humble beginnings. The top talent was not accessible to entrepreneurs, and if you're unable to attract that top talent, then it's very hard to build much."

"When we started, there was very little talent in the region that had experience of working at a large tech company, because we didn't have any large tech companies in the region," says Magnus. "So we had to try to convince people to come back, whether from Europe or North America. The people that joined us in the early days were brave, adventurous people, and oftentimes very young. I think at some point the average age at Careem was 25 or 26. It was a bunch of young people that just really believed in what we were doing and started doing stuff themselves, whether it was launching in new countries or launching new products."

Many who left the Middle East to study simply never returned. Whereas there were plenty of traditional jobs, even aspirational jobs within the private sector or government, where the public sector was employing anywhere between 14 per cent and 40 per cent of all workers in MENA by 2012,[40] the highest educated stratum of the population – the top echelon necessary to power innovation and entrepreneurship – saw little or no prospects for a career in MENA, which created a brain drain of considerable proportions.

The nascency of the ecosystem also meant that concepts like equity vesting and Employee Share Option Plans (ESOPs), which attract many employees to start-ups in the US and Europe and create an affordable talent pool for the start-up ecosystem, were not only not understood, but also unavailable from a regulatory perspective. Hiring talent was therefore virtually impossible.

Founders found creative ways to work around this significant scarcity: the creation of the distributed workforce, where talent is scattered across the world, in either fully virtual or hybrid working arrangements, came into being – out of necessity. Whereas remote working today is a choice for start-ups in mature markets, and one only recently exalted as the future of work, it is, and always has been, almost imperative in emerging economies. Not only does it allow founders to hire from a global talent pool, it also helps reduce costs – a priority in markets where capital is scarce. Necessity was indeed, the mother of creation.

"In the early days, we had to develop all our own talent," says Hosam, who grew up in Abu Dhabi and then returned to the region to found Namshi. "We also had to import a lot of talent. Now there is e-commerce talent, there is digital talent in the region that is experienced, that is trained, that has exposure. When you dig a bit deeper and you want fintech talent and proptech talent, things are still not where other markets are, but that's all part of the maturity the ecosystem."

Today, universities across the MENA region are increasingly recognising the transformative value that entrepreneurship can bring to regional economies and the pivotal role education plays in positioning the region on the global innovation stage. Institutions like Lebanon's American University of Beirut (AUB), with its Darwazah Centre for Innovation Management & Entrepreneurship housed within the Olayan Business School, are fostering entrepreneurial mindsets and bridging the gap between academic theory and practical innovation. Similarly, initiatives such as Berytech, rooted in Saint Joseph's University, exemplify a commitment to nurturing talent, offering comprehensive support through incubation, acceleration, and funding to empower start-ups.

In the UAE, the Sharjah Entrepreneurship Centre, known as Sheraa, as part of the American University of Sharjah (AUS), is redefining how students engage with entrepreneurial pursuits by creating an environment for innovation and design thinking and bringing the entrepreneurship ecosystem together. In Saudi Arabia, the Entrepreneurship Centre at King Abdullah University of Science and Technology (KAUST) plays a pivotal role in advancing graduate research aimed at finding solutions to some of the world's most pressing scientific and technological challenges.

FUNDING

Funding was the biggest mirage in the MENA region for the Originals. In 2010, the MENA region recorded a milestone in the quantum of funding raised by the venture capital funds thus far: $300 million

for the entire region – all 450 million people.[41] That same year, in
Silicon Valley, Better Round raised a Series B round for $350 million.
The entire MENA region's ecosystem was smaller than one Series B
round of funding for one investment in Silicon Valley. Where would
the Originals ever find the capital to scale large companies if this
was the size of the ecosystem?

"When we launched, not only was the tech and entrepreneurial
ecosystem very nascent, but the funding ecosystem was also very
nascent too," remembers Careem's Magnus. The founders were
lucky to have friends and family who were willing to invest, but
venture capital was something new altogether. "When we started
approaching more professional investors in the region, the question
was always 'what's my yield?' Because everyone was used to
investing in real estate. You put up a million dollars and then you
got six, seven, or eight per cent a year. That's it. But we were saying
there was a 99 per cent chance they would never see their money
again and a one per cent chance that this will go big'. That was very
different and very challenging."

At the time, there were only four or five venture capital firms and
the founders were rejected by all of them. STC Ventures, a venture
capital fund established by the Saudi Telecom Company (STC), also
declined in the beginning. "But then they came back and finally
agreed," says Magnus. "They led our first institutional round Series
A, and put in about a million dollars. Today, people do seed rounds
of a couple of million dollars, so it was very, very challenging. At
every subsequent round of Series B, Series C, Series D, you're trying
to make a strong case that there are investors lining up and people
are fighting to get in. In reality, there was always only one person
or one investor that was willing to invest, and when you're building
something this fast you're burning money. So, at every point of the
journey, there is a binary outcome – either you get funded and you're
fine, or you're dead. It was very close to that every single time."

The Originals tried going abroad. "It was extremely challenging
for a local brand to be benchmarked against peers on the New York
or London exchanges. It's like having to choose between investing in

a small regional brand and investing in Amazon. Given the dynamics of our region and the consumer behaviour in retail back then, that comparison would have been nearly impossible," remembers Ronaldo, the founder of Souq (now Amazon). "But when we went abroad, it was like a dating site. We had to educate investors about the region for a long time. Within a year or two, you had to prove to them that the company plans you shared early on have actually materialised, and only then do you build trust."

Capital was difficult to come by and the MENA region was a hard sell to international investors. At the time, the potential of emerging technologies was alien to most regional funders, including venture capital investors. The majority of available capital flowed into large-scale, capital-intensive infrastructure projects, construction, and the petroleum industry. Dubai was full of investors who were ready to support the building of a new mall or office space, but not a technology start-up.

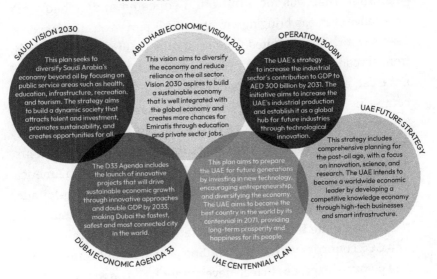

GCC DIVERSIFICATION STRATEGIES
National Economic Development Initiatives

SAUDI VISION 2030
This plan seeks to diversify Saudi Arabia's economy beyond oil by focusing on public service areas such as health, education, infrastructure, recreation, and tourism. The strategy aims to build a dynamic society that attracts talent and investment, promotes sustainability, and creates opportunities for all.

ABU DHABI ECONOMIC VISION 2030
This vision aims to diversify the economy and reduce reliance on the oil sector. Vision 2030 aspires to build a sustainable economy that is well integrated with the global economy and creates more chances for Emiratis through education and private sector jobs.

OPERATION 300BN
The UAE's strategy to increase the industrial sector's contribution to GDP to AED 300 billion by 2031. The initiative aims to increase the UAE's industrial production and establish it as a global hub for future industries through technological innovation.

UAE FUTURE STRATEGY
This strategy includes comprehensive planning for the post-oil age, with a focus on innovation, science, and research. The UAE intends to become a worldwide economic leader by developing a competitive knowledge economy through high-tech businesses and smart infrastructure.

DUBAI ECONOMIC AGENDA 33
The D33 Agenda includes the launch of innovative projects that will drive sustainable economic growth through innovative approaches and double GDP by 2033, making Dubai the fastest, safest and most connected city in the world.

UAE CENTENNIAL PLAN
This plan aims to prepare the UAE for future generations by investing in new technology, encouraging entrepreneurship, and diversifying the economy. The UAE aims to become the best country in the world by its centennial in 2071, providing long-term prosperity and happiness for its people.

Venture was a negligible part of the region's GDP, at a fraction of one per cent. Ronaldo had to identify financial backing outside regional borders. When he did, he found some investment appetite for tech-based companies in emerging markets, but it took a long time for investors to build conviction. In the early stages of attracting investment to the Middle East, companies had to address fundamental concerns about the region's safety, proximity to conflict areas (Ronaldo even had to explain how far Souq's warehouses were from ISIS and whether the market was large and technologically advanced). Just like in any other market, investors needed reassurance about the industry's viability and unit economics. Over time, these initial concerns have diminished, and the focus has shifted towards evaluating the business opportunities themselves.

His first backers were New York's Tiger Global, which had already made its first regional investment in Bayt, and South Africa's Naspers. What Ronaldo and every other start-up entrepreneur needed was commercial traction and a lot of luck.

Among the region's early investors was Oliver Rippel, a former chief executive of B2C e-commerce at Naspers. What he witnessed was comparable with other emerging regions at the time: a founder generation that was local but often educated and/or had work experience overseas, bringing with them well-proven business models. Teams were being recruited from established offline businesses and from abroad, as local tech companies with sufficient experience did not exist, and certain clusters of talent, such as tech development centres in Jordan, were being leveraged across the entire region.

"At Naspers, MENA was one of the markets we looked at closely for investment, especially for e-commerce related investments, alongside other markets such as India, Southeast Asia, Latin America, Europe, or Sub-Sahara Africa at the time," says Rippel, a co-founder and partner at Singapore-based Asia Partners. "We also thought the region had quite interesting characteristics. There were relatively rich GCC countries with high spending power. Levant countries that had plenty of expertise in tech development, and large North African countries with great long-term potential."

What investors identified in the MENA region was what they described as a low-level risk that was worth investing in, but there was little anticipation that any start-up that came out of the MENA would grow into unicorn status. What Rippel saw when he considered Ronaldo's pitch for investment was the same as every other VC had seen, but he took the risk anyway. From a population and GDP perspective the MENA region was already fairly sizeable in the early 2010s, offering the potential for good returns to investors.

Crucially, the region began recognising the importance of diversification outside oil-based economies and there was now greater macro-level investment in the required infrastructure that would make private capital investment interesting. Rippel also saw what had been identified in seminal books like Blue Ocean Shift – for investment companies like Rippel's the MENA region represented a new, relatively empty horizon of limited competition.

The region was less crowded compared to the red ocean that investing in the US, Western Europe, or China represented. "Our thesis first and foremost started with the right business model," explains Rippel. "At the time, we were big believers in B2C e-commerce (Amazon model), C2C classifieds (Craigslist model), and online payments (PayPal model), and we believed that in every region in the world, local or regional winners in these fields would emerge. Secondly, we believed in strong founder entrepreneurs that could scale such businesses over the long run. Thirdly, we were looking for proof points of long-term success, such as a clear market leadership position."

That is not to say that they saw something that others had not – the MENA region, particularly from a Western-centric perspective, had inherent warning signals of instability that many chose to heed. Where Rippel really made a point of difference in terms of investment, however, was how long-term he was considering success. He was looking at their investment as a marathon, not a sprint. He took into account geopolitics and the harsh realities of life in a region with deep historical ties, but one where the leaders and the people were committed to building the future. Naspers identified the region's demographical and digital potential, understanding how it could help transcend these barriers and leverage the significant market opportunities that lay ahead.

"We realised that market leadership needs to be defined more broadly, as often your competitors in the MENA region were online competitors from overseas (such as Amazon imports into especially the UAE or Saudi Arabia) or offline incumbents (such as strong retail groups) in the region. Companies were also rarely market leaders in every country in the region, and often it was hard to translate market leadership from a more developed market (i.e. the UAE) to a less developed market (i.e. Egypt), due to spending power and local infrastructure differences."

From Mona's experience, investors were hesitant about e-commerce, particularly in emerging markets. Globally, e-commerce was seen as capital-intensive, with more failures than success stories. The path to profitability was elusive even in mature markets, and in nascent regions, it often seemed impossible. Investors at the time, especially private equity firms and VCs, sought low-risk, high-return opportunities, and e-commerce didn't fit that mould. As one investor put it, "E-commerce was high-risk with slower returns. In a developing market, profitability can feel like an unreachable goal." It wasn't until the acquisition of Souq by Amazon that global investors began to take notice, realising that the market might hold more potential than they had initially thought.

To work around that, maintaining healthy economics was the result of creating an unfair advantage from the onset. She pursued exclusive deals with suppliers. As a first mover, she achieved better margins. She made sure to have very little inventory, and build a sticky customer base, which she achieved within the first six months of launching Mumzworld. It is that focus on profitability that allowed Mona to quickly convince investors of the potential of her business.

Eventually, Silicon Valley's time-honoured approach of 'growth-at-all-cost' faced a significant backlash, brought to light by a change in economic realities. When exponential growth supersedes profitability, the impact from economic slowdowns is magnified. As investors start to increasingly shift focus towards profitability, sustainable growth, maintaining healthy unit economics, and a positive ROI in financially sustainable businesses, the region's founders and companies begin to seem like increasingly attractive investments. Given the lack of capital historically, founders have been obliged to take a financially prudent approach to their growth, seeking high growth and financial sustainability from the beginnings of their journeys. This discipline is now being rewarded.

On the other side of funding lies debt. While banks in the region serve smaller enterprises, SMEs remain largely underserved, particularly on the credit side. The surge in venture debt across the world has slowly made its way to MENA, and today, the region is experiencing an increasingly sophisticated financial landscape, with the rise in venture debt and SME lending as investors are beginning to tap into opportunities within the unbanked mid-market. Though a relatively new concept in the region, introduced just a few years ago, this has gained significant traction in 2023, where approximately $757 million was raised as venture debt in the Middle East, an all-time high, up from $209 million in 2022 and $165 million in 2021.[42] The growth in appetite for venture debt is driven by the massive unbanked segment of the economy. Two major deals in 2023 that underscore growth in this space include Tamara's $400 million debt financing led by Goldman Sachs, and Tabby's $700 million receivables securitisation from J.P. Morgan.

In conjunction with the diversification of financing options and an increasing interest from international investors in the region – in Q3 2024, despite a decline in VC activity in MENA, for the first time in more than five years, international investors dominated the MENA region, accounting for 51 per cent of all invested capital – it is the sovereign wealth funds of the region that are playing a huge role in helping to boost venture activity.

Collectively, the Gulf's sovereign wealth funds manage around $3.7 trillion, with the region's seven largest funds holding more than $3.2 trillion in combined assets, representing 40 per cent of global sovereign wealth fund assets. Notably, as of October 2024, Abu Dhabi's sovereign wealth funds were valued at $1.7 trillion, ranking them as the largest in the world. In the first three quarters of 2024, Abu Dhabi Investment Authority (ADIA), Mubadala and

ADQ (Abu Dhabi Developmental Holding Company) invested $36 billion in deals across the world, which constituted 26 per cent of what all sovereign wealth funds invested in that period.[43] In the journey toward a thriving knowledge economy, public sector leaders are increasingly turning to seasoned start-up founders across the region, tapping into their insights to create a more welcoming ecosystem. This collaborative approach intertwines diverse perspectives, with government officials drawing on the hard-won insights of entrepreneurs to shape policies and programmes that drive innovation and growth.

This has been exemplified by the entrepreneurial journey of Mudassir Sheikha and Magnus Olsson, the co-founders of Careem, who have been pivotal in reshaping mobility across the region. Notably, Careem played a critical role in shifting perceptions for women to ride in a Careem and to later drive as Captinhas [female drivers]. "When we first entered Saudi, we weren't sure if women would even feel comfortable riding in our cars, especially since all our captains were expats at the time," Magnus recalls.

In the past, the MENA region lacked the pension and endowment fund models found in the US and Europe, which contribute to national development. However, the rise of sovereign wealth funds has provided a close equivalent. These financial institutions, with a global outlook, have not only generated substantial returns but have also focused on regional development. They are designed to foster job creation, drive economic diversification, and support initiatives such as decarbonisation. Saudi Arabia's Public Investment Fund (PIF) and the UAE's Mubadala are prime examples of funds that have invested strategically in projects that align with their countries' long-term visions, further solidifying the region's evolving role as a key player on the global stage.

INFRASTRUCTURE

During the early years of the millennium, the MENA region's ecosystem lacked the technological infrastructure needed to support its emerging founders. Building a business in the MENA region often required creating an entire ecosystem from the ground up. While the original goal might have been to launch an e-commerce platform, it would quickly become apparent that key components, such as payment gateways and logistics networks, are missing, leading founders to create those first. These essential elements, readily available in other parts of the world, must first be developed to enable the core business to function. In this environment, entrepreneurs often find themselves building not just their primary venture, but also the supporting infrastructure that makes it viable, making the journey far more complex and resource-intensive than in markets where these systems are already in place.

In many ways, this is not too dissimilar to the truly innovative companies in the US that are not focused on incremental change or chasing unique views, but are instead properly reshaping industries and the way we live, travel, and consume. Think of transitioning from an oil and gas economy to a fully electric charging network. Or think of the infrastructure required to support AWS or the size of the US e-commerce market. In many ways, the truly innovative and shaping companies need to re-invent from the ground up. In the US there are a select few that seem successful in doing that. In MENA, it is almost a prerequisite to succeed as a founder.

The Originals are unanimous in their recollection of how challenging it was to design technological products – especially looking back at that time retrospectively.

"We quickly realised that the two components needed for e-commerce to work well were logistics and payments," says Ronaldo of the early days of Souq. "There was a big gap in the region. The only delivery services were provided by third party players, and they were really geared to either document transport or big B2B transport across countries. There wasn't anything about last mile and B2C capabilities. Aramex was there and Fadi [Ghandour, founder of Aramex] was supporting us, but with cash on delivery, the lack of addresses, and the limited use of technology in delivery, there was a gap between where the cost of delivery, managing payment, and the speed of delivery needed to be."

By 2018, the Careem founders had built a successful regional ride-hailing platform and established the infrastructure necessary for its growth. They had created detailed location databases, constructed their own SMS routing and gateway systems, and developed a comprehensive customer service framework that included phone support and interactive voice response (IVR) technology.

Careem had also begun to expand its core services, diversifying into food delivery and digital payments. Exiting the business was not necessarily the primary goal for the Careem founding team. Their original motivation was to create 'something meaningful and big.' The limited availability of later-stage investors in the region eventually presented them with fewer options for scaling the company to the next level. With ambitions to scale Careem much further and having successfully gone head-to-head with Uber for years, the chance to join forces with Uber became the perfect opportunity to accelerate Mudassir's and Magnus' vision for Careem. The company was acquired by Uber for $3.1 billion in 2019 and the founders maintained Careem's independence, scaling it into the 'Everything App' we know today.

"We needed to accept credit card payments," says Careem's Mudassir. "Today, that is easy to set-up and founders now have options. When we first started, none of the payment providers that are ubiquitous today existed. There was a single provider. They needed a $30,000 deposit and a host of other requirements that we simply didn't have. With what we could afford, all they could give us was a POS machine. We took it. But every night, Magnus would sit down and process all the transactions from the device. Then, to get an office, we had to pay the year's rent upfront. We started with $100,000. After the credit card deposit, registration fees and the office rent, it was all gone and there was nothing left to build the business with. The ecosystem wasn't ready for this kind of venture."

For Ronaldo, it was the lack of logistical infrastructure and the challenge of acquiring and retaining customers that caused the most sleepless nights. When he was building Souq, the region had a rigid logistical environment that stood in stark contrast to those in more developed markets. Enabled by a zip code system, most e-commerce companies globally could rely on national postal systems, whether it was DHL, US Post, or UPS. In emerging countries, that service did not exist – and still does not. Last-mile logistics were made to a PO Box, which did not provide delivery convenience or accuracy, and home deliveries were almost impossible.

The region posed unique challenges due to its underdeveloped infrastructure. Deliveries were never as straightforward as sharing an address. Instead, a mobile phone number was required, and the delivery driver would call for directions. Streets usually lacked formal names or numbers, so navigation relied heavily on well-known landmarks and references of fast-food restaurants or recognisable stores. It was a process that required local knowledge, patience, and creativity to get deliveries to your door.

In the early 2010s, the lack of infrastructure also meant that Souq only had Maktoob, and very little else to drive customers to the platform. Those founders had to depend on an entirely different marketing strategy. In the absence of paid marketing, the only way was through organic channels – or through SEO. Back then, they would have to find search engine experts – or what Ronaldo calls a 'physicist' – and meet them in places as far away as Moscow to understand which algorithms to use and how the most basic tools of today work. The only lever was to build an excellent brand, a superior product, and unparalleled customer service. And to build the required infrastructure at the same time as building the company.

DEMAND AND MARKET

"The fact MENA is a fragmented market made matters worse and meant that tapping into the right products at the right time was difficult. Women in Saudi Arabia, for example, could not drive until 2018, so accessing basic mother essentials was a considerable challenge. It was an ecosystem where she simply could not access the right products, at the right time, at the right price, to feel empowered to make the most informed decisions for her family.

And so, I wrote the business plan for Mumzworld in 2011, with the objective of empowering the region's mother community."

To Mona, the region's fragmentation created an urgent need to build an e-commerce solution that consolidated a mother's universal needs into a holistic platform. The challenge wasn't just about what mothers needed but about navigating the region's complex logistics. Every country had its own requirements – separate licences, different bank accounts – and shipping from the UAE to Saudi Arabia, for example, often meant crossing borders where things could be held up for weeks. Each market was different too. A Saudi mother had her own unique preferences, which were unlike those of an expat mother in the UAE or a mother in Egypt. Even though they all spoke the same language, their lives, choices, and habits were shaped by different experiences. Mona saw that it wasn't just about providing products; it was about understanding the diversity of the region and creating a platform that could adapt to the needs of all these mothers.

For purely online services such as Maktoob, which provided email and chat services, the region could be considered relatively homogeneous, with the obvious exceptions of Morocco and Algeria, where French is predominantly spoken. It was a different ball game for companies involved in e-commerce.

"With e-commerce, transportation, and even real estate there's a physical component to what you do," says Ronaldo. "So scaling across geographies becomes very, very challenging. If you look at the big players – even the food delivery ones – they operate in five or six countries max. If you don't require heavy infrastructure, you can launch in a few more countries – Qatar, Bahrain, Oman, etc – because you don't have a big, centralised service centre. We needed a warehouse; we needed to have a certain amount of orders for that to work. And the regulation around importing is so different between countries. Differing regulations on importing, products, duties, and currency structures between countries added to the complexity of scaling."

For other founders, scaling was a challenge. In the early 2000s in MENA, the founders believed that the UAE was the only market where it made sense to start and grow an e-commerce business. This was due to a combination of factors, mostly on a macro-geopolitical scale. The challenges faced in the region were most acutely obvious in Saudi Arabia, which had yet to embark on the massive cultural and technological evolution we see today. In Saudi Arabia, the red tape – yet to be cut by the government – was a significant constraint for start-ups, while licensing requirements were both time-consuming and prohibitive. At the other end of the spectrum, the more liberal Egypt was a long-term game, and the rest of the region was far too small for meaningful scale. This combination of factors led many international investors to view the MENA region's challenges as intractable, deterring them from making sizable investments.

Expansion outside national borders into other regional markets was accompanied by significant time and financial costs as entrepreneurs tried to understand and comply with regulatory differences. More often than not, it was easier to maintain and strengthen a company's position in-country rather than undergo the cumbersome process of penetrating a new regional market, which created significant hindrances related to scaling.

What the Originals quickly realised was that the UAE stood out in this fragmented market as one country where it was possible to get started. The government was starting out on its journey to making itself globally relevant, and while they were still shaping the regulations that would best suit the country and make business easier, their geopolitical background and the fact that it was still such a young country, having only been formed in 1971, meant that it carried little of the historical baggage that weighed down its elder neighbours. Ronaldo had moved from Syria to Dubai to join Maktoob and later start Souq, and Mona realised that even if she wanted to go after the Saudi market, she would have to start on the other side of the border.

In the years that followed, the founders of Careem would tell stories of walking into pitch meetings and tell potential investors how enticing the region was. It had a population of 400 million people, the average age was 25, and smartphone penetration was exceptionally high. Not only that – just one per cent of the population was purchasing goods and services online, which meant a huge market was going untapped. If that one per cent could be grown to 10 per cent, that equated to a half a trillion-dollar online market. "But that only holds true if you can operate across the region, because if you look at it country by country it's quite small and not dissimilar to Europe," says Magnus. "That's why the US is so fantastic if you're a start-up, because you can build for one market. In Europe, it's quite painful because people operate differently in Germany versus France, for example."

"You don't need to work with one regulator, you have a regulator in every country, and in some cases, even Abu Dhabi and Dubai might have different regulators," explains Magnus. "The same in Saudi Arabia and other places. So the fact that there is fragmentation in the region is an ongoing challenge."

Whereas there are many similarities in building companies across the world, MENA is essentially the opposite of Europe: in Europe, there are many languages but no borders; in MENA, there is one language but many borders. The market exists, but it needs to be conquered – one by one. In operations, physical borders and multiple regulations exist – especially when shipping bits (physical goods) rather than bytes (digital services). For those that can master these challenges, the potential is tremendous, and a true competitive moat exists. However, for the region to accelerate its evolution toward a MENA where goods and services can flow freely, ensuring this continued prerequisite will be crucial. A big reason for China's accelerated growth over the past decades and the continued strength of the US economy can be attributed to the strength of their single market size with a significantly sized middle class with increasing buying power. There is strength in numbers.

CULTURE

"Suppliers did not understand the first thing about e-commerce," she recalls. "Mostly brick-and-mortar, they operated with primitive systems where thousands of SKUs were recorded either on Excel sheets or manually updated every few weeks. That's how they did inventory. The entire supplier infrastructure was very nascent. Our ambition was to build the largest and widest catalogue of products and so, to do things manually was simply not scalable." Mona remembers about the early days of Mumzworld.

In the early days of Namshi, 85 per cent of the company's volume was cash on delivery, with only a small percentage of customers electing to pay digitally via card or PayPal. "Our consumers preferred to pay in cash," says Hosam. "We tried to give consumers incentives – i.e. discounts to pay by credit card – but that would work while the discount was available and then stop working as soon as it was removed. We ended up just settling for disincentives – i.e. a cost to pay in cash – which consumers over the long term happily paid for. So we were charging a fair chunk of money for that service, yet consumers still chose it, largely due to a lack of trust in e-commerce."

In a nascent market where founders were striving to prove themselves but also convincing those around them of their ideas while managing the day-to-day operations, trust became a critical element for success. Earning the confidence of customers, suppliers, incumbents, and regulators was no small task, yet this buy-in from key stakeholders played a pivotal role in the success of the Originals.

Shifting the culture from one where suppliers only trusted name-brands, and customers didn't trust start-ups or e-commerce companies, with between 70 and 90 per cent of transactions being in cash, was imperative to the success of the Originals.

It was not just the culture of entrepreneurship that encouraged young talent to build companies that needed stimulating, it was also the culture of purchasing from these young companies and of inclusive growth of these companies into the ecosystem. As the Originals slowly built trust in the ecosystem as counterparties for supply and purchase, and as international investors deployed capital into their companies, the foundations of the culture were built.

One at a time, as each of the Originals reached their goals, their successes were celebrated by the community, slowly inching away from the concept that in order to be recognised, one must be a lawyer, engineer or doctor. The celebration of entrepreneurship began to change the culture from one where innovation was imported, to one where innovation is created.

Equally important is embracing culture in all its broader forms to enable a true entrepreneurial ecosystem. From embracing the acceptance of pivoting a business or possibly even failing as a founder, accepting not all investments are winners, accepting that the entrepreneurial success is not a reflection of the skills or reputation of the broader family. For many generations, people within MENA have been explorers, inventors, traders, alchemists, and scientists, all at the forefront of their respective industries. Many tribes within the region have survived the harshest of environmental circumstances, surviving for centuries in the deserts. Many other families come from war-torn regions where they had to leave everything they owned and built throughout their entire life, to re-settle elsewhere and start all over, from scratch. The region has proven to sustain a culture of survival. For centuries, the region has proven it is not necessary to have hope in order to be entrepreneurial, nor to succeed in order to persevere.

GOVERNMENTS

Supported by a new generation of visionary leaders and substantial financial capital, the Gulf has undergone a remarkable transformation, with national governments proactively nurturing the innovation economy. What were once markets with limited regulatory frameworks and developing infrastructure have now evolved into hubs at the heart of global and regional trade networks. Central to this evolution are the region's sovereign wealth funds, with the Kuwait Investment Fund, established in 1953, marking the world's first such initiative. Abu Dhabi soon followed with the launch of ADIA, now one of the largest sovereign wealth funds in the world, managing over $993 billion in assets.[44]

These financial vehicles actively contribute to the implementation of economic policy and act as engines of regional growth, deploying national wealth in strategic sectors of interest. Over time, they have championed industries of the future, increased regional visibility, and strengthened cross-border relationships. They have built local platforms in emerging sectors and created national champions, fostering an environment where entrepreneurship can flourish.

"The sovereign wealth funds, as well as local private or family offices, are investing in start-ups in the region, so funding has become easier," highlights Careem's Magnus. "Then there's the government support. The government has always been very progressive and we are huge fans of all the transformation that's happening in the region. Over the last ten years, this focus has shifted even more towards entrepreneurship, and particularly tech entrepreneurship. So, the cost of launching a business has gone down. The speed of launching a business has gone up. You see a lot of governments that are explicitly entering partnerships with start-ups. When we started it was very, very challenging to go to a government entity and say: 'Hey, we're a small, little start-up. Can we help you with something?' Now this is very actively being sought out and celebrated."

A prime example is Careem's e-hailing system, which has been seamlessly integrated with the Dubai Roads and Transport Authority (RTA) taxi management system. Through this partnership, users can now conveniently book official Dubai taxis directly via the Careem app, often with reduced wait times and at government-regulated fares.

Tech-forward initiatives remain at the forefront of the visionary leadership of countries in the region. A standout example of this is with the recent partnership between the Dubai Department of Economy and Tourism (DET) and Network International, who, in line with the goals of the Dubai Economic Agenda, D33, have signed an MoU to boost the digital payment infrastructure in Dubai and facilitate business access to finance and payment solutions, a move that will increase economic productivity by 50 per cent through innovation and digital adoption.[45]

Similarly, the enabling force of government in driving ecosystem growth is evident in the Golden Visa Programme. Pioneered by the UAE government, the programme is designed to catalyse innovation and attract global talent to the region. With the launch of this initiative, entrepreneurs globally are increasingly looking towards the UAE as an incredible location to establish and grow their ventures. As talent continues to flock towards the UAE, the ecosystem continues to thrive, all resulting in a firm step forward towards becoming one of the leading innovation hubs in the world.

The NextGen FDI programme, spearheaded by the UAE Ministry of Economy, further attracts global technology companies to establish or expand their operations in the UAE – the programme offers targeted support to companies in sectors such as ICT, AI, financial technology and blockchain, and offers benefits to companies looking to set up in the country, such as fast track services, infrastructure for growth and access to UAE ecosystems.

Further still, aligned with the UAE Centennial Plan, Area 2071, managed by the Dubai Future Foundation, is a dynamic hub designed to support entrepreneurs and drive innovation. Hosting initiatives such as the Dubai Future Accelerators, it serves as a launchpad for start-ups and global collaborations aimed at addressing complex future challenges. Located near the iconic Museum of the Future, the physical space of Area 2071 is another symbolic representation of the forward-looking development and investment in groundbreaking solutions and infrastructure.

Similarly, established in 2019 in Abu Dhabi by Mubadala, Hub71 is driving massive growth for the country's tech ecosystem by providing start-ups with access to world-class infrastructure, funding, and mentoring, along with access to key players in the wider ecosystem. The Hub is home to a huge and dynamic community of entrepreneurs, investors and industry experts, that are brought together through different initiatives and programmes, thereby facilitating active engagement and collaboration.

As part of Vision 2030, Saudi Arabia's PIF has focused significantly on domestic projects, including NEOM, which is taking shape across 26,500 square kilometres of the country's north-west at an estimated initial cost of $500 billion, and Qiddiya, a destination city close to Riyadh that will focus on entertainment and sports.

NEOM in particular is laser-focused on innovation and advanced technologies.

Whereas Gulf sovereign wealth funds are funders of the ecosystem's growth and regional development, the role they play as cultural ecosystem enablers is often lost. The direction of development and deployment signals well to the ecosystem the relevance and importance of different sectors. The culture of failure, as one example, has shifted massively as the sovereign wealth funds have begun to deploy into regional venture funds, build entrepreneurship hubs, and invest directly into start-ups.

These investment vehicles are not simply guardians of their countries' fortunes and crucial financial resources for present and future needs, but also serve as ecosystem builders and cultural shapers.

* * * * *

The nascency of the entrepreneurial ecosystem while the Originals were building their companies only makes their success that much more remarkable. As each of them journeyed into an ecosystem yet to be created, with little talent, no funding, a lack of demand and infrastructure, and a culture that encouraged them to continue with their corporate careers, their unwavering commitment to their dreams and their desires to build something meaningful created the foundations of what was to come for many years ahead.

Today, MENA has evolved to exhibit many of the attributes that laid the foundation for the continued success of Silicon Valley in the 1970s. By most frameworks, the region is converging to become an accelerator not just in traditional technology sectors like financial services, healthcare, agriculture, and supply chains, but most certainly also in the technology reshaping the world like AI and crypto.

"We are in an era of a great global unleashing of talent, ideas and building," remarks Christopher M. Schroeder, co-founder of the US-based HealthCentral and author of *Startup Rising: The*

Entrepreneurial Revolution Remaking the Middle East. "In many ways Web2 and Web3 were the warm up for the actual event – young people learned from global successes, they rose and fell in their first attempts, every market has a few juggernaut successes kicking out new talent who know 'how it is done' and how to scale enterprises. And in the midst of all this we are in the earliest days of AI and a myriad new technologies that seem more like magic. The winners will be where the talent and capital is, but also in places where policymakers and infrastructure lean in heavily to unleash them."

Today, MENA is setting itself up to win tomorrow.

CHAPTER 5

THE ADVERSITY ADVANTAGE

من علمني حرفًا كنت له عبدا

I am forever indebted to those who teach me.

– ARABIC PROVERB

THE ORIGINALS CREATED more than they initially set out to – they weren't simply building companies; they were forming the foundational elements of an entire entrepreneurial ecosystem. Unlike entrepreneurs in more developed markets who had access to established networks, capital and infrastructure, the Originals were forced to build these elements themselves, and in doing so, laid the groundwork for future generations of entrepreneurs.

Alex Lazarow applied this thinking in the context of innovation in emerging markets. Countering the Silicon Valley concept of 'disruption', he explains that it does not apply in frontier markets where there are no industries to disrupt to begin with. Instead, innovators in these emerging ecosystems create new industries by necessity, making 'creation' a more apt term to describe what is happening in those markets, and 'disruption' less relevant. Whereas they built much more than originally planned – or than would have been necessary in other markets with the ecosystem and infrastructure to support it – they did so with much less. In addition to the lack of talent and funding – both on the equity and debt side – there was also the lack of infrastructure, lack of demand, and the sceptical culture. Their ability to build companies with much less than their global counterparts has led to the creation of incredibly strong companies on every front: *the Adversity Advantage*.

HUMAN CAPITAL: FROM SCARCITY TO STRENGTH

The lack of local tech talent could have been debilitating. Instead, the Originals pioneered distributed workforce models that would later become global best practice. Unable to source talent locally, they created global teams, recruiting from multiple countries and building remote-first cultures. This adversity led to stronger, often vertically integrated businesses – designed to function seamlessly in environments where other companies might struggle. Additionally, the global nature of the talent base meant there was never a shortage of skilled workers, nor were they beholden to any single region or affected by rising costs of engineers in certain areas. Finally, their focus on talent development created a virtuous cycle: as the Originals continued to grow, they trained a generation of tech-savvy professionals who would go on to join or found other start-ups, gradually solving the very talent shortage that had once challenged them.

FUNDING: CAPITAL EFFICIENCY AS A COMPETITIVE ADVANTAGE

The isolation felt by the Originals on the talent front was exacerbated by the dire situation on the financial front, where severe funding constraints forced the Originals to build with capital efficiency that would ultimately become their strategic advantage. Without access to endless capital or fully developed ecosystems, the Originals created solutions that were not only financially sustainable but also uniquely tailored to their environment. Without the luxury of outsourcing challenges or relying on pre-existing models, they crafted their own solutions, often from the ground up. These constraints pushed them to be more creative and resourceful, needing much less funding to achieve similar milestones than their counterparts in more developed ecosystems, and reaching break-even points sooner; thus in the process, building companies with robust financial logic and foundations.

INFRASTRUCTURE: BUILDING ECOSYSTEMS FROM THE GROUND UP

Perhaps nowhere was the Originals' impact more profound than in the development of infrastructure. The absence of essential services – from payment systems to logistics networks – meant that in parallel to building their own companies, the Originals had to build entire ecosystems around their core businesses. In order to build an e-commerce company, Ronaldo had to first build a payment system and a logistics company so that the e-commerce company could function. As did Hosam, and every other founder at the time. Building their own infrastructure, and often spinning it out, in order to build their businesses, they left their successors with the foundational elements on which to create subsequent companies. International competitors, accustomed to operating within well-developed markets, found it difficult to enter the MENA region and compete, unable to replicate the agility and local insight these founders had cultivated. The very challenges that seemed like obstacles become moats, protecting these businesses from external competition. Through necessity, these founders have created companies with resilience built into their DNA, making them formidable competitors both locally and globally.

DEMAND: FROM FRAGMENTATION TO OPPORTUNITY

The MENA region's fragmented landscape – marked by varying regulations, diverse consumer preferences, and distinct business environments – posed a seemingly insurmountable challenge. It quickly became apparent to the Originals that a one-size fits all approach would not succeed in such a complex and dynamic market. What set them apart was their remarkable ability to navigate multiple regulatory environments, understand the nuances of local consumer behaviour, and develop solutions tailored to each country's unique needs. Local adaptation became the defining strength of the Originals, allowing them to build a deep, authentic understanding of the region's markets – an advantage that international competitors struggled to replicate.

This ability to tailor solutions to local demands laid the foundation for the landmark exits that would define the region's entrepreneurial landscape. Souq's acquisition by Amazon, Mumzworld's by Tamer Group, Careem's by Uber, Namshi's by Emaar, and Fawry's IPO marked an inflection point for the MENA region, giving it international significance and creating a ripple effect throughout the ecosystem. These exits not only validated the potential of start-ups in the region but also sent a powerful signal to global investors and entrepreneurs that the MENA market was ripe with opportunity. Each exit created a ripple effect throughout the ecosystem, attracting more capital, fostering innovation, and solidifying the region's status as a global player in the start-up world.

CULTURE: CREATING TRUST AND TRANSFORMATION

The Originals faced a business culture where e-commerce was viewed with scepticism, cash was king, and entrepreneurship was far from celebrated. Rather than experience this as an obstacle, they recognised that building trust would become their strongest differentiator. They focused on excellent customer service, superior products, and building strong brands when they couldn't rely on paid marketing channels.

"Great builders globally are strikingly more similar than different," says the American entrepreneur and investor Christopher Schroeder. "Put an entrepreneur in the same room from São Paulo, Cairo, Riyadh, Singapore and beyond, the conversations are the same – the problem solving, the hyper focus on thrilling customers, the sense that whatever is thrown their way you might slow them down but never stop them. I've been in such rooms as I invest across rising markets, and I see it regularly."

"Also, despite all the cultural and geographical differences, rising markets share similar challenges: educating customers new to technology and banking at scale; navigating rapidly changing and often unpredictable regulations; managing difficult last-mile logistics; and more. I watch them nod in agreement and share insights, often far more useful than those from Silicon Valley, due to their shared experiences. Each geography, with its distinct physical, cultural, and regulatory dynamics, offers unique approaches. But the women and men themselves – they are as one. They speak the same language. They finish each other's sentences."

LEGACY

Crucially, these MENA pioneers passed down DNA that is now quintessential to the contemporary Middle Eastern entrepreneur and is evident in other emerging ecosystems globally. The Originals also imparted valuable lessons on building businesses in resource-constrained environments. Operating under challenging conditions – where access to capital, skilled talent, and resources is limited, and uncertainty is a constant feature – today's entrepreneurs are always prepared for the worst. As a result, they build businesses that are resilient by design and follow a different playbook than their counterparts in Silicon Valley or Europe.

The successes of the Originals not only marked a turning point for the MENA region but also served as a powerful inspiration for the next generation of founders. Standing on the shoulders of these Originals, the new wave of entrepreneurs was empowered to look further into the horizon, dreaming bigger and aiming higher than ever before. Yet, as they reached for larger goals, they carried with them the invaluable lessons the Originals had uncovered – how to build sustainable businesses even with scarce resources. This new generation was inspired by the resilience and resourcefulness of their predecessors, learning that scaling a business required not just innovation but a deep understanding of local markets, trust-building with stakeholders, and an unwavering commitment to creating value, even in the face of uncertainty. They had learned how to build an Adversity Advantage.

SECTION II

A SHORT DECADE ago, few could have imagined the transformation that MENA's key industries would undergo, fuelled by technology and driven by a new generation of entrepreneurs determined to solve regional challenges.

However, progress isn't just about innovation; it's about creating the foundational pillars for resilient economies, sustainable growth, and a more inclusive society. Across global growth, there have consistently been five key sectors that have been instrumental to economic prosperity and growth around the world; financial services, healthcare, education, food and agriculture, and supply chains. In the fast evolution of the MENA region, as economies develop and grow, with technology being a fundamental enabler, these are no different.

In financial services, a sector once bound by cash transactions and limited access to formal banking, digital innovation is now opening doors to financial inclusion for millions. For decades, the region has struggled with limited financial infrastructure, leaving over two-thirds of MENA's adult population unbanked.[46] It is projected that financial inclusion could increase MENA's GDP by as much as 30 per cent by 2030.[47] By bringing millions into the formal economy, fintech is enabling small businesses to thrive, creating jobs, and fostering a more resilient financial ecosystem that can weather economic fluctuations. With more people participating in the formal economy, MENA isn't just solving financial inclusion; it's fostering economic resilience, strengthening the social fabric, and creating a pathway to sustainable, locally driven growth.

Healthcare, too, is experiencing a revolution. With a rapidly growing population, MENA faces rising demands for accessible, high-quality healthcare. In Saudi Arabia alone, healthcare spending is expected to reach $160 billion by 2030.[48] This growing investment in healthcare is crucial for economic productivity, as a healthier population is directly linked to a more productive workforce. It is estimated that a 10 per cent increase in life expectancy can lead to a 0.3 per cent increase in GDP per capita.[49] This means that improvements in healthcare not only enhance the quality of life but also drive economic growth by reducing healthcare costs and increasing the productivity of the labour force. In addition, as the region expands its healthcare sector, it creates job opportunities and boosts the economy through both public and private sector investment.

In education, digital platforms are preparing the region's youth for participation in the global knowledge economy, an essential step for nations seeking economic diversification. MENA's young population, with over 60 per cent under the age of 30,[50] represents enormous potential for transformation. According to a report by the World Economic Forum, MENA's education sector is expected to contribute $1.1 trillion to the region's GDP by 2030,[51] driven by increased investment in skills development and digital education solutions. When young people have access to quality education, they become a driving force in the economy, contributing to innovation in high-growth sectors, and building industries that add substantial economic value.

The evolution in food and agriculture is just as critical for national resilience. With limited arable land and water resources, MENA countries are harnessing agritech to improve food security and sustainability. Currently, MENA imports almost 90 per cent of its food needs,[52] a vulnerability that innovations in precision farming, vertical agriculture, and water-efficient practices are addressing. The agricultural sector alone is expected to contribute $33.6 billion to MENA's GDP by 2030.[53] This shift is more than just meeting local demand; it's about establishing food security and reducing external dependencies. With a sustainable agricultural framework, MENA can build economic independence, reduce import bills, create rural jobs, and improve the livelihoods of its people, all of which contribute to long-term economic and social stability.

In supply chains and logistics, advancements are connecting MENA to global markets like never before. The UAE Government is focused on more than doubling the contribution of industrial manufacturing to the UAE's GDP to 25 per cent, as highlighted in Vision 2021, Dubai Industrial Strategy 2030, and Abu Dhabi Economic Vision 2030.[54] Efficient supply chains and digital infrastructure are essential to realise this growth. The logistics sector in MENA is projected to contribute $40 billion to the regional economy, with a 5 per cent growth rate annually over the next decade.[55] Improved logistics, digital tracking systems, and infrastructure investments mean goods can move across borders more seamlessly, enabling businesses to scale beyond local markets. This integration into the global economy doesn't just drive growth; it attracts investment, strengthens local industries, and creates jobs. With streamlined logistics, MENA becomes a reliable hub for trade and investment, enhancing its economic profile on the world stage and reinforcing its position as a competitive player in international markets.

In each of these sectors, technology and progress, enabled by innovation, is not just a response to local needs – it is the bedrock for economic growth and regional stability. By investing in financial services, healthcare, education, food and agriculture, and supply chains, MENA is building a future where each sector supports the other, creating a dynamic, interconnected, economy that is prepared to face future challenges and lift the quality of life for generations to come. These efforts are more than just modernisation; they are laying the foundation for a prosperous, sustainable future, redefining what's possible for MENA's people and its place in the world.

CHAPTER 6

IN THE ABSENCE OF FINANCE

البحصة بتسند خابية

A pebble can support a barrel.

– ARABIC PROVERB

CAIRO, EGYPT
ISLAM SHAWKY – PART 1

Islam ran as fast as he could, dodging the cars as he crossed the Cairo streets. His mind willing his legs to go faster and the clocks to slow down. He couldn't miss the exam, yet it didn't seem like a real possibility to make it on time. After all those hours and years of studying and fighting to get into this university, he had never imagined this moment might end in failure. He felt the weight of his parents' hopes, his friends' encouragement, his teachers' pride – everybody who had vouched for him and supported him throughout the years. All those who were so proud of him and eager for him to graduate next month and start on his career path. The pressure to make it on time felt insurmountable.

Despite his best efforts to rush and get there, Islam knew he would never make it, and despite everything, he knew it was his fault he was late. He had gotten carried away with his company – with the idea that had taken hold of him and refused to let go. He had poured his heart into it, imagining all the ways it could impact the world. While building, he had lost track of time – he had forgotten about the exam – and now, he was paying the price.

As he arrived, too late to start the test, he began to realise that though it was hard to face, there was a silver lining – without the pressure to graduate immediately, he would have more time to build his start-up, to make his vision a reality. His subconscious had made his decision.

With this realisation quickly dawning upon him, Islam called his friend Alain El Hajj, and together, their search led them to Mostafa Menessy. "After bypassing the security firewall of the university, Mostafa had become a rockstar on campus, and so when I had decided that I wanted to start a company, he seemed like the perfect fit. Mostafa was on board with the plan immediately. He said, 'Super!' and off we went with Alain." It had been that simple. Yet, now, it was so hard. There was so much at stake. He had missed the exam at the expense of his dreams of building a company. There was no way he could fail at building the company. Islam started to feel the weight of the pressure on his shoulders. This had to work. At this point, they had already pivoted twice, and had yet to really start.

In the early days, they had been convinced that in tech, there was only one sure way to succeed – Bitcoin. So they set out to mine the cryptocurrency and thought they would work at night when the university was quiet because of the large amount of energy they would need. They soon encountered a slight problem – they discovered that the university powered down the grid overnight to save energy. Undeterred, they came up with another idea. "This time we got super-excited about e-commerce after I read that 80 per cent of purchases happen through recommendation, not ads. People were becoming ad-blind, so I asked the guys how we could allow people to monetise their presence on social media. Instead of just ~~likes~~, how could they make money instead?" They invented ~~the~~ idea that if you liked a product and someone bought it based on your recommendation, you would get a slice of the price.

It was a brilliant idea. However, as they started building, despite the demand for their product, they needed an end-to-end payment infrastructure that allowed for pay-ins, accepted a variety of payment methods, and integrated APIs to push payments to affiliates in real time. Islam, Alain and Mostafa scoured the market for a partner bank that could service the needs of the business.

"One of the bank representatives laughed his heart out when we told him what we needed," remembers Islam with a chuckle. "He said: 'You boys from the American University in Cairo think you're in the US? This is not PayPal, and we are not Silicon Valley.' He offered us a 400-page cumbersome integration guide that came with a long list of set-up and maintenance fees and required us to open a bank account – which would take weeks. When we asked him how many merchants they could onboard using this process, he proudly shared that they were the biggest and most efficient, onboarding six merchants a month. Our goal was to serve merchants in the millions."

A debate ensued among the three co-founders: was SocialTab that important, or was there an even bigger opportunity in payments? The commitment to the idea of SocialTab was significant, but it was quickly apparent that the existence of SocialTab would never happen unless they tackled payment technology first. After six months of trying to resolve the issues around payments, they realised that solving the real problem of payments was much bigger than the e-commerce dream they had. And much more daunting. They were going to take on the banks and infrastructure providers. They pivoted again; and Paymob was born.

They had full conviction but no proof of concept yet. But now, having missed the exam, and failing to graduate, Islam and his co-founders had another academic year to prove this could work.

"If we were bullish about e-commerce, we should be bullish about digital payments," says Islam. "We asked ourselves what is going to change and what isn't? What was going to change was that millions of people are going to build their businesses online, whether a start-up or a psychiatrist or a home office business, and they are going to want to be paid remotely and digitally. The second predicted change was that there would be fragmentation in payment methods because the Egyptian population is mostly unbanked. What was not going to change was the need for a variety of payment methods – pay-as-you-go models with no barriers, seamless onboarding and transparent payment systems – and to be paid quickly. If we built an entity that stood between tens of payment methods on one side and hundreds of thousands, maybe millions, of businesses on the other side, we could build a company that would revolutionise e-commerce in Egypt, and beyond."

When Paymob first started in 2018, less than three in ten Egyptians had a bank account.[56] Of those who did not, 65 per cent were unemployed or out of the money economy, with women making up more than half of the unbanked population.[57]

Financial Inclusion
Citizens with a Bank Account (%)

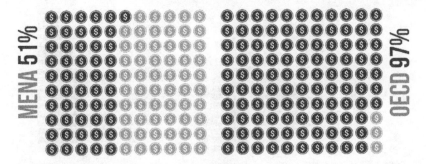

Source: World Bank (Most Recent Data)

A number of factors explain the historic lack of financial services. The first is that banks across the MENA region tend to cater to affluent or the more 'bankable' groups. Incumbent banks exclude a large portion of the population by adopting stringent underwriting requirements and limiting access to a suite of financial products. Many countries in the region do not have a credit bureau, meaning the information typically available in other markets to determine whether or not an individual is eligible for a loan is non-existent. Compounding this is the fact that much of the population operates in the informal economy, meaning they exist beyond the bounds of the formal financial system. In Egypt, 85 per cent of SMEs are thought to be informal, with the black economy employing approximately 10 million people.[58]

The numbers involved were daunting, but the social issues were even more intractable. How could this fearless trio provide a service which would attract those in the unbanked sector to join the digital age? Not least because, despite its importance, credit was expensive. At an average interest rate of 7.3 per cent,[59] it was prohibitive for the average Middle Eastern consumer. Overall, credit card penetration rates stood at 7.6 per cent, compared to the US (82 per cent), Europe and China (38 per cent).[60]

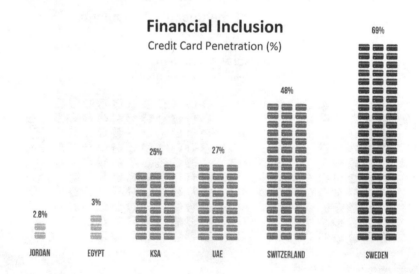

Financial Inclusion
Credit Card Penetration (%)

JORDAN 2.8% EGYPT 3% KSA 25% UAE 27% SWITZERLAND 48% SWEDEN 69%

Source: World Bank (2021)

Those who do manage to open a bank account face endless friction and inefficiency that costs time, money, and effort. Until the early 2020s, most banks in the region did not have a mobile app and required in-person banking for the majority of their users. Some banks still do. For example, in Egypt and Syria, some customers still have to go into a branch to complete the necessary formalities to open a bank account. It can then take up to three weeks for the account to be activated.

Across regional economies, cash still plays a significant role. In Saudi Arabia, 38 per cent of payments were made in paper money in 2021.[61] In Egypt, 40 per cent of cash-based transactions take place in the informal sector, making it almost impossible to gauge the scale of cash transactions as a whole, although the figure is no doubt significant.[62] In Morocco, the world's most cash-reliant country, 74 per cent of transactions are in cash currency.[63] Although e-commerce had seen an exponential surge over the last few years, buying products online is still relatively new, since only a subset of the population have the financial products to participate in the digital economy. When building Souq and Mumzworld, Ronaldo and Mona had to incorporate cash transactions (Cash on Delivery: CoD) within their check-out points and payment infrastructures because a majority of customers were uncomfortable buying products they could not physically see or touch.

SMEs are particularly underserved when it comes to their financial needs. According to the World Bank, formal SMEs contribute up to 40 per cent of GDP and around 60 per cent of total employment in emerging economies.[64] In the MENA region specifically, they account for 90 per cent of registered companies. If we include informal SMEs, which comprise 96 per cent[65] of businesses in the region, these numbers are significantly higher. Yet, these companies receive a mere 7 per cent of total bank lending,[66] and the total financing gap for SMEs in MENA is estimated between $210 and $240 billion.[67] By comparison, small businesses in the US receive 36 per cent of total lending.[68]

The needs of merchants and small business owners have been largely ignored. To Islam, Alain, and Mostafa, that gap was astounding and they spent months trying to understand where to start. The depth and breadth of the challenges meant that there was plenty for financial technology to solve, from building financial infrastructure and payment rails, to B2B solutions and consumer-focused products across payments, savings, and credit. Ultimately, it became clear: building the payments capability was non-negotiable.

Islam's head was still turning with the numbers that the bank executive had shared with him: onboarding six merchants a month with a 400-page manual. No payment infrastructure for SMEs. None of it made sense to him. Yet, he knew Egypt. And he knew its people and its strengths. He was going to have to dig deep and see how he could leverage the uniqueness of the market to build a company nobody had built before.

He would have to ignore that more than seven out of ten adults were unbanked, that 65 per cent said they would need help using an account at a financial institution, and two-thirds relied on family and friends for borrowing.[69] He would have to focus on the strengths: 96 per cent of the population had a smartphone, and 82 million were internet users – and those numbers were growing.[70] In addition, they were all young and unattached to the names of the big financial institutions.

But the questions loomed: how do you build an all-encompassing platform that accounts for that level of fragmentation in payment methods? How do you create a solution which offers speed, interoperability, and optionality in the absence of banking rails? How do you develop underlying payment technology that captures and services a fast-growing e-commerce industry, while accounting for local realities in financial literacy and access?

The answer... from scratch.

With the highest levels of enthusiasm, the young and eager team started building the solution they wished had been available when building SocialTab: an online payment interface and solution for SMEs. However, the need to integrate banks into the platform became glaringly obvious very quickly. If their first experience with Egypt's financial institutions was any indication, this was going to be far from straight-forward. There were four banking partners they could work with, so they excitedly approached the first with their proposition of becoming the interface for SMEs and integrating with the bank's system. The "no" was quick and resolute. The second potential partner informed them that this was not a valuable market segment and they should stop wasting their time. The third rejection was the scariest since it left only one potential final partner.

They approached this one differently and with much more data: fifteen memoranda of understanding (MOUs) from the bank's existing merchants who had expressed interest in Paymob's payment offering. The bank representative paused, recognising the strong demand and the possibility that the founders might collaborate with another financial institution – potentially leading to the loss of merchants – and took them seriously.

As the bank considered the opportunity, Islam couldn't help but wonder if this was just a long no. It had been three months since the meeting, and then six months, and now it was fourteen months after the first meeting and they were still negotiating the deal. The company was surviving off the $350,000 they had raised from their seed investors and from cash they were earning by selling bank software to financial institutions. The potential partner bank was killing them with new clauses every time they met, and Islam wondered whether this was their strategy – to keep them lingering until they died.

He had almost lost hope when the deal finally came through. Islam's sigh of relief was short-lived. The deal had significant handcuffs and required Paymob to use the bank's bulky and legacy platform and documents to onboard merchants – they could not onboard merchants alone. This meant they could only onboard two or three merchants a month. They were, effectively, the bank's SME onboarding team. An incremental improvement to the 400-page process. No real technology. No real solution to the SMEs.

The team had had it. They were done. After fourteen months of negotiations, this was the result, or no deal. They took the deal, but Islam wasn't sure what to do. He had given up everything for this company and was convinced that there was something they could build that was meaningful, but they couldn't get going, and they were starting to run out of money. Had he really given everything up only to become part of a sales team of a bank?

DUBAI, UNITED ARAB EMIRATES:
HOSAM ARAB – PART 1

Hosam was restless. He had already founded and exited an e-commerce company, Namshi, the Middle East's online destination for fashion and lifestyle, to Noon in a successful transaction. Being someone who lives, sleeps and breathes ideas, he now felt stuck. Everywhere he looked, there were ideas and opportunities that were disturbing his desire to take some time off after building his last company.

But his mind was off to the races. He knew he wanted to do something in the fintech space since those had been the largest challenges he had encountered as a founder. Yet, even after narrowing it down to fintech, there was so much to do! The opportunities were endless! And there was so much competition – there were an infinite number of fintechs in the MENA region now, each one tackling one of the multitude of problems the industry presented.

"My initial idea had been to take some time off. However, it was all down to timing as it was before the summer holidays and the kids were still in school so I couldn't just set off and travel on my own. I did some thinking and one of the ideas was Buy Now, Pay Later (BNPL). I had discussed it with a few people then I got this random call from a friend who said there was an investor in town who had already put money into BNPL solutions in other markets and they'd like to meet you," he says with a smile. It took one more meeting in New York and the deal was done.

Before he knew it, Hosam was back in the throes of entrepreneurship, building Tabby. But this time, as a second-time founder – and it was different: investors were happy to commit capital from the beginning, it was easier to attract talent, and the pitfalls of building a company were known to him. Additionally, he was convinced that this time, given the agony of entrepreneurship regardless of the size of company he was building, he was going to insist on building something huge. He was out to solve a big, audacious problem.

Hosam had already surveyed the MENA region and its potential for digital growth. He made three observations that were true to global digital consumer behaviour but acute in a region like MENA that had been historically underserviced by traditional selling options. The first was that online consumers were looking for shopping experiences that allowed them to be more in control of their finances. The second was that highest potential online consumers lacked alternative financing in the absence of credit. Thirdly, he observed that an estimated 65 per cent of e-commerce transactions were cash-based even though it was already clear in 2011 that there was an overwhelming desire across the region, from North Africa to the GCC, to move away from a reliance on cash. Ten years later, in 2021, this demand had not been fully satisfied and consumers still expected to pay for online deliveries with cash. So, he set up Tabby to enable digital payments.

"Can we provide consumers with a reason to ditch their cash and start using digital payments?" wondered Hosam. His belief was that free, easy-to-access instalments would be the solution.

Although the initial idea was to provide an alternative to paying in cash on delivery of a product – a problem he was familiar with from building Namshi, the real intention was that if they provided an incentive, like a BNPL solution, customers would hopefully move away from cash and begin to use their debit or credit cards. This would help retailers who struggle to manage cash transactions reduce the risk of fraud and streamline their payment processes. If they achieved this, merchants would be happy and so would consumers, who would benefit from a more convenient and secure payment method, quicker transaction times, and an enhanced shopping experience.

"However, over time, we realised that cash was just one problem. The bigger problem across the region is access to credit. There was a major credit gap in the region, which was underserved by the banks. We thought we were very well placed to address that, so that was the opportunity we believed was really worth going after. How do we provide consumers with an alternative that addresses that gap, is also a much friendlier alternative, and allows us to scale effectively?"

BNPL was not a new concept either globally or in the MENA region. A form of short-term financing that allows consumers to make purchases and pay for them in instalments at a later date, the concept taps into the desire for convenience and provides easy access to credit at zero interest. In Sweden, Klarna has built a customer base in excess of 150 million. Start-ups offering BNPL command some of the highest valuations in the world, including Klarna ($20 billion) and Australia's AfterPay ($14.76 billion). However, despite these success stories, the BNPL concept has failed the test of building sustainable models in many growing markets. With inflation and rising interest rates, many of the BNPL start-ups struggled with increased default rates because customers had less money to spend on what they needed, let alone on what they wanted. This financial strain has impacted the ability of BNPL companies to maintain profitability and liquidity, as many rely heavily on transaction fees and late fees, which are only viable when default rates remain low. The consequences placed BNPL under increased regulatory scrutiny and made headlines as BNPL start-ups consecutively announced either liquidation, bankruptcy, contractions or downsizing, and saw their share prices plummet. Take Canada-based PayBright, for instance, which struggled with mounting financial difficulties and eventually filed for creditor protection in 2020 before Affirm stepped in to acquire it. Or, Klarna, which hit turbulent financial waters in 2022, leading to a series of layoffs as it scrambled to adapt to the changing economic landscape.

However, this was different for the MENA region. The low credit card penetration rates and low access to credit meant that this was a novel offering to consumers. This was their first exposure to credit. The GCC had one of the lowest debt per household as a percentage of GDP than any part of the world. This was a completely blue ocean in which Hosam would be launching.

While BNPL is a way for customers to spread out the costs of products and services and for sellers to increase their average basket size, it serves an entirely different purpose in the context of the MENA market. It is less about the convenience that the BNPL model creates

– extending the time between full payment and consumption – and more a necessity given the fact that credit is either non-existent or, in the pockets of the region where credit is available, is inconvenient or predatory. By going for a BNPL option, they could access credit and avoid the loan sharks. In addition, it meant that customers would pay online, rather than in cash.

"That looks like it really shifted the need and moved the needle with consumers. Today, across most of the merchants we work with – and the feedback that we get from merchants – cash is sitting around the 15 per cent mark, so a significant change since Covid-19. In 2019, cash was still around 60 to 65 per cent of e-commerce payments."

What remains true even today, when the region had turbocharged its online economy, is that there is still widespread under-penetration of credit across the MENA region. The UAE has the highest percentage of credit card ownership at 26.8 per cent, but that figure drops to as low as 2.8 per cent in Egypt and 1.1 per cent in Morocco.[71] Although credit card ownership stood at 25.4 per cent in Saudi Arabia in 2021, that figure differs dramatically to the US, where 66.7 per cent of the population owns a credit card.[72] Across Europe, credit penetration is similarly high, standing at 62.1 per cent in the UK and 57.9 per cent in Italy.[73] Such low regional figures can be partially explained by the hugely complicated, laborious, and time-consuming process of acquiring a credit card. From initial application to the final delivery of a credit card, the process takes at least two weeks, and up to three months, in some parts of the MENA region. In the absence of data on credit history, the verification process is tedious, as each individual application needs to be reviewed at multiple levels in any banking organisation. The credit card system simply didn't work.

In addition, there are also social and cultural factors that dissuade people from adopting credit cards as a way of making payments. Many credit products don't comply with the rules of Islamic finance, also known as Shari'ah, which prohibits the charging of interest on a loan or deposit. As such, in a predominantly Muslim region, credit cards, in their current form, do not carry relevance or applicability and are not part of many people's vocabulary. A significant portion of the population is also intentional about avoiding debt and largely prefers debit.

In fact, a majority of BNPL users repay their short-term loans using debit. In Saudi Arabia, 90 per cent of Tabby users pay their instalments with a debit card. In the UAE, it is 60 per cent, and this is down to a combination of both religious factors, but also because of a general mistrust of financial instruments that is exacerbated by their opacity. This is particularly true of the new generation of customers – the Millennials, Gen Z, and Alpha – who are sceptical about current banking systems and pursue transparency and honesty in all of their interactions, including how they participate in the financial system. For these generations, traditional banks – often criticised for their confusing fine print and lack of transparency – are increasingly seen as untrustworthy.

In markets where credit cards are ubiquitous, BNPL is a less suitable credit model. In the MENA region, however, BNPL solves the problem of the lack of credit accessibility. Its interest-free feature also makes it Shari'ah compliant, which significantly broadens the product's total addressable market. While BNPL works at the consumer level, it also carries wider-ranging benefits for e-commerce as a whole. Cash is the enemy of e-commerce. The product-market fit was therefore instant. Within two years of launch, Tabby became the first or second largest payment method on any e-commerce website regionally. Merchants witnessed their sales increase between 20 and 40 per cent soon after being onboarded. The value of the product was clear. It was easy, quick, and transparent with no hidden costs or fees. In many ways, it was the antithesis of the traditional banking model.

From the outside, it looked as if the product-market fit was perfect, the consumer and retailer uptake was astronomical and the growth was unsurpassed by any fintech in the region. It looked like Hosam should have nothing to worry about, and that everything was perfectly on track to tremendous success. But there was one thing nagging him: how was he going to fund the growth? There had never been such a fast-growing and large fintech in the region before. Nobody had been able to scale like this yet, and he could see, as his comparable companies around the world struggled and folded, that this would be a journey requiring significant equity investments, and an even more significant balance sheet.

Hosam started racking his brain: who would do this? The region's banks were uncomfortable lending, and struggled to understand the business model, and the international banks and investors struggled to understand the region, and how this business model could be sustainable and grow quickly in MENA despite it having failed gloriously elsewhere. Who could he turn to? Hosam was curious: would it be easier to convince the regional banks about the new business model or the international banks about a new region?

KARACHI, PAKISTAN
OMAIR ANSARI – PART 1

Omair knelt down on the dirty and dusty floor one more time and carefully ran the gluestick over the edges of the paper. Once satisfied, he stood up and meticulously stuck the poster onto the wall. "Let's see what happens" he thought sceptically as he walked down the hallway and into the sticky humid heat of Karachi, with a part of him wishing he was still at his comfortable and clean desk at Morgan Stanley back in Manhattan. But before he could make it to the door, his phone beeped. After a quick glance, he looked over his shoulder. There was a man reading his poster and messaging him requesting the service. Then the phone beeped again. And again. And again.

"Do you struggle with the late payment of your salary? Contact us and we can square it for you."

"Just with that and no other advertising, we soon had 40 per cent of that company's workforce transacting with us. So I said to myself, if I don't need to spend a lot of money to convert someone, this has got to be a product that people want. It's the easiest way to build your user base before you go into anything." It was certainly exhausting, but it paid huge dividends.

The disbelief of the workers and the smiles on their faces when they receive their salaries on time were all it took for Omair to keep building Abhi, which all started from a simple observation. "Wage payments in Pakistan were taking an average of thirty-five days and inflation was running at 13 per cent, with real inflation closer to 25 per cent. People's purchasing power was diminishing daily, yet by the time they were paid, they had actually lost income. I just thought that it was incredibly unfair. The whole premise of our business model is that: if you work today, you deserve to be paid today. That applies globally, but in markets like Pakistan, it is a matter of survival."

This has a knock-on effect when it comes to needing to pay for basic amenities like water, electricity, phone and internet bills. It makes trying to get a mortgage or a loan for a car difficult to the point of being impossible. And of course, there is no recourse – you cannot sue your employer if your salary is late. For many of Pakistan's 65 million salaried workers, this is a daily reality.

Omair is truly a global citizen. Born in Pakistan, he was constantly on the move, living in Nigeria, France, Singapore, India, the UK, Canada, and the UAE. While he was never in one place for more than five years, Pakistan was always where he called home. After graduating from the University of Toronto, he began working with a hedge fund based in London and Hong Kong, before moving to Renaissance Capital, a leading independent investment bank, where he oversaw research and helped to expand the company's footprint into Sri Lanka, Bangladesh, Pakistan, and Vietnam.

During his two years with the company, Omair's hands-on experience of emerging markets was astounding, focusing specifically on financial technology and the evolving ways in which financial services are delivered and consumed outside traditional banking institutions. In 2016 he joined Morgan Stanley as an investment analyst. For five years, he helped the firm run its first frontier market fund focused on consumer technologies and telecommunications, before launching a second fund purely focused on financial technology across emerging markets. Acutely aware of how many millions were locked out of the existing financial system, he was convinced financial technology enabled growth and inclusion in these markets, which fed his desire to be part of the story and, where possible, create socio-economic change through fintech.

When he was researching the Pakistani market, he was stunned by some of the data. The country had a population of 240 million people, but only three out of every 100 had access to credit. Microfinance only served 11.5 per cent of a potential market of 27 million people, and there were only ten bank branches and eleven ATMs per 100,000 adults. What struck him like a bolt of lightning was that at the same time, the nation had a fast-growing internet penetration rate, which stood at 21 per cent in 2021.[74] Even more convincing was that more than eight out of ten had a mobile phone.[75] Yet, despite the visible opportunity, little was being done about it.

Omair knew fintech – and credit specifically – could be the key to unlocking the huge potential of a market as huge as Pakistan. To paraphrase Douglas Adams in *The Hitchhiker's Guide to the Galaxy*, he had the answer, and he now needed to work out the question What existing models in credit and financing could he potentially adapt and bring to Pakistan? What manual pain points could be effectively addressed and digitised? He quickly realised that there was no cookie-cutter solution that he could just drop onto the Pakistan market. The market needed, and he wanted, to build a solution to allow ordinary workers in Pakistan access to finance and credit that was tailor-made for Pakistan. So he went back to the place he was born to explore and a friend connected him to Ali.

Omair entered the coffee shop looking for Ali. Glancing down at his phone to see the WhatsApp profile of what Ali looked like, Omair tried to match one of the faces in the coffee shop to the image on his screen. "Nobody knows the start-up scene here like Ali," his friend and soon-to-be investor had told him when introducing them over WhatsApp. Omair sat down and waited – he was still becoming accustomed to the fluidity of time here.

When Ali arrived, Omair quickly identified that Ali's strong operational background and in-depth understanding of the Pakistani market could be a complementary force to his own skills and knowledge. Over many coffees and teas, they narrowed the opportunity they wanted to pursue to one where the credit challenge was solved using salaries. They would build a platform to provide access to credit for their target audience down to the challenge of providing access to salary advance and small and medium enterprise (SME) credit.

They met with over fifty company representatives, and asked them a few simple questions.

- *Are your employees asking you for salary advances?* The answer was always yes.
- *How often does this happen?* Every month.
- *What percentage of your employee base is asking for such an advance?* Between 20 per cent on a low month and 100 per cent on big occasions.
- *When they do ask, how often do you provide this service to your employee base?* Three to four times a year though we try to keep it at a minimum.
- *Why?* It's a manual annoyance but also, we have other uses for our working capital.

The beauty of applying these kinds of questions was that it quickly became apparent that they were far from unique challenges. Omair and Ali had seen this work in other markets. Minu, from Mexico, founded in 2019, now valued at $60 million. Xerpa, Brazil, founded in 2015, valued a $70 million. Refyne, from India, worth $450 million. The examples were many. Before deciding to quit their jobs and pursue this, Ali and Omair ran a quick test on a primitive minimum viable product (MVP): their poster.

With the poster all over the walls of a 450-employee company and 40 percent of the employees transacting with Omair and Ali, the idea was validated. They ran the test for about three months, assessing the stickiness and frequency of use, and found that the employees kept coming back. Even more, they were increasing the frequency of their transactions.

Abhi went live in July 2021. In a few short months, it had 400 users transacting on the app and a 50 per cent transaction rate where half the customers who had downloaded the app were requesting and receiving loans. By August, the start-up had completed $25,000 in transactions. By September that figure had risen to $300,000, followed by $1 million in October, $2.5 million in November, and $10.4 million in December. By January 2022, Abhi was cashflow positive.

The beta-testing that they had trialled earlier that year was conclusive. Given the right information, and the right level of transparency, the market was willing to trust the financial vehicle that they had created to access their salary on a regular, stable basis. It was time to scale it in the largest ready-made audience they knew – Pakistan. "The math is straightforward," says Omair. "There are 65 million people in Pakistan who are salaried individuals, and the average monthly salary is about $150, so we are looking at a payroll market of about $9 billion a month. Even if you factor in the cash economy and cut that in half, you are still talking about $4.5 billion to $5 billion every month, so you need a market share of just one per cent to get to $50 million every four weeks."

Employees loved the platform, but, much to the frustration and irritation of the founders, the employers weren't as convinced. Despite Omair using all his skills of persuasion, employers agreed that salary advances were a pain point, but not enough to justify using their stretched working capital when it could be better spent on other business expenses. They were unwilling to enable the scaling of the business and could not see the benefits of paying their employees on time.

Omair was beyond frustrated. He didn't understand how this problem could exist in the first place, and how companies could not pay their employees for months, leaving them stranded with no money to pay for food or shelter for their families. Now he had provided a solution for this, they were unwilling to play ball. He had to find an incentive for them. After seeing the impact Abhi was having on all the employees, stopping was not an option. What could he do to compel the companies? How could he convince them to give up their precious working capital to pay employees on time using his platform?

RIYADH, SAUDI ARABIA
NAIF ABUSAIDA – PART 1

In the yellow light of a hospital ward, Naif could only wonder what might have been. Until he was diagnosed with stage three colon cancer, he had been a happy family man with a successful career in banking then marketing and communications. Now, lying with a drip in his arm and the steady bleep of monitors for company, he had begun to reflect more deeply about his purpose in life and what he could do to make a lasting difference. The scourge of cancer had thrown his whole way of thinking into turmoil. Major surgery followed by weeks of debilitating chemotherapy gave him plenty of time for reflection.

"That was the period I thought about my life. Everything had changed. Reality had changed. What would I leave? What would be my legacy? What about my family and kids?" He thinks deeply before he speaks. "What is my motivation? I want to build something different, something valuable to me, my family, my investors, my shareholders, my employees. That's what I identified – I wanted to do something meaningful while also making money."

Born in Cairo to an Egyptian mother and Saudi father, Naif grew up in Riyadh and spent his life in the capital city. He began his career as a banker, working in operations for cash management in corporate banking, before transitioning to financial and operational risk. After seven years in the financial services industry, he thought it was time for a change, which led him to marketing and communications. He worked for General Electric, ACWA Power, and PIF Projects, before his illness pushed him to months of reflection on the meaning and purpose of his life.

Pondering different ideas and trying to combine his understanding of the unbanked communities with his experience in banking services, Naif's mind went from idea to idea. As his friends came to visit him on his recovery journey, he realised how much he appreciated the cultural commitment to community in the region, and how much community provided in caring for each other.

His mind travelled to other functions the community had previously, and still currently, serves – including banking and savings.

How does a community become a bank, or savings platform? The same way it has for hundreds of years in many different countries. Savings groups are not unique to the MENA region, but characteristic of many societies across the Global South whose populations are, coincidentally, largely excluded from the formal financial system. They are academically referred to as Rotating Savings and Credit Associations, or ROSCAs, but better known by their local indigenous names: Susu in Ghana; Sandooq in Sudan; Chits in India; Kye in Korea; Tanda in Mexico, and Jameya in Saudi Arabia and other parts of the MENA region. While they have different names, the concept is the same from one country to the next: members come together voluntarily to pool and share money based on an agreed set of rules. The objective is for members to support each other cooperatively through a democratic savings-and-lending system.

The concept of people coming together to pool economic resources has been a reality even before people started using fiat money. In ancient Mesopotamia and Egypt, the concept of cooperative lending took shape through communal grain storage. In these societies, surplus grains were carefully stored and shared, acting as a collective economic resource. During lean years or poor harvests, this communal reserve ensured that no one would go without food.

ROSCAs do not exist as an alternative to formal saving systems but is a saving system in its own right. In many markets, these structures were, and still are, a necessity for the socio-economic well-being of the communities they serve. It is not that the underbanked population does not save. It just saves the same way it has for thousands of years. Saudi Arabia is a case in point.

Traditional Jameya consists of a group of people (usually friends, neighbours, or colleagues) who agree to deposit a certain amount of money over a certain period. The host may briefly hold onto the collected cash during each meeting until it's time to distribute it to the member whose turn has come that month. Each person then receives the full amount in rotation. For example, if ten people agree to pay SAR 1,000 ($265) a month for ten months, every month one of the groups receives the full amount of SAR 10,000 ($2,650). "By the end of the ten-month period, no one owes anybody anything," says Naif AbuSaida, the founder of Hakbah, his brainchild to contribute to alternative financial savings in a digital way. "Jameya is based on a very simple economic principle – money, or time, versus needs. One person's need for money may be in June, another's in July. So let's swap the needs around without losing anything."

Traditionally, the community comes together every month over a traditional, large meal and the pooling and sharing of resources is one more reason people convene. Over a shared meal, people save and support others – creating even deeper bonds and ties.

As Naif thought about these ROSCAs and his legacy, two goals came to mind: "The financial security I wanted to build for my family and the impact I wanted to create on society." He reflected, "Little did I know that the first would ultimately lead me to the second. Financial security was ultimately a matter of saving enough money, so I started thinking about savings which is when I realised it was a complete whitespace, with significant potential that I became determined to capture."

He carried out market surveys, travelled to Belarus, London, and Geneva, and began to develop four products, one of which was related to Jameya, the Saudi Arabian name for the ROSCA. One of his advisors encouraged him to not to concentrate on the Jameya product, which had no clear model neither clear ROI. Other start-ups had concentrated on wallets, payments, and lending, but no one had delved into the world of savings. The opportunity to digitise and modernise the most common savings mechanism in a country where 70 per cent of the population did not have emergency funds was too large to ignore. And it is a blue ocean with hidden gems. As an ex-banker, deposits (savings) are the core of banking.

But how do you take a tradition and savings ideas steeped in thousands of years of tradition and community-building practices and turn it into a tech start-up? How do you not lose the fundamental essence of what a Jameya is by doing that?

Naif observed how the young used their phones and started with people's online social networks. Just as historically this had worked in-person, it could now work digitally. "For the first year-and-a-half, only family and friends could create groups on the app." This worked well, and Naif had cracked it, beaming. "We were doing something meaningful and making money, so it's not a charity, but also innovative. We own the technology. There was no white-label solution for Jameya, so everything had to be developed from the ground up."

The technology was incredibly strong and people were excited, but this network was limited to people's own relationships. Would it be possible to extend this to others? Perhaps those that did not have such extensive networks and still wanted to save? Many people were in multiple Jameyas saving in multiple groups that were equivalent to different amounts and timelines. What if someone wanted to add one but could not find one?

Naif's head started spinning with the possibilities – but this was all relationship and trust-based. Would it be possible to scale this beyond the human relationship that endorsed trust? What would happen to the platform if it expanded beyond that? How could you vet people's track record and ensure that they contributed as promised? Or should the ROSCA stay small and serve only its direct community as it had for thousands of years?

* * * * *

CAIRO, EGYPT
ISLAM SHAWKY – PART 2

Back in Cairo, it was a chance encounter with the Central Bank that reignited Islam's spirit. Two years after reluctantly agreeing to work with a partner bank, Paymob received a payment facilitator licence from the Central Bank of Egypt, which allowed them to onboard merchants directly.

From that moment on, it was all about 10x-ing (achieving a tenfold improvement). For example, *if banks could onboard six merchants a month, then the founders would aim for sixty*, which was achieved a few months after launch. Within six months they had onboarded 600 merchants, and 6,000 by the end of the first year. "We didn't think these numbers were possible, but Paymob's total addressable market was much larger than we ever imagined," says Islam. By 2022, Paymob had over 100,000 transacting merchants. Today, it has over a quarter of a million.

Islam and the team were on a mission to reach as many SMEs as they could, which meant expanding the payment acceptance solution to include virtually every channel. At that point, merchants could complete transactions online, using mobile wallets, credit and debit cards, and payment links. They could also complete transactions offline at kiosks and through cash on delivery. They hadn't yet figured out the hybrid: *making payments face-to-face but digitally.*

Hard POS (point of sale) was the way to go in other parts of the world, such as the US and Europe, where people could swipe their cards in a machine. In places such as Egypt, however, the economics did not make sense because of the size of the country's SMEs. Not only were only three of every ten Egyptians banked, but the average POS hardware costs between $200 and $300 – a cost that SMEs could not justify considering transaction volumes are that much smaller. Did this mean that their market size was capped at the number of SMEs who could afford POS hardware? Islam refused to believe this. They needed to build something different. Something unique. He looked around the world, and there were no solutions on offer to emulate. They needed to innovate, or die.

In an effort to leverage the region's strength – mobile penetration – and to grow 10x again, Islam and the team set out to decouple Paymob's growth from hardware. So, in partnership with Mastercard, Paymob became the first in the region to launch a tap-on-phone payment solution. What would be viewed as an incremental innovation in some markets was in fact an act of leapfrogging in emerging economies, simply because it was an imperative, mass market, need. That innovation, in turn, became better than anything else being built globally.

The ability to turn any mobile phone into a payment receiver was huge. It created an entirely new market: suddenly, any SME that had a mobile phone could download the Paymob app and start accepting payments. There was no longer any need for a hardware device that could cost more than an entire month's revenues. The creation of this market was a game-changer and excited Islam and the team more than anything before. This innovation was truly new and ahead of anything in the world.

Paymob's success continued, built on strong fundamentals, a bit of luck, relentless perseverance, and the urge to constantly innovate. In those early days, they faced a vast market with little competition – a business landscape ripe for innovation. Engaging legacy banks was just one step along their journey, as they demonstrated to these institutions the value of collaborating with emerging tech players. Over time, banks began to recognise the transformative potential of new technologies – not just for their customers – and understood they couldn't navigate this alone. Paymob played a pivotal role in driving this shift, the Originals might not have experienced firsthand, but for which they had undoubtedly helped to lay the groundwork.

By 2023, Paymob was a significant regional success story and had processed half a per cent of Egypt's entire GDP. Since its founding (and many iterations) in 2015, the company has raised $90 million in funding from investors, including PayPal Ventures and EBRD VC. Handling over 1.5 billion transactions in a year, empowering over 40,000 merchants on a yearly basis, Islam and the team reflect on the early days and think about their future as they grow into the UAE and other markets – continuing to serve the SMEs, the backbones of the economies.

DUBAI, UNITED ARAB EMIRATES
HOSAM ARAB – PART 2

With a few deep breaths before the call starts, Hosam adjusts the Tabby pitch depending on whether the focus is bringing an international investor up to speed on the region or a regional investor up to speed on BNPL and the business model. His next call proved to be successful, and resulted in a meeting. Then a subsequent meeting, and finally a term sheet – he was relieved! The next week yielded another term sheet, and funding stopped being his fundamental concern. Slowly but surely, Hosam built the balance sheet required to scale Tabby into the first fintech unicorn in the MENA region, raising a total of $1.7 billion in equity and debt from global investors including J.P. Morgan and Mubadala.

While other credit providers have taken advantage of late payments by charging hefty interest fees – especially on credit cards – Tabby was adamant they should be paid on time. The money that investors had put in was not going to be allocated to a growth-at-all-cost strategy but getting the unit economics right in a model where they had the potential to go very wrong.

Within four years of its launch, Tabby was highly profitable. Tabby also introduced a payment card to tap into offline retail and offers monthly pay later options on grocery delivery apps, leaning into the regional needs and demands.

Today, Tabby serves 15,000 merchants across Egypt, the UAE, and Saudi Arabia and processes around 5 million transactions every month. Tabby's journey proves that an emulative model, imported from abroad but localised to the regional context, can create a more fundamental shift in markets where its application resolves a deep market pain point, rather than acts as an additional product feature.

"When we first came into the market there were a lot of questions from consumers around, 'hey, listen, I don't really need this. I can buy what I need, right? And if I can't, then I won't buy it'," says Hosam. "But I think what has shifted is the fact that it's so seamless and so convenient for consumers. The question then becomes why would I not use it if someone's giving me that flexibility? And the fact of the matter is it is easily one of the most flexible and seamless payment solutions that there is out there. You don't need to re-enter your card every time you go on a different website. Your card details are saved. So once Tabby recognises you, you are able to transact in many places with a click of a button. But then you're able to also spread your dollar over a longer period of time at no additional cost to you. So I think that goes a very long way." As does his company.

KARACHI, PAKISTAN
OMAIR ANSARI - PART 2

Omair and Ali were, once more, working through the night. The solution they had devised for these business-owners might be able to solve the problem; but it would mean a grander strategy and larger vision for Abhi. They were going into the invoice factoring space – a financial service of paying a company's unpaid invoices to keep their operations running smoothly to avoid delays in payment. Suddenly, they were not asking companies for help – they were providing help to companies. They were offering both the companies, and the employees, a service. Nobody could say no. It was a game-changing moment, and Omair suddenly realised he was building a real business and needed a strong balance sheet.

That offering catalysed Abhi's uptake. Helping a company with cashflow, as it turns out, is a prerequisite to granting employees earned wage access. That was the decision that tilted the supply and demand equation, leading Abhi to a point where it had more demand than supply, in terms of credit capability, for the local market.

Omair often reflects on this catalyst "When I started out, I'd say yeah good idea but who the hell is going to back me? To be honest I didn't even back myself because my idea of an entrepreneur was just not me." A thoughtful look clouds his face. "It was something which I treated as a challenge, a personal challenge. When I was sitting on the other side as an investment banker, you always pretend you know what you are doing, giving out all this advice to entrepreneurs who are actually building companies but you haven't ever put your hat in the ring and actually done something."

The founders continued to add to the offering. While they were allowing their users to gain early access to their salaries, the money was still locked in the digital world because there were no bank branches or ATMs nearby. So they introduced Abhi Bill, which allowed users to settle bills with registered institutions, such as hospitals, banks, or schools. They also wanted to offer an option for those who wanted to borrow or send money to their friends, so they launched Abhi Dos – the Venmo of Pakistan.

Omair and Ali never planned to stay local, but they also had not imagined the opportunity to expand would happen so soon in the company's lifecycle. What transpired was that their idea had multi-national demand. They watched in awed delight as their first foreign opportunity came and they grabbed it, acquiring an earned wage access (EWA) player in Bangladesh and expanding internationally. The Gulf was next in line. The company already had a foot in the door in the UAE and Saudi Arabia, both of which are considerable markets for the underserved workforce when it comes to salaries and remittances. They maintained their main operations in Pakistan but went to live in the UAE. Within a year, the co-founders had expanded their company, acquired another one, raised rounds of capital, and were already profitable.

Financial success is one side of Abhi's impact. Socio-economically, this is a business that has not only helped people rebuild their homes. It is also a business that has allowed urgent and critical surgical procedures to take place without worrying about the medical bill. Abhi is working toward promoting financial wellness and alleviating the stress of living paycheck to paycheck, or loan shark to loan shark. Access to advanced wages does more than ease financial strain; it allows families to cover essential needs like healthcare and education, building a foundation for long-term stability. With this flexibility, they can afford timely medical care without falling into debt and support their children's education, from tuition to supplies and activities.

Abhi raised $25 million of funding over three rounds followed by $240 million in debt funding and is now valued at $128 million.

RIYADH, SAUDI ARABIA
NAIF ABUSAIDA – PART 2

Naif's mind was made up. He walked into the office with the answer and directive: Hakbah would serve everyone who wanted to save in groups or importantly, want to do something with the money saved through the groups. It's a very strong financial instrument. "We launched a marketplace, where customers could form groups by supplying half of the members themselves (such as family or friends), with the remaining members provided from Hakbah's own marketplace. "For the third phase, which is where we are now, you don't need to know anyone," says Naif. "Just come by yourself with your commitment and you will find the Jameya for your needs. If you don't find it, put it on your wish list and we'll create it."

Groups are created based on various data points, including the number of participants, their backgrounds, KYC (Know Your Customer) information, income levels, and geographic location. Additionally, the creation of groups takes into account seasonal needs. For example, there is often an increase in spending on food and drink as families prepare daily iftars (dinners where they gather to break their fast during Ramadan). Similarly, in September, before children return to school, expenses typically increase. Using the example of ten people paying SAR 1,000 a month for ten months, anyone using Hakbah not only gets the SAR 10,000 in rotation, but additional saving rewards, too. The only criteria for that reward? Don't miss a payment.

Hakbah is more than a savings platform, or a means to an end. It's a story about achieving financial inclusion using a grassroots, centuries-old practice that is an opportunity to revive and modernise a fully functioning financial system that helps millions of people realise their financial aspirations. Hakbah shows that the 'alternative' is actually not one, but a necessity that can achieve comparable financial inclusion outcomes as markets with a history of industrialisation, or those adopting the fintech-for-financial-inclusion playbook.

Hakbah now has 1,000,000 registered users, of which +110,000 are active customers. It is home to 14,300 savings groups and has helped over 110,000 of its customers save more than $1 billion over four years and turn to profitability in the third year of operation, which is not a common reach in fintech at this stage.

As for Naif himself, his annual check-ups have revealed no issues since the original diagnosis and treatment. He says that, *inshallah*, his life will continue to be driven by the same sense of purpose. Certainly, he has earned a very honourable place in the ranks of the Originals.

* * * * *

The absence of legacy incumbent banks, leaving an underbanked population and SME market was one of the key reasons for the lack of financial inclusion in MENA. It was also the reason of the incredible adoption rates of these technologies. In the absence of banking, credit, or savings, consumers could embrace the solutions these founders offered as new and impactful problem-solvers, rather than incremental improvements to existing providers. There were no switching costs – just onboarding. There were no attachments to the previous way of doing things – just new, real and complete digital solutions to persistent long-established problems.

For consumers, these founders solved the challenges of financial inclusion, salary payments, access to credit and savings. For SMEs, the backbone of the economy, they enabled the acceptance of digital payments and working capital facilities, expanding their potential reach. For the banks and infrastructure, they grew the potential client base and increased efficiencies dramatically.

The ability to understand, in a deep and meaningful manner, the day-to-day problems and limitations of the ecosystem translated to the development of solutions that were applicable and practical to reaching the end-goal. Whether it was the cost of the POS for Paymob, or the social element of savings for Hakbah, understanding the culture and the regional nuances of finance were key to solving some of the large societal challenges lack of financial inclusion had created.

Their ability to identify and leverage the region's largest asset – youth and smartphone penetration – to build solutions that lean into the region's key strengths in order to provide solutions for all has transformed commerce and lives. Today's founders have payment providers, retailers and e-commerce companies have credit solutions increasing their basket sizes, and employees are paid on time enabling them to contribute to the economy and pay their bills on time. For those who want to save, a platform enabling them to save in a communal way that generations have done exists and can serve them the way they need.

Whether Paymob started as a social platform but ended up as a digital payment provider, or Tabby started to provide digital payments but ended up as a BNPL credit solution, the solutions and resilience required by these founders to achieve the levels of success is humbling, and their ability to pivot and change course, and ultimately build infrastructure, not just consumer solutions is eye-opening to what was genuinely required.

When each idea was conceived, the region provided no infrastructure and little, if any, regulatory framework. Each of the founders was able to visualise massive opportunity that their idea could grow into – from payments to savings to credit. By collaborating with the progressive regulators and financial institutions, they were able to identify and explore new huge potential markets, with Tabby illustrating how some business models that were suboptimal in other markets would actually be ideal for MENA as they solved more fundamental problems within the ecosystem – not just marginally improved existing solutions.

Their struggles and victories, however, are not limited to fintech. The path forged by these fintech companies has enabled the evolution of other sectors in an accelerated and exciting manner. Platforms that integrate payment solutions with educational tools are making it easier for students and institutions to manage tuition fees and access resources; agritech platforms are helping to overcome the financial woes of small-scale farmers; and entrepreneurs are addressing the challenges of access, quality, and cost in the field of healthcare by providing advanced digital health solutions to millions of people who have never had it before.

Combined, the businesses which these aforementioned founders have each built mean that an estimated 6 million people now have access to finance and credit who were previously excluded from the finance ecosystem. Their efforts translate to 130,000 small and medium-sized businesses and more than 400 million transactions worth over $16 billion. Along with financial inclusion, a stated aim for all these founders, the figures represent a substantial financial boost for the region.

These are some of the inspirational stories that are driving forward the spirit of regional entrepreneurship while simultaneously providing financial rewards for investors around the world. It is truly remarkable to see founders work alongside progressive regulators to create a financial infrastructure that addresses the needs of today's economy and population. In less than a decade, and each with their unique offering, Islam, Hosam, Omair, and Naif have contributed massively to MENA's financial services landscape by bypassing outdated systems and forging new paths with their start-ups – from payments, to credit, to savings, while emphasising the importance of a mission driven goal.

CHAPTER 7

ENABLING ACCESS TO CARE

الصحة تاج على رؤوس الأصحاء لا يراه إلا المرضى

Good health is a crown worn by the
healthy; that only the ill can see.

- ARABIC PROVERB

BEIRUT, LEBANON
NADINE HACHACH-HARAM - PART 1

Huddled at home in war-torn Beirut, glued to the television, which infuriatingly stopped and started with the intermittent and rationed electricity, 14-year-old Nadine felt outraged and powerless at the same time. It was 1996 and Nadine's heart was breaking for the 106 dead women and children and their families in Qana, a Southern Lebanese town under fire in the war with Israel. This was her holiday home – she had spent endless weekends and holidays with her family in Qana. Her mother and grandmother had grown up in this town.

As a young teenager, seeing that first-hand was quite traumatising," says Nadine of the attack. "I distinctly remember a girl in our school who was burned from top to bottom. No fingers, no hair, but she managed to be the life of the party at school. Within her trauma, I saw the beauty of people helping and coming together and how that could help you almost overcome that trauma." The attack made Nadine determined to devote her life to improving the lives of others. How could she help all these people? "The lack of medical care was obvious and frightening. The feeling of powerlessness created a seed – there had to be a way to reach them, to help them, to heal them."

Her mind kept returning to Qana and the 800 civilians that had come under fire, leaving hundreds dead and wounded. The contrast with her early life, until the age of 10, could not be starker. Her early memories were of a comfortable and largely peaceful time in the prosperous Californian city of San Diego – until her mother decided to return to their native Lebanon to care for her elderly parents, shortly after the long and brutal civil war had ended.

In a fundamental change for the whole family, they returned to a country still recovering from years of bloodshed that led to over 150,000 deaths and forced over a million to seek refuge elsewhere.

"It was quite a stark difference going from that very beautiful, idyllic sort of life in California, to a country where you didn't have clean water every day for showers," remembers Nadine. "You had to buy your water in tanks. Electricity was limited and every other day there was a new value to the Lebanese lira against the dollar. Growing up in that chaotic, messy environment was quite a culture shock for us. In hindsight, it was probably the best thing my parents ever did. Whilst it had all these negatives, the positives were that it really taught me the importance of community, the importance of family, and relying on each other. The importance of people helping each other in those really difficult times."

Qana's shock was deeply personal for Nadine, as it was her grandmother Leila's home. Leila had been a rock for Nadine – her role model, her inspiration. They had grown close over the years, and Leila's infinite compassion for others moved Nadine.

A philanthropist and charity founder who dedicated her life to helping others, granny Leila encouraged Nadine and her sister, Noha, to be compassionate and caring. Together, they would pack food parcels during Ramadan, play with children at the local orphanage, and be of service wherever and whenever they could. Leila's impact on Nadine would be profound. She instilled resilience, independence – and entrepreneurialism. She gave her the hunger, desire, and capacity to think bigger. To be fair and independent, loving and strong.

After Qana, and inspired by her grandmother and her own need to help others, Nadine, only 14, asked a surgeon who was a family friend if she could attend one of his surgeries in the southern Lebanese city of Saida. "Shockingly in hindsight, he agreed," she laughs at the idea that someone would agree to that, "And that was how I first entered the operating theatre, observing intently everything he did, and absorbing it like a sponge. I was fascinated and knew I had found my calling."

She distinctly remembers a young girl with a contracture – the shortening of a muscle – in her foot which had made it impossible to walk normally. Following a simple plastic surgery, the girl was able to walk again. Nadine was mesmerised. Nadine ran home and excitedly told her mother she wanted to be a reconstructive plastic surgeon.

Eight years later, while studying medicine in London, she volunteered with medical missions abroad, travelling and helping with reconstructive plastic surgery. Always at the back of her mind was her grandmother's voice telling her to be of service to others. These medical missions continued during her career with the National Health Service (NHS) in the UK. She was now able to help others and live up to her grandmother's high ideals.

In 2009, she graduated from the London School of Medicine as part of Queen Mary University and became a qualified doctor. She stayed in the UK to advance her training, and at a basic level she says she felt really good about the work she was doing. As well as her full-time job as a medic, she was flying to different parts of the world, first with 'Facing the World' craniofacial charity working in Asia and Vietnam. Then she specialised in cleft lip and palate reconstruction in the Middle East as part of the 'Global Smile Foundation'. For the next decade, she spent eight weeks a year in Southeast Asia, South America, or the Middle East.

But something was bothering her – eventually releasing the latent entrepreneur in her character. She began to look at the cost of these missions. How many lives were they really touching? Was it really the most scalable way to help others? How effective were they? The thousands of people they could never reach troubled her. The young girl wanting to help all the wounded in Qana began to haunt her. What more could she do? It was obvious that what was being done was not enough, nor would it ever be.

On one of these Lebanon trips in 2015, as she was preparing for a cleft lip palate mission (to invite doctors and patients from Iraq and Syria to train them and provide knowledge and expertise so they could locally operate), Nadine came across a report that validated her thoughts. The Lancet Commission had just revealed that 5 billion (of 7.3 billion) people worldwide lacked access to safe, affordable, and timely surgery. Not only did the report highlight significant global disparities in surgical care – this figure equates to two-thirds of the world's population – it also called for urgent action to improve surgical access and quality, particularly in low and middle-income countries.

Doctors were due to fly in from London and Boston; the media was on standby, and everything was in place. It was meant to be the start of the campaign to put all the report's promises into action. Sadly, geopolitical events overtook the best laid plans. The security situation, which had only heightened the need to make these programmes work, deteriorated to the point where safety of the medical staff was at risk. The Syrian and Iraqi doctors cancelled and only a few Lebanon-based patients were able to make it to Beirut.

Nadine was devastated. All of the mission's hard work had come to nothing. The upshot was – in the classic style of a potential pioneer – she and a few of the other doctors sat down and brainstormed. What if they used technology instead?

Nadine recalls they asked each other some basic questions: "Couldn't technology help us virtually collaborate, live stream what we were doing, and help these doctors learn the steps of the procedure without having to physically be in the room? Because surgery for so long was dependent on physical co-presence, could we disrupt that?"

It was the kind of solution that might have eventually arrived in the medical field, but it took an event outside everyone's control to catalyse its consideration. One of the mission's team members had a Google Glass. Although a cutting-edge wearable device at the time, as it was still in the early days of development, it was still better than nothing.

In another effort at adapting whatever was available, the team taped an iPod to the operating room ceiling. The Google Glass was switched on and the team live-streamed the operation, so Iraqi and Syrian doctors could watch and learn from the relative safety of their own homes. It was a ground-breaking experiment.

"We were streaming this case and showing, through augmented reality (AR), that you could mark a patient, you could guide someone through the procedure whilst they weren't in the room with you," remembers Nadine.

When the excitement of their achievement died down, Nadine and the team concluded that while it was a great experiment, it showed operating rooms were not in tune with an increasingly online digital world. What if they could change that, she thought? What if operating rooms became digital, connected, and collaborative? What if the way healthcare workers carried out procedures could be changed dramatically?

Nadine started to imagine a world where operating rooms across the globe were intelligent – where doctors, anaesthetists, and nurses could connect and activate operating theatres beyond their physical borders. If that could be achieved, then disparities in access recorded by the Lancet Commission could be overcome. Back in London, Nadine returned to the report and set about understanding the specific challenges in the MENA region that required addressing if her vision was to be achieved.

Although the number of physicians per 1,000 people varied significantly from country to country, 1.72 physicians per 1,000 was the average across the MENA region. By contrast, for countries within the OECD, the average was around 3.34 physicians per 1,000, rising to a high of 7.1 in Sweden and 5.6 in Portugal.[76] This disparity was compounded by significant rural populations, especially in remote areas of the Arabian Peninsula, North Africa, and the Levant. Then factor in that access was often denied to women in rural areas and in conflict zones.[77]

Access to Healthcare
Physicians per 1,000 People

MENA 1.72   OECD 3.34

Source: World Bank (2021)

These disparities are shocking and highlight a critical challenge for the region's healthcare ecosystem. An estimated 43 per cent of the world's physicians are available to just 20 per cent of the global population. This 20 per cent lives – unsurprisingly – in countries with a very high Human Development Index (HDI).[78]

Conversely, 12 per cent of the world's population lives in low HDI countries with access to just one per cent of the world's physicians.[79] Such physician-to-population ratios are deeply distressing and hammer home the severity of the MENA region's healthcare inequities, revealing a system strained by both insufficient medical resources and the profound challenges of delivering care to some of the world's most vulnerable populations. Resolving this issue was at the forefront of Nadine's thinking.

Smart operating rooms could enable the scaling of expertise and reduce variation in the quality of healthcare provision. They could also accelerate the pace at which the quality of operations improves, increasing the chances that every patient has the best access to care. And what if she could virtually scrub in (the process of preparing for surgery) into any operating room in the world and share best practice? It became an itch she needed to scratch.

Returning to Beirut, in 2015, she set about building a prototype. Nadine wanted to create a platform extending the reach of a surgeon's expertise.

"I envisioned an immersive experience that enables collaboration and digitises a surgeon's footprint to make their skills timeless. Our platform would be a borderless operating room where surgeons can capture, share, and analyse life-saving knowledge, from anywhere."

This telematics technology was self-funded at first – because, at that stage, there was little to no access to finance for digital healthcare – and her solution had to be accessible on any device. That included low bandwidth to handle poor internet connections, which was the reality in most markets and environments where this was most needed.

Nadine reached out to friends and fellow surgeons who she had worked with in different countries to help introduce the prototype in challenging environments, such as Peru, Gaza, Lebanon, and Vietnam.

The prototype was so successful that, in 2016, a study in Peru revealed it had not only helped to upskill local teams; it gave them confidence, increased their speed of work, and enabled the training of others. Nadine was excited – she had proven the concept with a makeshift prototype! She could now enable the provision of care where before it would have been impossible.

Back in Gaza in 2016, Nadine was preparing to use the prototype to help reconstruct a blast injury at Al-Shifa Hospital. Then CNN called. They had discovered her work and wanted to cover it – they asked for the name of her company.

"What company?" remembers Nadine. "At that point, this was a project and I was focused on proving we could save lives and help people around the world without having to fly there. We wanted everyone to have access to help when they needed it." But now, she needed a name.

Around a traditional Middle Eastern dinner that night, she was eating with a few colleagues and they brainstormed a name: Proximie.

The next day the CNN article came out. 'Could this technology be the future of surgery?' it asked. Immediately, investors took interest. Nadine was thrown headfirst into the world of start-ups, fundraising, and pitch decks. "I had no idea where to turn and what to do. I hadn't set out to build a company, but this was incredibly exciting!"

Nadine began to build Proximie from the ground up. That meant setting up a business and devising the right financial model to raise funding. True to her family roots, she did so in Lebanon. The company's first employees were all based in Beirut, and its first funding came from the region. Even today, one of Nadine's proudest achievements is that Proximie was born and built in Lebanon, with a third of its 100-strong workforce still based there.

"What was clear, as I started doing my research around surgical discrepancy, surgical disparity, and variation in surgical care, was this was a problem the whole world was facing. Historically, people try to pigeonhole this as a problem of the Global South: they don't have enough surgeons; they don't have enough care. But as I started to look, even in the UK's NHS and in the US, you have the same problems. Not every patient has access to the same quality of surgery or gets the same outcome, and not every procedure is being done to the highest quality it should be. Technology could play an incredible role and revolutionise how we digitise operating rooms and deliver care."

Nadine's instructions to the engineers set to roll out the equipment were simple: make it easy to use and cheap to buy. The end-to-end platform had to work anywhere; on any device; on low bandwidth; operate with a federated data platform and be capable of evolving as the need arose.

Proximie's aim was to build a highly adaptable, universally accessible platform that could integrate existing data systems and grow rapidly, making advanced surgical care more widely available. These initial goals would ideally enable Proximie to scale swiftly and begin democratising access to surgery. To succeed, it would need to reach the most remote locations and provide support during operations.

While not a pressing necessity for some of the region's wealthier countries, for the low-income and lower-middle-income countries such as Egypt, Iraq, Syria, and Yemen it was desperately needed. Those countries faced major limitations in healthcare funding and infrastructure.

For Proximie, the challenge was less the technology and more the need for fundamental behavioural changes. It is a familiar challenge for would-be disruptors. In this case, it was how to persuade a profession of highly talented and skilled individuals to alter its working ways. Nadine and her team had to make clinicians feel comfortable with the idea of digital operating rooms (ORs) and remote collaboration as a priority.

They initially focused on a single application – telepresence. The technology allowed doctors to virtually 'scrub in' to any OR, anywhere in the world; collaborate in real time, and share best practice. But how to enable real time development and collaboration and real time data transfer, while layering AR over various devices?

At the time, existing technology was clunky and prohibitively expensive. Yet, the vast majority had a mobile phone, tablet, or computer, irrespective of location. A hardware-agnostic platform capable of working within a multitude of contexts was therefore required. They had to start almost from scratch but once built, the application allowed any doctor, globally, to join a case, see and hear everything taking place in the OR, and walk someone through the procedure. They could even draw on the screen.

The beauty of Proximie was that it didn't just capture video data, it captured device data too, including anaesthetic or imaging information. This data was shown on the screen and could be recorded and archived for future consultation. The more operations captured, the better the data set doctors and surgeons could draw on. But there was nothing there to start with, and traction was difficult to garner.

This was far removed from anything others were doing in the space between healthcare and mobile technology. In 2016, the MENA region was growing its first generation of healthtech entrepreneurs, but most were in the very early stages of enabling patients and providers to remotely capture health and wellness insights from a range of devices and smart sensors.[80]

Egypt and the UAE led the way in start-up activity, but capital being pumped in was low. Seed funding tended to be under $500,000 and various challenges, including the difficulty in conducting clinical trials, opaque health regulations, and talent shortage were holding them back.[81]

Nadine set about winning hearts and minds. For the next few years she toured the world attempting to build something which until then was in its infancy. For investors, the fact that this was completely new made them nervous. There were too many unknowns. What would happen if the technology lagged? Where would the responsibility of a mistake lie? Could engineers sitting in Lebanon really build something world-class? Nadine kept hitting one wall after another. Despite the CNN publicity, raising $2 million was illusive and was taking too long. Maybe this was a dream that would never transpire.

On one flight back home from another investment pitch where she was told that there is no way this would work, and that no hospital would ever use this technology, Nadine's self-doubt felt insurmountable. "Maybe I am wrong. Maybe I should just go back to the OR myself and help one patient at a time. I feel like I am completely wasting my time." She was ready to give up.

AMMAN, JORDAN
JALIL ALLABADI – PART 1

Jalil pretended he was still asleep as his father was trying to wake him up. He hated visiting the Jordanian refugee camps near them, and resented his father waking him up early on the weekends to go and visit them. The poverty, the smells, the conditions in which the refugees lived all made him uncomfortable.

Abdulaziz kept insisting and finally Jalil opened his eyes and reluctantly got dressed. One more time to these camps as a young teenager. One more time watching his father, a highly-respected

German-trained surgeon, educate patients about the importance of managing their health, explaining their diagnosis and what was being done to treat them. And one more time realising that nobody was listening to his father – nobody cared. Nobody understood.

Yet, could it be possible that people did not care about their health? How was it possible that they did not want to understand? Jalil could not help but reflect on these moments many years later, in 2008 when his father called him excited that he had finally completed his twenty-year project of writing the first Arabic medical dictionary. Until then, even diabetes, a condition most prevalent in the Middle East, had no medical explanation for the Arab-speaking layman.

Jalil's father had a request; his many years of work building an Arabic medical dictionary seemed doomed in a world of the internet. He had started this project in 1988, when the internet did not exist to the average person. Now, in 2008, nobody bought dictionaries. What should he do? Was all this work pointless?

His father's despair led Jalil to call a few friends and start exploring. During their research, they discovered that whereas dictionaries weren't selling, online healthcare websites such as WebMD were popping up and doing a roaring trade. So they thought carefully and took a similar approach. They digitised the entire book, created a website, and launched altibbi.com in 2011. Job done. Or was it?

Jalil, who had studied industrial engineering in Italy before entering the manufacturing side of the pharmaceutical industry, was suddenly thrown into the world of entrepreneurship. Whereas this was first a project, with the initial focus being digitising his father's comprehensive medical dictionary, a broader vision started appearing in his mind.

"I suddenly had this strong desire to provide reliable and accessible healthcare information in Arabic to everyone." His memories of the refugee camps and the lack of understanding of his father's patients came flooding back. These were the people who needed this information. These were the people who needed somewhere to turn to, to learn from, to provide them with basic health information.

Five per cent of internet users spoke some form of Arabic in 2011 as Jalil decided to tackle this problem, yet only one per cent of all online content was in the language.[82] This posed considerable problems for any entrepreneur trying to break through in their native tongue. The lack of content meant high-speed broadband connections were low on the priority list for most Arabic speakers, while talent and funding were in short supply for healthtech start-ups. Even today, and despite more Arabic speakers online, Arabic remains one of the most under-represented languages in web content.

Content scarcity stemmed from several factors. Many operating systems had limited support for Arabic fonts. Early versions of HTML offered limited support for right-to-left text, making it difficult to create web pages to work well with Arabic content. Even the limited variety of Arabic fonts had a negative impact. Aesthetic limitations restricted the ability to reflect the language's rich typographic heritage and discouraged creators from developing Arabic content. These challenges combined to make content hard to absorb. More pertinently – for the world of medicine – the paucity of information and resources in any Arabic dialect restricted the ability of healthcare professionals and patients to access critical information.

"Back in 2011, it was still the beginning of the internet revolution in this part of the world," explains Jalil. "Start-ups were not a thing yet. It wasn't glamorous like today, and you had to try and convince someone working for a big company to take a risk. I needed someone with significant experience – because I didn't have any – to join me. That was a big risk for anyone. I spent six months recruiting a person who would bet on the company, quit their high-paying job, and come join someone who didn't have any experience in this field."

Jalil had just launched the world's first medical website in Arabic from his home in Amman. Initially, it had 16,000 pages of content and he set himself the target of hitting 500,000 page views a month – just because an advertising agency had given him that number. If he wanted Altibbi to make money – 500,000 views was the threshold for advertisers to start spending. He was performing an urgent need

– creating medical content in Arabic in a world where Arab users wanted the internet to be relevant to them; but persuading web developers to join Altibbi was not easy.

Within three years, the number of pages grew to 1.5 million, and Altibbi was looking beyond being a simple repository of information. Jalil, like many others in the field, had become acutely aware of the fundamental issues facing healthcare provision in the MENA region: access, quality, and cost. He wanted to do something about it, but what? The problems were enormous and seemed unsurmountable.

In many parts of the GCC, the public health sector has sought to address the challenges of access, quality, and cost by mandating universal healthcare, controlling prices, and encouraging providers to adopt smart healthcare initiatives. These strategies include increasing investment in hospital infrastructure; leveraging international healthcare brands via public-private partnerships (PPPs); and implementing policies to ensure healthcare delivery aligns with international care standards.

And yet, as with fintech and the unbanked, the solution to availability is not merely to build new hospitals or to enter into PPPs – important though that is – but to innovate around how we improve access by other means. How do we streamline the industry to enable high-quality care for all at a lower cost, and improve patient outcomes in the process?

Such questions are especially pertinent in the MENA region, where advanced digital health solutions offer the opportunity to deliver primary care to millions who have never had it before. Unlike in developed markets – where healthtech works to improve the patient experience – in large tracts of the MENA region entrepreneurs are seeking to provide a patient experience for the very first time.

In addition to rural areas in the MENA region being underserved by bricks and mortar healthcare facilities, many countries – including Syria, Libya, and Yemen – were in the midst of conflicts that had devastated their healthcare systems. There may have been hospitals, but many had been shelled and were barely functioning. Outside these war zones, inequities based on income, gender, urbanisation, and age persisted. To take just one example of many, an urban woman was twice as likely to have a skilled attendant at birth, and access to contraceptives, compared with her rural counterpart.[83]

MENA governments were also spending far less on healthcare than other parts of the world, on average only eight per cent of national budgets compared with 17 per cent in OECD countries. Households were making up the difference themselves, with out-of-pocket expenses reaching 40 per cent of total health expenditure, compared with 14 per cent in OECD countries. Consequently, many people were foregoing or delaying medical care because of the unaffordable and impoverishing nature of the costs.[84]

For many, this financial burden causes the abandonment of medical treatment altogether. In contrast, immediate intervention, supported by comprehensive insurance coverage and a robust healthcare safety net, is the norm across North America. In Sweden, the national guarantee of care (Vårdgaranti) aims to keep waiting times for a primary care physician below seven days.

Jalil's quiet and pensive nature led him down one rabbit hole of exploration after the next. There was so much to be done. "The more I learned about the industry, the larger I realised the gap was. It was incredibly overwhelming to consider what people needed compared to what was available. I had to think carefully about where to start and what unique assets the region had that I could leverage."

The answer lay in the region's incredibly high rate of mobile phone ownership and the fact that most of his users were coming onto the platform to research ailments – he already had a huge funnel of patients. Given that the fundamental challenge was basic access to a doctor, and the low number of doctors per person, why not build a telehealth company?

By 2015, total unique subscribers to mobiles stood at 334.1 million across the MENA region – a penetration rate of 59 per cent.[85] This was higher than the global average (51 per cent) but lagged Europe (78 per cent) and North America (70 per cent).[86] The following year, mobile broadband (3G and above) accounted for over 40 per cent of all connections, while smartphones were 42 per cent of all mobile connections.[87] With such a high rate of ownership, mobile phones began to connect people to the care they so sorely needed.

For Jalil, the answer was combining his knowledge of medical practice and patient requirements, with an understanding of using market data gleaned from his web platform. For him, MENA's healthcare system problems could be solved through telehealth. He envisioned a world where patients could be connected in person online to a network of certified healthcare providers twenty-four hours a day, helping to overcome the problems of inequitable access to primary care.

Initially, Jalil began with a simple question and answer forum, allowing users to ask medical questions and receive answers from healthcare professionals. "I needed to convince someone who was busy – and making a lot of money, as doctors do – to come in and offer their time for free answering questions on our website. That was a big, big challenge. And it was a big milestone when I got my first doctor to come in."

The idea became a runaway success and revealed the overwhelming need patients had for interacting with doctors. Altibbi's offering therefore evolved to include video consultations, including a mobile app that enabled users to access health information, ask questions, and book appointments.

Specialty consultations were added too, but at every step of the evolution process, the patient's needs were prioritised. For that to stay true, it was essential the platform was as accessible and comprehensive as possible to everyone in the region. It also required the provision of consistently universal high standards of care, at an affordable price.

In Jalil's own words: "You could get doctors to answer patient questions, but quality was the real issue. We had to work hard to ensure quality was the same across the board, regardless of the doctor and country. That is why we started using AI. As we scaled, it became very expensive to control the quality. So we started building many tools to make sure we were controlling every single aspect of the journey – and controlling the quality level for the patient."

For Jalil, AI helped to solve an acute problem – the inconsistent quality of patient care across different doctors and countries. By applying AI's functionality to the platform, it meant the platform could transcribe conversations, highlight key points, suggest possible diagnoses, and offer treatment recommendations during virtual consultations.

The introduction of AI also meant the platform could suggest supplementary lines of questions to doctors to elicit more precise answers from their patients, ensuring comprehensive assessments and enhancing the overall care quality. The platform could even look for red flags during a consultation that were so subtle that even the most attentive doctor might not have noticed. For example, a moment of silence or changes in the tone of patient's answers to sensitive questions might indicate misunderstanding, tension or even cases where the patient was not answering the question completely truthfully for fear of embarrassment. It would then produce a summary of the consultation, helping to reduce the time needed for paperwork from ten or fifteen minutes to a maximum of fifty seconds, while maintaining quality.

Altibbi was revolutionising telehealth. It was democratising access to healthcare and simultaneously improving primary care quality. In Jordan, women living in remote areas faced accumulating costs (energy, time, money) to attend doctor appointments in neighbouring villages or towns. In many cases, they had to take a day or two off to travel sometimes considerable distances, for ailments easily diagnosed by phone.

"We don't do everything – it's primary care – but we can follow up with 60 per cent of what these women are suffering from," says Jalil. "And that reduces all that waste by 60 per cent. And, yes, that is a revolution. We are driving real impact here, touching people's lives."

But Jalil wanted to move beyond increasing access – with better quality and lower costs – to prevention. The MENA region was strained under the burden of non-communicable diseases (NCDs). Six Arab countries (Bahrain, Egypt, Jordan, Kuwait, Saudi Arabia, and the UAE) were in the global top twenty for obesity, with four (Bahrain, Kuwait, Saudi Arabia, and the UAE) among the top countries globally for diabetes. Depression was a leading cause of illness for women, and tobacco was a major killer, especially for men. In Egypt, an estimated 11 per cent of annual premature excess deaths could be prevented by a comprehensive tobacco control programme.[88]

Coronary heart disease is now the leading cause of morbidity, mortality, and disability in the MENA region and was classified as a pandemic by the National Library of Medicine.[89] Importantly, all four principal NCDs – cardiovascular diseases, cancers, diabetes, and chronic respiratory diseases – share behavioural risk factors such as tobacco use, physical inactivity, and poor diet.[90]

By leveraging machine learning, Altibbi could offer personalised health recommendations based on user data. Not only would this include reminders for medication, but suggestions for lifestyle changes and preventive care tips tailored to individual health profiles. In Jalil's mind, prevention was the key to the region's health crisis. However, what the company was trying to do had not been attempted anywhere else in the world.

"What we were – and are – trying to do is be the family doctor for the patient, not the doctor you only call when you're sick. The doctor checking on you constantly, predicting and helping you avoid things in the future. That is built on a lot of data. We have to have the best data infrastructure ever. We have to collect a lot of data from patients, trigger a lot of data input, and use that data to help that patient conduct a healthier life."

But would people be happy to share their data? What about data privacy? Can an AI doctor be just as good as a regular doctor? Would people trust the AI? Did they have a choice given the lack of other doctors? Who was liable if the AI hallucinated or made a mistake?

As Jalil contemplated these issues, and began to build the AI algorithm, he couldn't help but imagine a new world. He found his current business relatively obsolete – it was, he thought, the equivalent of the dictionary his father had completed in 2008, only to find that discover that the world no longer needed dictionaries.

DUBAI, UNITED ARAB EMIRATES
NADIN KARADAG AND SUNDEEP SAHNI – PART 1

The machines held Sundeep back as he was trying to get up. After three weeks in the ICU, he was tired of being in the hospital. He wondered what life lesson he was supposed to learn here, and was eager to leave, convinced he was cured from Covid-19, and get back to work. At 36, he was too young to slow down. Knowing full well that the reason this had affected him so badly was his poor health, Sundeep promised himself he would do something about improving his own health. If he could find a convenient way.

As the community started to check in and make sure he was okay, he reconnected with Nadin, one of his close friends from many years earlier at INSEAD. Nadin was worried for Sundeep, especially considering he was suffering from long-Covid symptoms. Nadin introduced Sundeep to Jamie Richard who had been her health coach for several years. He had helped her tremendously when she was suffering from her own health challenges: prediabetes and early arthritis. Jamie, through nutrition, supplements, and regular blood test checkups, was able to reverse Nadin's prediabetes without any medication. Similarly, Jamie also succeeded in reversing Sundeep's long-Covid symptoms by recommending lifestyle changes, blood testing and supplements.

Nadin's own health challenges had come from years of working in a stressful environment, while being a caregiver for her mother who was battling Multiple Sclerosis. From a young age, she had to navigate the silos of healthcare, which was inconvenient, confusing and non-integrative. Nadin had been trying to change her mother's diet and supplement intake in order to hold the condition at bay, and had succeeded in improving her mother's state with a new combination of diet and supplements. These results were the outcome of an independent search from answers, with no support from the healthcare system. As a result, Nadin's personal background and experiences drove her to engage in a deeper conversation with Sundeep.

Reminiscing about their INSEAD times over breakfast at Jones the Grocer in Dubai, Sundeep and Nadin's conversation turned from the good old days to growing old. Or feeling old. Why did they feel this way? Who could help them? They didn't want to go to traditional doctors, who would prescribe medication. They didn't want medication. They wanted care. Healthcare. Somebody to guide them to become healthier and stay healthy.

A long search yielded nothing, so Nadin and Sundeep decided to team up and try to build something themselves. They were clear on the values to eventually guide their decision. Their north star was creating something to foster a positive, inclusive culture and to make a real difference in the world. They channeled their shared challenges into creating Valeo. The vision behind it was deeply personal – rooted in their journeys through a healthcare system that had often let them or their families down.

Something they would want to use as customers. Valeo was born. The idea was to create a platform that would place preventive healthcare at the top of its agenda, dubbing it 'longevity' and emphasising the goal of optimising wellness in all aspects of our lives. Valeo even introduced a longevity score – an in-house algorithm for users to track the progression of their health markers and blood work over time. It can also shine a light on the intricate connections between lifestyle and biomarkers such as inflammation, cholesterol, hormone levels, blood sugar etc. The higher the longevity score, the longer a customer stands to stay healthy.

With the understanding even something as disruptive as the pandemic can offer opportunities to the entrepreneurial mind, it catalysed developments in healthtech. Faced with unprecedented challenges, it presented the industry with the opportunity to demonstrate its collective healing potential. As Sundeep says, "It was a time when everything healthtech was booming".

Again, technology played its part. The launch of a raft of devices including Apple watches, Oura and Whoop encouraged people to take ownership of their health. By closely monitoring personalised health data they could make better informed decisions on dietary requirements, exercise and sleep, plus visiting the clinic whenever they felt data was alarming. While previous initiatives weren't as successful in translating that change, the accessibility, gamification and ease of engagement with these tools and platforms started striking behavioural changes in how we view personal health and well-being.

In 2021, a PwC report found that 84 per cent of respondents in the UAE, Saudi Arabia, and Egypt were more focused on taking care of their diet – an increase of 44 per cent on the previous year.[91] It also revealed a keener interest in mental and physical well-being. The appeal of wearable tech had soared, allowing users to monitor their physical activity, heart rate, blood pressure, and the oxygen levels in their blood. This increase was mirrored globally, with the world's consumer wellness market valued at $1.8 trillion in 2024.[92]

Nadin and Sundeep were from financial and entrepreneurial backgrounds and looking to build cutting-edge technology, but they saw the need for the convenience of home testing and a return to the tradition of home visits in a world striving to be healthier.

In other markets, home testing involved pricking yourself with a needle and filling a tube with drops of blood. Cultural considerations meant no one was going to do that in the GCC. However, they would welcome a nurse into their home. Home delivery was – and still is – deeply ingrained in the Middle Eastern culture. The relatively low physician-to-population ratio (1.72 per thousand compared with the OECD average of 3.34) and lower labour costs also meant the price of sending a nurse to someone's villa or apartment would be much less than in Europe or the US. Importantly, the infrastructure to make this happen was already in place due to Covid-19.

The founders began by offering at-home blood testing, allowing users to schedule appointments and receive results-based advice. When the company launched, advanced tests for men and women cost $400. A year later, they were selling the same tests for $135, with a 40 per cent margin. Results were stored in the Valeo app, allowing users to access their health records, monitor biomarkers, and track improvements. They could also be matched with a health coach, who would provide advice on everything from meal plans to fitness and supplements.

"The limited size of the UAE market, however, meant at-home blood testing alone was insufficient for the company to grow. What really stood out in a review of the data was that around 80 per cent of the people were deficient in either a vitamin or a mineral," according to Nadin. The MENA region, particularly countries with warm climates, experienced high levels of vitamin D deficiency, largely due to the tendency to avoid sun exposure because of the intense, year-round heat. Iron deficiency was another significant concern, driven primarily by the region's diet which was deficient in iron.

"We realised that a lot of the advice we gave was for supplements, and a lot of people were ordering their supplements from the US, from the UK, or they were flying back with them from their home countries," says Nadin. "We thought: 'Why are we doing this?' There's an opportunity here. We need to be able to deliver high-quality supplements the very next day."

But as the company grew, customer segmentation became apparent. Some prioritised longevity and sought to optimise their health. Others worked long hours and had less time to take care of themselves, so embraced the convenience of at-home and at-office testing. New mothers, too, were short on time and favoured Valeo's convenience. And there were those with specific issues (hair loss, weight, performance) who wanted the guidance of personalised journeys.

The founders discovered that if one member of a family ordered, others followed, with parents also buying for their teenage children. Such behaviour mirrors cultural traditions, with decisions (especially regarding health and well-being) often made collectively in a region known for its youthfulness.

The founders were marketing Valeo Health as a wellness company, meaning monitoring and providing advice on weight management, sleep, energy levels, fitness, stress management, and digestion. Supplements could not replace a balanced diet and regular exercise but were recommended as suitable complements to a healthy lifestyle. Soon, at-home doctor consultations were introduced, as were skincare solutions, food intolerance tests, physiotherapy sessions, IV therapy, and weight loss programmes.

Valeo Health was becoming a super app for health – was that even something people wanted? What would happen once the world stopped being as concerned about Covid-19 and other health concerns? Would the business continue to grow and thrive or was this simply lucky market timing fit? Sundeep and Nadin considered all the opportunities ahead of them, and tried to focus – which ones would be key to growth over the long term? Could they create something for everyone? Where should they focus? Or was this a temporary moment in time? Their gut instinct and personal experiences told them this was hugely needed, but they also knew human behaviour is difficult to change, and they were trying to build so many different strategies at once. Would they fail at everything if they didn't focus? How would they know what to focus on?

CAIRO, EGYPT
KARIM KHASHABA – PART 1

The pharmacist insisted that the medicine he was selling Karim was as good as the one the doctor had prescribed. "They are all the same – just take this one." he said, "Trust me." Karim Khashaba stared in disbelief. This was not the same medication as the prescription commanded. Nor was it the first time this had happened. The pharmacist then presented him with some cash. Karim left the medication on the counter next to the money and left.

Walking home confused, and with his head in a daze, he couldn't make sense of what was happening. His family had been in the pharmaceutical industry for years, he was a management consultant at Booz & Company, and had worked in Munich and Dubai, recently returning to Cairo. Now, in this busy, noisy, bustling city, he was learning how different things were. He needed a friend; a guide; somebody who could help him sort out his thoughts. He called Yasser.

Busy at his job in a digital studio, Yasser heard the phone buzz and looked to see who it was. He never missed a call from Karim, especially not since the autobahn incident in their university days when Karim and another friend were stopped by the police in northern Germany and had no valid IDs with them. This time, though, it was different. Karim was calling in confusion and excitement "The way it's done doesn't make sense, and I have an idea – join me?" The answer for Yasser was a resounding yes, without even knowing the idea. Karim was brilliant and Yasser knew it. Sherief El Faky, a software developer who would later become the company's chief technology officer had the same reaction, and the three of them got together and founded Yodawy – which means 'to heal' in Arabic – launching the company's first informal MVP six short months later.

"We went straight to the ultimate model," says Karim, "We wanted to build a platform that supports insurance companies in terms of automating approvals, managing that back office, and digitising prescriptions, but at the same time served as a fulfilment channel for customers. We also wanted to provide a greatly improved customer experience."

That would also eliminate insurance fraud, which is how it had all started for Karim. 45 per cent of all insurance claims were also subject to fraud. People were entering pharmacies with a prescription and walking out with either cash or an entirely different product. This required complicity from the prescription holder and the pharmacist. The customer experience could also be horrendous. A patient would visit a doctor, be given a handwritten prescription, walk to a pharmacy, wait forty-five minutes for insurer approval, and then be told the medication was unavailable.

The network of insurance companies was also very small, so only certain pharmacies could be used for claims. In many cases, people with medical insurance simply weren't using it or preferred to pay out-of-pocket to avoid the headache. Those most affected were patients with chronic illnesses, who had recurring expenses for medication and had to regularly run the gauntlet of pharmacy and insurer.

Historically, Egyptians (who now number 116 million) have paid for their own medical care because of the public healthcare system's poor quality. It is underfunded, understaffed, and most avoid it – causing disparities in access to healthcare services. The country has one of the world's fastest-growing populations, placing immense pressure on the nation's healthcare system, with only 0.71 physicians per 1,000 people in 2021. Those who could afford it were shifting from a cash model to insurance cover. Karim discovered the growth rate for insurance was double-digits, but from a low base. However, infrastructure to support that growth was missing.

Karim considered how to address the problem. He was a fan of the US pharmacy benefit management (PBM) model, where third-party administrators managed prescriptions on behalf of health insurers. PBMs built networks of pharmacies, automated approvals and established seamless connections to the back office of insurance companies for real-time approvals. However, they consolidated in the early 2000s, leading to improved efficiencies in prescriptions delivery and services to consumers.

The long-term goal was building a product providing easier consumer access, and substantially more savings for the insurer. However, the platform began as a relatively simple app for ordering medications. Users could select their medication, and orders would be routed to the closest pharmacy for fulfilment. The founders realised the digital health sector wasn't as easy as they had anticipated, and partnerships were key to moving forward. The founders' strategy was simple: pharmacies had to be on board before any insurance companies could be approached.

When enough pharmacies had signed up, they started to contact insurers. It took a year-and-a-half of weekly visits to persuade the first to join the platform. That insurer was the French multinational insurance company AXA. Seed funding of $1 million followed shortly afterwards, and by the end of 2019 the three founders had begun to work full-time at Yodawy.

"Before that we were just part-timers," says Karim. "Everyone had a job and was doing this on the side. But we were fully committed to the company by the end of 2019 and really started to build the company throughout 2020, which was a good time to start building a product because when Covid-19 happened, we were the only medication delivery service linked to insurance companies in the country."

By the end of the year, the company had secured 60 per cent of Egypt's insurance market. But its supply chain was dependent on others, and it was only as strong as its weakest link. The co-founders were struggling to keep up with the demand. The company was growing too fast to be supported by the weak ecosystem around it. In order to fulfil his objective, Karim would have to think to the stories of the Originals – does he have to build the infrastructure for the company before he can grow the company? Was that a requirement or a distraction? What was his biggest limitation to capturing the market and continuing to grow? The demand was there – how could he meet it? Karim's head was spinning searching for a solution.

* * * * *

BEIRUT, LEBANON
NADINE HACHACH-HARAM – PART 2

Qana's memories kept Nadine going just that little bit longer. Enough to raise a little bit of money, then a little bit more. Her reputation as a top surgeon enabled her to convince a few surgeon friends to try the technology, and a few hospitals to allow it. At least in markets where the need was dire and it was a question of using the technology, or no care at all.

"It was a very benign way to open up their eyes to the possibility. To get them to try it. To get them to even listen to us. If I had walked in on day one into a hospital in California and said, 'you have real issues with your variability of care and your quality of care and how you guys work together and how you train and teach', I don't think we would have had the same success. So in a way we had to start from the markets who needed it most first and then grow into the West."

And the company did. By 2024, Nadine had raised over $118 million in equity and debt from investors including Mubadala, ᵈvent Life Sciences, Global Ventures, and Emerson Collective at a valuation exceeding $250 million. The technology has been deployed in 800 facilities across over sixty countries and over 80,000 procedures. There are 15,000 users engaging with new and historic cases. Each case is recorded, anonymised, and sits in a secure cloud-connected library, providing a contextual view of ORs during any given procedure.

Proximie's commercial success, particularly in the US and Europe, hasn't shaken the commitment to providing global health. Proximie's largest market, currently the US, illustrates the ability of building in areas where there is acute need, such as Lebanon, to solve a real problem, without industry limitations, and then exporting to global markets. Proximie was unique to the region and the world. It was pioneering the use of AR applications in surgery – which were significant advances in the evolution of healthtech.

The answer, of course, lies in critical need. A home-grown solution, developed in a region where the problem was most acute, instinctively provided a more effective and tailored product. Proximie's success highlights how proximity to a problem can lead to a more impactful and relevant innovation than one imported from a remote market.

"My vision is that eventually every room and every procedure will be powered by technologies like Proximie, and every room will be connected and data-driven. We will be far more transparent and digitally collaborative in these rooms, and this will help us accelerate care. We have shown we can train twice as many healthcare workers in half the time and deliver the same quality, if not better, using these kinds of platforms. And we'll continue to build evidence around what we do."

AMMAN, JORDAN
JALIL ALLABADI – PART 2

"I've solved it!" Jalil thought as he finally figured out how to harness the power of AI for Altibbi. It had to capture every ounce of information and apply it for the benefit of the patient. Any medical data from a conversation between a doctor and patient was automatically captured and added to the patient's profile. AI algorithms then analysed that data, plus health records and lifestyle information, to help users adopt healthier lifestyles.

Developing algorithms to help patients make informed choices about their diet, exercise, and other habits was not easy. It required an understanding of all Arabic dialects, understanding of medical contexts, and knowledge of any issues relating to a specific patient's medical profile. Protecting patient data was also a crucial concern. Today, however, Altibbi's AI use has become a virtuous loop with data-informed doctor training leading to improved care quality and preventive advice given to patients.

In Altibbi's early days, the website had 5,000 unique daily users. By 2024, that figure had reached 1.6 million, with an estimated 120 million page views a month. By comparison, only 5,000 copies of the paper version were sold – the digital platform achieved 320 times the reach of what the physical book could have achieved.

Altibbi also has 2.2 million pages of medical content, 20,000 active physicians, and performed 2,000 daily telehealth consultations. Since launch, it has carried out over 6 million primary care telehealth consultations. Together, these statistics mean not only that Altibbi is the number one Arabic medical website in every country across the MENA region, and number eleven globally in website traffic – enabling doctors to manage their time and diagnosis better and allowing people to take ownership of managing their health, but that all this data can be combined to create AI-led care, and indeed, as Altibbi has created, the first LLM (Large Language Model) AI for healthcare in Arabic.

Through this LLM, Altibbi is able to aggregate all patient conversations, decipher the Arabic dialects and guide doctors to higher success rates when addressing patients. The reach Altibbi achieved through digitising the Arabic medical dictionary would have been unimaginable without the shift to an online platform. What started as a traditional resource transformed into a powerful digital tool, unlocking access to millions that a physical version alone could never have reached. In a world where we will never have enough doctors to serve our population, this solution ensures that we can still have care.

As Jalil reflected on the beginnings, the mornings he was reluctant to join his father at the refugee camp tours, he realised that his purpose and drive were seeded in the most unlikely places decades ago.

DUBAI, UNITED ARAB EMIRATES
NADIN KARADAG AND SUNDEEP SAHNI – PART 2

Meanwhile, Sundeep and Nadin reached a conclusion – to focus on their core. "We strongly believe that people want to take care of their health, but it is something people compromise or delay because it's not convenient," says Sundeep, who grew up in Kuwait. "Organising a booking, going to the doctor... we want health to become so important that preventive care is the future and sick care is actually a corner case. Today, healthcare has to be the solution before people get sick. We want healthcare to focus on how to stay healthy."

"The teenagers of now are going to be the healthcare customers of the future, and they will expect their services to be delivered in a particular way," says Nadin. "When they are in their 20s, they're not going to go to a hospital or clinic to buy something, they're going to download an app and do it that way. We see this young population as a huge potential market."

Much of that potential is already being realised. Valeo has carried out over 20,000 tests, has a total customer base of 30,000, and adds over 5,000 customers a month. It has also taken over 200,000 orders, and supplements have become 50 per cent of Valeo's revenues. With four offices in Dubai, India, Saudi Arabia, and Lebanon, it was set to hit an annual recurring revenue of $10 million in the second quarter of 2024.

With a sense of relief, Sundeep and Nadin reflect on the early days, and today, and realise that yes, it is indeed possible to build a health superapp that can cater the overall needs of peoples' health at large. Just because it hadn't been done before, it didn't mean it wasn't possible. And this is still the beginning.

CAIRO, EGYPT

KARIM KHASHABA – PART 2

As for Karim at Yodawy, the subsequent year, the company focused on building its own supply chain, fulfilling orders for chronic prescriptions, and then went on to build the country's first approval automation engine for prescriptions. From there, the company built capability after capability, until it became the de facto prescriptions partner for insurance companies across Egypt.

Yodawy set up a robust logistics network to efficiently handle and fulfil orders, particularly focusing on prescriptions for patients with a chronic illness and developed the country's first automated engine for approving prescriptions. This came with its own set of problems.

Low digitalisation in the insurance sector meant integrating insurers into the platform was long, painful, and arduous. Karim remembers one insurance company still doing everything manually, sending chronic patients a printed and stamped prescription by mail every month.

"Whenever someone did not really have a digitalised back office, we had to work with different optimisations. We still gave them our systems up front. So what the customer was seeing was that the insurance company was digitalised at the pharmacy, despite the fact that the back office was not digitalised. In some cases, we had to maintain their data and manually update the information on a weekly or monthly basis on our systems. We (kind of) haggled our way through these difficulties. But now a lot of them are on the platform, whether they're digitalised or not, and using us as their system for medications."

Nevertheless, Yodawy has rewired Egypt's medical ecosystem, connecting medical providers and insurance companies and offering consumers a convenient and frictionless way to order and receive medication. Today, it accounts for an estimated 95 per cent of Egypt's insurance market, serves almost 300,000 patients a month and has a 50 per cent share of the medical insurance market for approvals. It has also shown insurance companies that by shifting fulfilment to Yodawy, the price of medications can be reduced by up to 20 per cent and insurance fraud is nearly eliminated.

But Karim is not yet finished. Today, Yodawy is taking those savings further, launching a micro-insurance service in Egypt and expanding into Saudi Arabia, where demand for the company's intellectual property is high. The micro-insurance offering will take Yodawy's services to the uninsured, specifically those with chronic diseases, providing price reductions for a small annual fee. Karim thinks about the future, "Customers with pain points and who want medications delivered frictionlessly, exist everywhere. So expansion possibilities are infinite."

* * * * *

First and foremost, the ability to passionately care for others and the drive fuelled by such a strong desire to serve were fundamental to the journey of Nadine, Sundeep, Nadin, Jalil, and Karim in building their companies.

But the real accelerant and inflection point for each of these founders was the timing and combination of the lack of healthcare and medical infrastructure, the acute, identified human need for solutions and the advancement in technology, specifically the proliferation of smartphones.

The ability to leapfrog, due to the lack of industry incumbents, in the case of Proximie, was paramount. The choice between a new and virtually-enabled surgery, or no surgery, is an obvious one for those living without access to any care. However, had this been in markets with a different option – perhaps waiting a few weeks for your surgery or accepting a virtually-enabled one – the option for virtually-assisted surgery would have never been selected, and the product never proven. The lack of choice for patients, and the lack of healthcare infrastructure enabled the development of what has become a global success story in healthcare provision.

The need for such innovation will only further increase in nations torn apart by conflict and civil strife. In 2023, the MENA region was home to over 16 million displaced people, with around 6 million Syrian refugees living across Turkey, Lebanon, Iraq, Jordan, and Egypt.[93] In Yemen, Syria, and Libya, public health infrastructure has collapsed, leading to higher morbidity and mortality rates. In such circumstances, healthtech can, and is, offering transformative solutions to the pressing and lifesaving questions of accessibility, availability, and quality of care. It is providing the means to leapfrog conventional solutions, delivering scalable, accessible, and efficient healthcare solutions in conflict zones and addressing the most critical of health needs.

However, even beyond conflict zones, the region faces a series of public health challenges, particularly in addressing NCDs. Tackling the underlying behavioural and environmental risk factors of NCDs requires prioritisation of prevention over treatment. In Saudi Arabia, where the direct costs of managing NCDs are predicted to increase by 63 per cent by 2030, prevention will be critical.[94] The increase in costs for diabetes in the Kingdom alone will be $2.4 billion,[95] while a growing, yet ageing GCC population emphasises the urgent need to promote healthy lifestyles and prevent chronic disease onset. In 2020, the UAE's over 60 was just 3.1 per cent of the population. By 2050, they will be nearly one in five.[96]

Regional governments have initiated reforms to address these issues, prioritising early detection, treatment, and management, but success has been limited. In many cases, the capacity of national healthcare systems to deliver comprehensive NCD services is simply not there.

The early traction of companies like Valeo and Altibbi have given hope in this area – where such a large part of the population is still young. With Valeo embracing cultural practices of home care first, yet using technology to manage and influence better health outcomes; and with Altibbi's AI platform using analytics to improve efficiency and manage care, there is a visible shift in the move from treatment to care.

Leveraging the region's youth and tech-forward population, these healthtech start-ups have helped revolutionise healthcare on a global scale. They have addressed the profound inequality in the fundamental right to healthcare and significantly improved access to essential medical services for underserved populations. Such inequities have historically not only impacted overall health outcomes but exacerbated existing social and economic divides. Addressing these challenges has been crucial in moving to a more equitable and efficient healthcare system – one harnessing technology's potential to provide accessible, quality care for all.

Observing Nadine, Jalil, Sundeep, Nadin, and Karim identify, address, and tackle such large and complex challenges is not only inspirational but potentially transformative to all societies. Combined, they have delivered care to more than 20 million patients and enabled more than a thousand hospitals. Their ability to precisely identify and solve the lack of varying pain-points from health education, primary care access, pharmaceutical access and fraud has been game-changing. Ultimately virtual surgeries using the world's best technology will bring hope to those who – even now – lack even basic healthcare or could potentially even be deployed and further advanced within more developed yet grossly inefficient Western medical systems. They also provide inspiration to those seeking to address similar large, complex and daunting challenges in ways not yet tried – radical, not incremental, eventually perpetuating and further cultivating the region's culture of entrepreneurship through disruptive innovation.

CHAPTER 8

TEACHING THE YOUNG

العلم في الصغر كالنقش في الحجر

Learning while young is akin to etching in stone.

– ARABIC PROVERB

AMMAN, JORDAN
HAMDI TABBAA – PART 1

Hamdi hung onto every word his grandfather spoke. The young boy was always mesmerised by the older man's stories and tales. The stories of the 'days gone by' and the importance of education, aspiration, and hard work were shared one after the other on the long Friday family lunches. "If done well," the wise man uttered, "education is not only a service that can change lives, but also one that can make money."

Hamdi remembers that simple piece of advice as if it were yesterday. Yet, it remained a distant memory for many years as Hamdi pursued his own education at the London School of Economics, subsequently taking a role with Uber and becoming incredibly busy enabling its scaling across Jordan, Lebanon, Qatar and the wider MENA region. As an entrepreneur, he was left bruised but undaunted by a failed supermarket venture and a fledgling tech-enabled platform that helped children with their physics and economics studies.

In his fifth year at Uber, with an incessant desire to continue learning and growing, he was taking a course at the Harvard Business School Online and was struck by how much learning was possible through a well-built online platform. "It wasn't so much a single light bulb, it was more like a lot of small light bulbs along the way showing me that you can achieve even more impact in the region if you combine education with technology," he said reflectively. "The great thing with technology is that you can deliver the best quality at scale and help another generation on their way up."

As he reflected, he had already established that Jordan performed poorly when it came to the Programme for International Student Assessment (PISA), which measures the ability of 15-year-olds to use reading, mathematics, and science to meet real-life challenges. In 2022, the country had a mean mathematics score of 361 points, which placed it significantly below the OECD average of 472.[97] It was fourth from bottom globally for reading (342) and only marginally better at science (375). To Hamdi, the scores were a damning indictment of the sorry state of the country's public school infrastructure. These disheartening results were replicated across the region, even in Saudi Arabia, where reading stood at 383 and science at 390, much below the OECD average.[98]

This was true not only for Jordan, but for all MENA countries, particularly those in the Levant. Hamdi also knew that Jordan had a rapidly expanding population that had more than doubled from 5.2 million in 2003 to 10.8 million in 2020.[99] It also had a birth rate of 2.83 births per woman – almost double that of the European Union (1.46 births per woman)[100] – and an estimated 710,000 refugees, primarily from Syria and Iraq.[101] The other Levantine countries also had similar population trends and growth rates.

Combined, for Jordan, the country's population growth, high birth rate, and refugee influx had placed considerable strain on Jordan's infrastructure, including its antiquated education system. With 63 per cent of its population under the age of 30 – an estimated 33 per cent of whom are school age – public schools were buckling under the pressure.[102] In many cases, public schools were operating one, two, or even three shifts, resulting in fewer learning hours per student.

Government expenditure on education as a percentage of GDP was also alarmingly low. In 2022, Jordan allocated only 3.2 per cent of its GDP to education, a trend reflected in other countries across the Levant and North Africa.[103] Egypt dedicated 3.9 per cent of its GDP to learning, while Lebanon's investment was a paltry 1.7 per cent.[104] The situation in Egypt was, and is, especially dire.

Despite the implementation of a multi-shift system to address the shortage of classroom space, an estimated 1.5 million children were still out of school in 2021. Around 250,000 new classrooms are needed to accommodate the school-age population (only 15,000 are built annually),[105] and there is an estimated shortage of 320,000 teachers.[106] The disparity between educational expenditure and the high percentage of school-age children is stark. The countries around him were in a dire state, all very similar to one another.

In contrast, in 2019, Saudi Arabia allocated a substantial portion of its budget to education, amounting to $51 billion. This represented 21 per cent of fiscal spending and 7 per cent of total GDP.[107] Such investment placed the kingdom above the EU, where average expenditure was 4.7 per cent in 2022.[108] In the UAE, despite education spending accounting for only 3.9 per cent of GDP in 2021, the private sector plays a substantial role in catering to the educational needs of all age groups. However, across the board, the education results when students tested were below their international counterparts – education had a core problem.

The temporary solution that had been developed in local communities had resulted in the substantial growth and proliferation of the after-school tutoring sector. In Egypt, an estimated 40 per cent of private educational spending flows into this sub-segment. Almost 60 per cent of 15-year-olds across the MENA region spend their early evenings and weekends in overcrowded tutoring centres, placing incredible financial strain on parents who choose to supplement their children's education.[109] Although these centres can significantly boost a child's chances of academic success, they point to the deep challenges of quality and underfunding faced by public schools.

"I reached a point where I felt that the region was falling behind due to low-quality education regardless of investment," says Hamdi. "I felt a responsibility to address this gap, especially for middle- and lower-income populations who lack access to good education and school infrastructure. A genuinely effective tech solution could transform the way students learn, offering them a better chance to either pursue higher education or enter the workforce, ultimately leading to a more prosperous future. I thought back to my grandfather – what would he do if he saw these numbers?"

Addressing access is about more than building additional schools or hiring more teachers; but rethinking how education can reach more people meaningfully – teaching them the way they want to learn. Perhaps the answer is a complete reimagining of education – one including hybrid, blended, and alternative models, all powered by technology. Technology is the key to opening doors for more students, bringing education to them in ways that are flexible, engaging, and closer to the lives they already lead.

From access to content and approach, the educational challenges faced across the MENA region are exacerbated by a demographic bulge, heightening the need for immediate solutions. In the MENA region, 47 per cent of the population is under the age of 24.[110] By contrast, the percentage of the population aged 15 and under in OECD countries stands at 17.3 per cent.[111] Further still, it is expected that the population in MENA will increase to 724 million by 2050, almost doubling from that of 2018, which is likely to further exacerbate the problem.[112]

Globally, lack of access to education disproportionately affects those from disadvantaged backgrounds, especially in rural and remote areas of impoverished nations. In 2023, the number of out-of-school children stood at 250 million globally – an increase of 6 million from 2021.[113]

In the MENA region, where roughly half of the population is under the age of 24, nearly 15 million children between the ages of 5 and 14 were out of school in 2016.[114] Very little had changed by

2023, when 14.9 million children and young people were failing to receive any form of education in North Africa and Western Asia.[115] That figure represented 12.2 per cent of the school age population. Conflicts in Syria, Iraq, Libya, and Yemen, where more than 8,850 education facilities had been collectively destroyed by 2015, greatly exacerbated access disparity.[116] In Sudan, the country's ongoing civil war has left 90 per cent of the country's 19 million school-age children with no access to a formal education.[117]

SCHOOL-AGED INDIVIDUALS
School-Aged Individuals, from 0 to 24 Years Old (%)

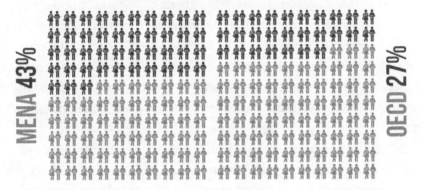

Source: UN Population Division (2024)

When Hamdi met Hussein Alsarabi, the founder of Instructit, an edtech SaaS start-up on the brink of failure, in 2019, he was suddenly inspired to try, yet again, to build another start-up and focus on the education space. Previously a product development director at the online platform Mawdoo3, Hussein was the technical co-founder Hamdi had been searching for. The code he had developed at Instructit provided a foundation to build upon, leading to Abwaab's launch in late 2019. They were soon joined by Sabri Hakim, the general manager of Careem (later Uber) in Jordan, who was initially Hamdi's direct rival and later turned partner/co-founder, and they set out to disrupt education, founding Abwaab.

Initially, they raised $2.4 million in pre-seed funding – one of the largest investment rounds in regional edtech at the time – to build a platform that would teach school students everything offered in their national curriculum, online and at affordable prices, with the goal of improving student scores and providing access to basic education. The goal has been to replace the high dependence on tutoring. Pre-recorded video lessons and performance tracking allowed secondary school students to learn at their own pace, test themselves, and receive tuition. The focal point was math and science, but that would evolve over time to include math, biology, chemistry, physics, Arabic, and English for students in grades seven to twelve.

Then, when Abwaab was just six weeks old, the Covid-19 pandemic began. Schools were about to face an immediate lockdown, and the governments needed help. When Hamdi met with the Minister of Education, he was faced with a decision of stepping in to offer the distance learning replacement to students across Jordan, at such a young age of a start-up. He took the bold decision to do it, which was costly to the start-up, but also pushed them to scale very quickly and gain awareness.

The meeting was hastily concluded and Abwaab was identified by the ministry as the go-to solution for existing schools, with only forty-eight hours to put something together. Although a distraction from the product roadmap the founders had originally planned for, this meeting propelled Abwaab into the distance learning front line almost overnight.

The company went from serving a few thousand students to millions as the country grappled with the pandemic's fallout and the accelerated transition to online education. The collaboration dramatically boosted Abwaab's reach and importance, enabling it to build a comprehensive ecosystem that changed the way students learned, and equipped them with the tools to succeed in life.

However, in order to keep up with the demand, more funding was needed. Hamdi's ability to build a team, a product, and a company had massively impressed investors, and the clear demand for the product, regardless of circumstances, was clear. In 2021, Abwaab secured $5.1 million in seed funding, followed by a $20 million Series A round later that year. With these investments, the company expanded its offerings to include video and live lessons, an assessment engine, and a gamified experience – all of which complemented its curated library of educational content, interactive learning tools and resources, and personalised learning paths based on student progress and performance. This was all based on the way in which this new generation was learning and interacting with the platform.

Hamdi's original fear of his early failures subsided. He now saw that with the right product, market and team, he had reached significant metrics and success. However, something was missing.

On analysis, Hamdi started to realise that renewal rates were not as high as they had hoped for – and parents, who were responsible for their children's purchase decisions, were too far removed from the platform's offering. Analysis of Abwaab's user base also revealed a predominance of highly capable students, which meant those who required guidance, and didn't have access to education, were not being catered to. As a result, a greater degree of human interaction was necessary.

The question was: how could that interaction be provided at scale? Was it worth building something so significant if it was only serving the capable? Why were those that were most in need not using the platform? What was he missing? Despite the success metrics of funds raised, students reached, and hours spent, Hamdi felt that the platform was underperforming and not reaching a fraction of its potential. But everybody else seemed to think that the company was amazing! He wasn't convinced that they were measuring the metrics that mattered, or reaching those who needed them.

LAHORE, PAKISTAN
FATIMA RIZWAN – PART 1

The shriek of the dial-up modem connecting to the internet was her cue. She raced into the living room and stood silently behind her father, watching him intently and memorising everything. This was the highlight of her day, every day. After school, hours of homework, dinner and chores, she was permitted to observe her father using his computer and accessing the internet. Despite the intermittent power, cutting the electricity every so often, Fatima was steadfast in her desire to learn.

These memories of her childhood came flooding back to her as Fatima started down the Web3 rabbit hole. Wow! She couldn't believe the opportunity that this technology would provide the people around her. The equaliser it could become. The companies that could be built. Fatima's mind went into overdrive thinking of all the things that Web3 could do, where Web2 hadn't. The lack of Web2 development for Pakistan meant that people could build relevant companies straight onto Web3. This was amazing! But who? Who would know how to do that? Who would build these projects? How could her community participate in this new technological age if nobody knew how to build on the Web3 platform?

Suddenly, her calling became clear: she was going to build something where everybody could learn and build projects on Web3. Without paying upfront. She knew that nobody around her could afford to take time off, or pay money, to learn a new technology. She had to incentivise them to learn. She had to promise them a job, or 'project', if they could learn to build the protocols. "Imagine," she thought, "being paid to learn the newest technology and build a project."

This was very different to her first company, TechJuice, a platform for writing about start-ups and entrepreneurship in what was the increasingly febrile and dynamic market in Pakistan. Its success was phenomenal and surprised even Fatima, let alone her family and friends. "When I started, my target was to get a million people to use this product and if they are going to use it, that's going to be life changing. Once I'd achieved that milestone, I started thinking that maybe my dreams are just not big enough." So, she dreamed bigger.

Fatima would be the first to say she has always been the odd one out. The sixth child and one of five girls in a family of seven, she knew from childhood she would take a very different path from the others. "I was the first one to take a stand and tell my family that I wanted to study software engineering because, growing up, I was fascinated by the computer," she says with a rapt look of intensity, "My mother is a homemaker and all my sisters are married and none of them had ever gone into business. Yet, by the time I graduated, I had been exposed to so much of what was happening in the world, thanks to the internet, I was determined to start my own company."

Growing up in Lahore, Pakistan with no obvious female role models to look up to, she needed all of her intelligence and determination to establish herself and be taken seriously in the predominantly male world of technology. When she was done with Techjuice, she had everybody on the edges of their seats: what was next?

What Fatima had realised early on, was that with the marked lack of Web2 platforms in emerging markets whether in fintech, healthtech, or other areas, there was much yet to be built online. The question she asked herself was why would anyone want to build on Web2 if Web3 was a better solution for certain sectors and companies? The ability to leapfrog straight to Web3 was something that struck her. A true entrepreneur, she recognised that the underlying problem was a lack of properly skilled individuals to make it a reality.

Her background in software engineering enabled her to see an opportunity to create an integrated social network for developers – one where they could learn, build, and eventually be funded by a community of investors and mentors who shared her vision for the future of decentralised technologies. Her research revealed an estimated 40 million developers were operational worldwide, but only 42,000 were active in the Web3 space. If she could create a platform that enabled the next 10 million developers to enter the Web3 ecosystem, she could build a company with the potential to generate meaningful impact.

She launched Metaschool in February 2022 to allow teachers and subsequently developers to learn their skills online. On a platform that was completely gamified. The small team identified communities of developers – either online or offline – and approached them via mass messaging or personalised requests for feedback. "I mean we had to hustle so much." They also attended conferences and adopted old school pamphleteering, simply to raise awareness of what they were doing. Metaschool's unique selling point was that it was not a platform for courses, but for projects.

"Blockchain and the technology in the Web3 ecosystem is very different and I would say the polar opposite to what a developer has learned so far in their life," she says gamely. "It can be overwhelming for a developer when they enter the Web3 space and we say 'hey, just build it and take it to a level where other people can interact with it'. That kind of confidence I don't feel you can get when you are taking a course where there is so much theoretical content." Fatima's aim was to give others the confidence she had shown herself, but equally to make sure the platform stayed relevant in a rapidly changing world.

"It's always day one at Metaschool," she says cheerfully. "We have so much to do, there is so much we need to solve, there are so many bigger problems that we want to tackle. We have validated the business model. We know there is a clear-cut demand for what we are building. But with the rise of AI we see that in the next ten years there are going to be 1 billion people who will be enabled to create their own software. So imagine going out and one in every ten people you meet is a developer. One billion developers out there in the world are going to be creating 10x more software.

"With this huge amount of creation, the problem is not going to be who can solve a problem – the problem is going to be who has access to the right capital. The vision we have for Metaschool is we want to become a platform where developers learn, build, and are funded by the community. This is how we close the loop. A lot of developers are coming onto the platform, they are learning and building, but right now we haven't been able to support them. So learn, build, and fund are the three key words we are going to be continuing to chase as more developers enter the world." And she was one of them.

As she started to build and scale the platform enabling others to learn how to code and then complete projects and start to earn income, Fatima herself had to find funding. But where?

A Pakistan-based female founder for a Web3 education company was going to be a hard sell, even for the most risk-loving investors. Fatima's mind started wondering – she knew there was an answer, but what was it?

CAIRO, EGYPT
FADL AL TARZI – PART 1

Fadl laughed out loud. Of all his crazy ideas, this was definitely the craziest and most unlikely. There was, of course, no way it would work. Nobody could just decide to build a university. He was sure plenty of people would want to, and had thought about it, but nobody actually *did* it. But while he was dreaming about what it would look like, why not build one that actually helped people get the skills they needed for real jobs? And maybe partner with the companies to ensure the skills this university teaches are actually what employers were looking for then when people graduated, they could apply for employment? Oh, and make it accredited yet more affordable than anything else. Now he was really laughing. But the thought wouldn't leave his mind. It wouldn't be the first time he tried something crazy.

Fadl was in his last year of high school in Egypt when he founded his first company – a website for tourists offering trustworthy information on places to stay and sites to visit. The classic example of a founder who cannot sit still, by the time he moved on to college he had sold the business and moved into advising other companies on digital transformation.

"You know it was only really with hindsight that I realised that college doesn't really help you to identify what you need to learn based on what you want to do," he says with a sigh. "So you sit with an advisor who actually has very limited experience of industry because it's impossible for anyone to know about every career in the world. And the advice they give you is very theoretical and therefore not very helpful."

He happily admits that even as a hugely ambitious undergraduate, his first thought was not to found a university. Instead, he set his mind on creating a software platform which would help young people discover what they needed to study based on what they ultimately wanted to do.

What crystallised Fadl's vision was his next venture. SocialEyez which started as a Dubai-based social media listening agency he founded in 2012, under the wider umbrella of News Group while he was COO there. SocialEyez disrupted the consumer research industry, replacing the long hours and resources needed for consumer surveys with a social listening tool, allowing for the same and even more accurate insights collection, The company grew to become a full-fledged digital engagement agency with clients ranging from the US State Department to New Balance and Etisalat. From a single client and a solitary employee, the company grew to over 100 people, largely due to its strategic approach, innovative use of tech, and the ability to deliver measurable results for its clients. This was when his restlessness kicked in again. At the end of one particular year, he remembers his team printing out a poster highlighting the agency's accomplishments. It showed the number of new cars sold on behalf of a client, the increase in the customer base and the volume of app downloads. Everyone was thrilled, except Fadl.

"I thought to myself we sold more cars, people downloaded more apps, they bought more songs, we sold more chocolate, hotel rooms... so what? Is the world a better place now?' To an extent, I thought it was probably a worse place. We persuaded people to spend millions of dollars buying stuff they didn't need, increasing this culture of consumerism. Companies made more money as a result, but I don't think it made the world a better place in any way."

On the other hand, a few clients with strong missions stood out for Fadl. One was the World Government Summit, which brought together leaders, policymakers, and subject experts to discuss the future of governance. Others included Hope Makers, a yearly initiative to honour exceptional humanitarians, and the Arab Reading Challenge, a project promoting reading among students across the Arab world, both operating under Mohammed bin Rashid Al Maktoum Global Initiatives and the Emirates Public Diplomacy Office. All three, he strongly believed had one unifying pillar

– education. If the lack of education was a contributor to many of the world's challenges, surely its provision held the solutions.

In Egypt, for example, the country's growing population crisis was directly linked to a culture of women dropping out of education as soon as they married. In 2017, one third of women aged between 25 to 29 had married before the age of 18. Many had stopped attending school early – to take up traditional roles in the household. It meant frustration for those who wanted to carry on their education and a huge talent drain for the entire country.

Education was long understood to be the key factor in breaking poverty cycles, unemployment, and social inequality. This was as true across MENA, as in the US and Europe, but the challenge had never been addressed directly and consistently by successive governments. Improved education could help to counter political instability, child labour, gender inequality, and the degradation of the environment. At the time, the MENA region had one of the highest youth unemployment rates in the world. It still does. Almost one in three people aged between 15 and 24 are not in employment, education, or training, with young women particularly disadvantaged.[118] Without urgent interventions in both education and employment, UNICEF predicts this will increase by 11 per cent by 2030.[119]

According to a fifty-year study by the World Bank published in 2023, the return on education is clear – each additional year of learning translates into a 9–10 per cent increase in annual earnings. But the impact of education reaches far beyond the income boost. Education broadens horizons and expands life choices, giving individuals the ability to pursue varied opportunities. It also serves as a powerful vehicle for passing down social values through generations. As a practical man, Fadl was fascinated by what was needed.

He also recognised his own good fortune in having a family who could afford to send him to college – making him very much in a minority. The cost of sending a child to university (tuition fees, accommodation, textbooks, and other expenditure) is prohibitive for families across the world. In the US, the average price per year is $38,270, meaning a four-year degree can cost in excess of

$153,000.[120] Such costs are traditionally covered by a combination of family contributions, student loans, and, if applicable, grants and scholarships. In the majority of cases, students emerge from university burdened with considerable debt.

Everything he had achieved so far made him certain he was doing the right thing when he founded Nexford University with the aim of achieving greater economic and social mobility through quality, affordable education. This education would, ideally, better meet potential employers' needs and place their requirements above the rigidity of academia. It would be a system where students would have the flexibility to pick and choose, to learn at their own pace and be taught the needs of the digital age, accessibly and practically.

Not only were there significant concerns about access, affordability, and the quality of education, but there was also a critical issue of relevance. At SocialEyez, whenever Fadl and his team looked to hire marketing graduates, they found that new recruits had little or no knowledge of digital marketing. This wasn't just a problem in Dubai; it was a global issue. The root cause wasn't necessarily the subject matter but rather the material and approach to teaching. Universities and colleges were still emphasising theoretical learning and academic research over practical, hands-on applications. Teaching methods were outdated, unaligned with the digital economy's rapidly evolving demands. Graduates entered the workforce lacking the real-world skills needed to contribute effectively from day one, especially in dynamic industries like marketing and business.

"Education is one of the very few industries that doesn't follow market economics," says Fadl. "It's just so ingrained in society that whatever your university tells you is what you've got to do. People don't really question that. You're pre-programmed to graduate high school, to go to college, get a job, and just do what you're told in college. The saving grace for education is the social value of a degree, but as that diminishes over time, it's going to be very difficult for colleges to continue offering something that doesn't have any ROI to it."

During the course of his research, Fadl visited markets across the world to gain a deep understanding of the education landscape, he recalls the Philippines in particular, where he discovered students were still working with a programming language that had fallen out of use in the mid-1990s. He asked them why. "They said, 'what do you mean? That's what we were told'. So no one really questions the way things are done. And they get away with it. It's almost like getting away with murder, because you're literally making people pay for something that's not going to deliver value."

Fadl saw a glaring mismatch between graduates' skills and those demanded by digital economy employers. "The disconnect between conversations on bridging the gap between employer needs and higher education, and the action taken to address it, can largely be traced back to three core issues. First, there's the matter of incentive. Universities, particularly public institutions, lack the motivation to evolve as quickly as industry demands. With funding structures and tenure processes that reward stability over rapid change, the drive to adapt just isn't there. Then there's resistance – a formidable barrier. Faculty and administrators often resist shifts in curriculum or teaching methods, particularly if those changes threaten traditional academic practices. Even if there are change agents within these institutions pushing for progress, they face an uphill battle to influence entrenched systems and mindsets."

His conclusion is damning of the current system. "Finally, there's the model itself. The entire higher education industry operates on a framework that often prioritises academic distinction over practical outcomes. Take, for example, university rankings. These rankings emphasise the volume of research papers published, among other factors, rather than measures that reflect how well universities prepare students for the workforce," he reflected morosely. In simple terms, there is a disconnect between the buyer and the seller across higher education, the buyer thinks they are investing in a service that will help with career outcomes, while the seller doesn't necessarily intend on delivering that.

It was a challenge he was determined to address. Unsatisfied with the impact SocialEyez was making but still deeply convinced of the platform's potential, Fadl asked himself, "Why not replicate this model in the education sector? Simply using open-source data such as published job vacancies, the software could thoroughly analyse millions of data points thereby removing the subjectivity of what is being taught across curricula. Those needs would be presented to universities, whose curricula could be adjusted and aligned accordingly. By first understanding the needs of employers, Fadl was able to reverse-engineer the educational gaps preventing people from being fully prepared for the workforce. This approach allowed him to pinpoint skills and knowledge lacked by new hires, providing insight into how education systems needed to adapt.

That idea only lasted a few weeks.

Fadl remembers attending a conference in Wisconsin along with his co-founder Mohamed Rayes, where delegates were discussing the gap between employer needs and higher education. At various sessions, he would ask how long this issue had been debated. The answer was decades. Papers had been written, but nothing had been done. Fadl was shocked. How could there be so much discussion about one of the world's most pressing challenges, yet so little action from universities and policymakers to meaningfully reshape the education landscape? He realised this was a far more deep-rooted issue than not knowing what employers needed. It was an issue of bureaucracy and faculty resistance.

"It's like any industry that's evaded disruption or is awaiting disruption. It's just so deep rooted and entrenched in legacy. Things have been done in a specific way for decades and decades and it's very difficult to bring innovation from within. It's like traditional banks versus fintechs. Why are fintechs able to do what they're doing, whereas the banks that had every resource in the world weren't able to?"

This wasn't a problem that was fixable with a software solution. And if the world wasn't ready to replace a college degree, Fadl knew he had to build a university, one that addressed the shortcomings he had observed in higher education over the years. It had to be affordable, accessible, and provide quality learning focused on meeting employers' needs.

By offering competency-based learning and practical skills relevant to the workplace, his university would enable greater social and economic mobility. Southern New Hampshire University and Western Governors University had started addressing a similar challenge, almost setting the groundwork for inevitable disruption, but he knew he had to build something beyond those, one that also caters to the region and the rest of the world in fact.

At the time, two-thirds of youth in the Levant did not believe their education system was adequately preparing them for jobs of the future.[121] That included everything from advanced manufacturing technologies such as 3D printing, robotics, and automation, to data analysts and scientists. Fadl saw an opportunity to bridge the gap between education and employment by leveraging technology and innovative learning methods to better prepare students for the realities of the modern workforce. His goal was to create a university that educated *and* empowered individuals worldwide to achieve their career aspirations. To do this, he needed accreditation.

His research revealed that US and UK universities were held in the highest regard globally in terms of accreditation, so he had to choose between one of them. Building a higher education institute is an exercise in brand building, reputation, and accreditation mattered, particularly to the populations of emerging markets, who prized and valued their education above everything else as they sought to build their future – it is how people "value" their tertiary education.

After surveying thousands of students and potential students globally, Nexford set out to identify which countries were in highest demand for higher education. They took a deep dive into Google search volumes, analysing a range of keywords related to studying abroad, and found clear trends in student interest across different regions. But the choice of where to focus wasn't just about popularity – it was about practicality too.

They looked closely at US and UK regulatory requirements, comparing the process for obtaining an educational licence. It quickly became apparent that while both paths were challenging, the US offered a clearer, shorter route to proper accreditation. A US licence also promised greater long-term value, as the UK equivalent held little weight across the Atlantic. Knowing they wanted to eventually target the American market, they saw the US as a strategic choice, offering an accessible path and significant potential upside.

"A lot of folks discouraged us at the time, especially investors," recalls Fadl. "We had some VC calls that were literally five minutes. Even lawyers told us to plan for five years if we even stood a chance. I thought: 'This is ridiculous, we're never going to get licensed in the first place. Who builds a university?' So, there was a lot of discouragement. But we knew that this was the path that we'd have to follow. It's a challenging, long-term path, but if we want real impact, you've got to pursue that challenging road."

Nexford University finally received its US license in November 2018 and launched in February 2019, probably a record time in the higher education industry from idea to launch in less than two years. After being licensed by the Higher Education Licensure Commission, Nexford then became fully accredited in the US in 2023. As an online-only institution, it rendered geographical barriers obsolete. It also turned the concept of a time-bound curriculum on its head. Why should a curriculum be based on certain number of months if the learning is online and flexible? Fadl decided to experiment: could Nexford launch a subscription-based monthly learning plan? Could this provide access to learning to those that don't have it in an affordable manner anywhere in the world?

He had a mission: he wanted to allow students to access courses from anywhere in the world; providing flat-rate tuition fees of $80 a month for a bachelor's degree and $120 a month for a master's degree; and offered flexible enrolment. The latter ensured students could make the most of multiple start dates and begin their studies at a time that suited them best. Tuition fees were also capped, which meant the cost of a four-year bachelor's degree did not surpass $4,000 – less than a tenth of the $153,000 paid by students in the US.

Fadl held his breath as the first students enrolled in early 2019, signing up for undergraduate degrees in business administration.

Its curriculum, which featured specialisations in business analytics, entrepreneurship, digital marketing, supply chain management, AI (before AI became a thing), product management, digital transformation, and international business, had been designed to fulfil the needs of industry.

"I remember us saying to ourselves as a team: 'If we don't do anything else, but we graduate folks with zero debt, we've succeeded. And if we've enabled folks across the world to get access to education, which they never would have been able to get, again we've done a good job."

But would people complete their courses? Would they graduate, or drop out? Would their salaries increase as a result? Fadl was eager to find out, and the survival of the company depended on students engaging and staying enrolled and completing their classes and courses. Their education was at stake, as was his company. However, there was no expediting time. Everyday Fadl watched the dashboards indicating whether students were spending time online and passing their classes and tests.

RIYADH, SAUDI ARABIA
MOHAMMAD SUHAIL AL MADANI – PART 1

Nine-year-old Mohammad raced out of the car as it pulled into the gas station, leaving the door wide open behind him. As he counted the coins he was pulling out of his pocket, he knew he would only have a few minutes to make the photocopies before his father would call him back to the car to continue the drive to school. "Hurry up, hurry up" he begged, "If only this photocopy machine would go faster!"

Finally, the machine stopped. Mohammad picked up copies of his hand-made, short-form science fiction comics and sped back to the car. Eight. He would sell eight comics today. Tomorrow he would be ready to leave home earlier, he promised himself.

The 9-year-old creating these comics could barely have imagined that he would end up in medical school and become a doctor. His desire to help people had driven him to that pursuit, but it wasn't long before he transferred to industrial engineering. At this point in his life, he had decided that what he really wanted was to create something which would touch the lives of millions – not one at a time. "I wanted to do something more powerful, with better meaning," he says. "So, I asked myself: 'What would be something I could be proud of? Something that I would enjoy but would disrupt at the same time'."

While still in the US, he launched Classera with Mohammad Alashmawi, one of his old college friends and they moved to Silicon Valley to build a platform that could transform the learning experience for the world. For Mohammad, that meant heightened engagement, which in turn necessitated an approach to education that was inspiring, personalised, and collaborative. "I wanted to be the one who would disrupt education using technology," he says. "We wanted to make it inspiring using gamification, personalised using AI, and collaborative using social learning. All to create better engagement, and therefore a better learning experience."

Soon, Mohammad began to see that Classera, an integrated Learning Management System (LMS) covering every aspect of the learning journey – from school admissions and daily activities to digital libraries and exams – could make the greatest impact in emerging markets. These regions faced critical issues of affordability, quality, and access were especially pertinent, and where the greatest opportunities for impact lay. In the MENA region, physical and cultural barriers, political conflict, infrastructure challenges, and affordability stood in the way of many children's access and right to education. And with 2 billion more learners expected globally between now and 2050 – the majority in Sub-Saharan Africa and South Asia – Classera could have a substantial impact on improving educational outcomes and accessibility. It could also help bridge the digital divide and provide quality education to underserved regions. From then on, Classera would be MENA-focused.

"We thought using the latest technology could be one of the fastest ways to improve education rates in the region, which needed it the most and even more than other places," explains Mohammad. "And that's the punchline we keep using with ministers of education in the region. Yes, we have many ways to improve education, but one of the fastest ways is the effective use – not just the symbolic use – of technology. That is what we have proven."

Classera's growth was steady if unspectacular. Then in 2018, it began working with the Ministry of Education in Saudi Arabia, enhancing the digital learning experience for students and educators nationwide. It was a pivotal moment. Such large-scale deployment of the platform allowed the company to significantly expand its market presence, leading to further contracts with the Ministries of Education in Egypt and Jordan. It also developed partnerships with multinationals such as Microsoft and HP, powering HP Classeasy and integrating with Microsoft 365 and Microsoft Teams. When Covid-19 broke out, the company launched Learning Never Stops, an initiative to help schools quickly transition to remote learning by providing free access to its platform for six months.

Everything snowballed from there. A game-changer was the launch of Classera's Learning Super Platform (LSP), an advanced tech solution designed to transform the learning experience across various educational sectors, including K-12 schools, higher education institutions, and corporate and government training.

Rolled out in 2020, the unified, cloud-based platform featured an integrated learning environment, gamification, comprehensive analytics and reporting capabilities, mobile accessibility, and support for multiple languages and content types.

"The LSP is a full ecosystem that fully serves educational and training institutions," explains Mohammad. "You can think of Classera today as a layer of SaaS (Software as a Service) that includes a gamified LMS using AI and social learning. Additionally, it features an ERP (Enterprise Resource Planning) system specifically tailored to the education and training sector to meet their needs. This means that for any educational institution, we offer a complete value chain, covering even their back office, HR, finance, and everything else required. We've also added two engines to enhance the ecosystem and provide better value for our user base: a payment gateway and a marketplace."

Suddenly, the growth was unbelievable. With this, Mohammad recalls, came the big question: how long does it last? How do we fund it? Classera had always been self-funded and never raised outside money. It had grown slowly and steadily and was achieving all of its goals. Was that not the point? How could fundraising help? What if the growth became unmanageable? Or did Mohammad have an obligation to grow as quickly as possible in order to help as many students as possible? Would any investor even look at a company that had grown to this scale without external funding? Mohammad had so many questions, and so few answers. Everybody he asked seemed to have a differing opinion.

* * * * *

AMMAN, JORDAN
HAMDI TABBAA – PART 2

The cognitive dissonance between the impression of success, and the actual success towards what Hamdi believed he wanted to achieve kept him analysing and testing new solutions. It wasn't just one change that was required. Hamdi was going to transform the entire platform. The risk associated was tremendous, but deep down, he had a gut instinct and knew it had to be done.

Abwaab was transformed from an online learning platform that replaced school tutoring into a structured, guided learning experience. Students who enrolled would now join a cohort, receive personalised academic guidance from an advisor, and progress through their studies with regular feedback. Parents would also receive progress reports, and those students who requested it would be offered psychological support. The results were immediate. Engagement levels increased, parent satisfaction soared, and renewal rates grew sixfold.

"The ultimate goal is to be able to personalise the experience and curate a learning journey for every single student based on their learning cognitive abilities, preference of modality, what they want to learn – making learning an adaptive learning experience," says Hamdi.

The platform now works with 3 million students spread across Egypt, Iraq, Jordan, Saudi Arabia, and Oman, with Egypt accounting for a big bulk of Abwaab's user base. The rest of the students are almost spread equally between the other countries. The age group of its students ranges from 10 to 18 years old. Remarkably, Iraq emerged as one of Abwaab's strong markets in terms of revenues, underscoring its significant impact where schools are less available. Meanwhile, Saudi Arabia and Iraq show promising growth in monetary terms, while Egypt drives expansion in terms of student numbers.

Hamdi envisions a future where blended learning will be the norm, where the majority of content will be consumed online and outside of school, placing an emphasis on proactive and independent learning. However, offline experiences, such as group problem solving, will transform the learning dynamic. This is already being trialled in Iraq and Saudi Arabia, where traditional classroom instruction is being integrated with digital and online media.

"The approach that we've taken is to try and craft a commercially feasible model," explains Hamdi. "Create a business that's generating a lot of cash flow to start changing the world. I would take over every single school. And this is our long-term vision. We believe that if we make it, this is what we'll do. We'll become the largest educational institution in the region, where we turn schools into collaborative workspaces, where you solve challenges with your teachers, are given room to discover things on your own, and are given tasks at home to think about and then apply at school. In other words, we'll provide a blended or hybrid learning experience."

LAHORE, PAKISTAN
FATIMA RIZWAN – PART 2

"That was why about five years ago I realised that I needed to be in a different economic environment and a different place – because what I wanted was to build a humongous, I mean humongously big company," she said with a broad grin. So she took the tough decision to leave the comfort of her family environment and move to Singapore.

Fatima admits it's been a tough journey. "I'm a solo founder, right? So, you know it's like a roller coaster ride. One day you are very excited because you've closed a big deal, the next day you are firefighting in the office, and you have to figure out what is not working. I feel it's been like coming to a new country where I don't see a lot of women who look like me or even women from other nationalities who I can look up to and see they have made it in life. You're trying to look for someone who is a role model or hero and there aren't many in this space. I talk it over with female founder friends who are at the same stage, and we tell each other, maybe we will become those role models in time if we grow these companies. Yeah."

From the US to Vietnam, over 150,000 learners have found their way to Metaschool, where more than 33 million hours have been offered to help them master Web3 skills. Along the way, they launched over 40,000 projects and explored a growing library of twenty-nine-plus courses, each one pushing the boundaries of what's possible in blockchain.

What lies ahead for Metaschool is even more thrilling. Having already established a strong foundation for tech-focused developer education, starting with blockchain, the journey is just beginning. As AI reshapes industries, Metaschool is ready to explore new technologies and expand its curriculum, redefining how tech skills are taught and developed.

CAIRO, EGYPT
FADL AL TARZI – PART 2

Fadl was in disbelief as students completed classes, courses and degrees. Over 10,000 students from over 100 countries have completed more than 30,000 courses at Nexford University. The impact of the programme on graduates' careers was unmistakable.

Nexford University has beaten a pioneering path. By creating a university with no campus, no set schedule, and no high fees it has democratised higher education, making it more accessible and adaptable to the needs of a diverse, global student population. A lack of obstacles accelerated market entry, while Fadl knew adoption would be strong if the curriculum aligned with industry needs.

Within just six months of graduation, half of the students got a promotion. By the eighteen-month mark, 81 per cent of graduates experienced a salary increase as well. These outcomes painted a compelling picture: the programme wasn't just about acquiring knowledge – it was propelling graduates up the career ladder, equipping them to achieve professional growth and financial stability faster than they, or Fadl, had imagined possible.

RIYADH, SAUDI ARABIA
MOHAMMAD SUHAIL AL MADANI – PART 2

Mohammad took the leap of faith. Two years after the launch of LSP, Classera raised $40 million in a Series A funding round. For a company with no prior funding, it was the largest edtech Series A to date. The company used the capital to continue developing its LSP, to expand LeadXera, a corporate and government training system launched in 2021, and to accelerate its global expansion, especially into Asia Pacific, via direct sales, channel partners, and acquisitions.

It was a big relief. "There were many times when we were almost broke," admits Mohammad. "Sometimes I would take out personal loans to cover the costs. They weren't small loans either. Sometimes they were close to a quarter of a million dollars. I took big risks. But I believed in what I was doing and took some calculated risks. You're always going to face challenges, but you can overcome them if you have the right determination, and the right consultation."

His greatest challenge, however, was not financial or technical. It was negativity. "'Oh, you're going to fail.' 'You're too young, you cannot do it'. 'You're an Arab in the US, there's no way you're going to win. Just forget it'. When we started focusing on the region from the US, it was, 'Oh, you're crazy, you're not going to win here, just go back to the US'. We proved them wrong. And then when I started with the government, I was told we're going to fail again. It was of course challenging but we ended up winning. Nothing is impossible."

Mohammad and his team were proving that they did not have to emulate what was global in order to build a company for MENA. They could create, innovative and build world-class solutions from the region and export them to the world. It had, however, been a far from easy ride.

Classera is now the largest edtech company in both the MENA region and Sub-Saharan Africa, educating millions of learners in over forty countries. It employs 300 people across ten offices and works with governments across the MENA region and Southeast Asia.

"We don't want to be just the best in the region, we want to be this global force that focuses on emerging markets. We want more and more countries to trust us and to set a good example. We would also love to be an inspiring example, proving that great entrepreneurs from the region can have global success. That's a big dream for us. We want to be one of those companies that has global impact."

* * * * *

Tomorrow's workforce are digital natives. Today's learners are fluent in a world of screens, seamlessly navigating online environments and engaging with information in ways education has yet to fully embrace. They bring distinct learning styles, interests, and ways of processing information, all shaped by the digital age. Yet, education still tends to remain rooted in traditional structures, focusing on *what* is learned rather than *how*. In many classrooms, content takes centre stage while delivery methods lag behind, leaving students without the adaptive, interactive experiences reflecting their lives outside school.

The youth comprise such a large part of the population in the MENA region, making the innovation in technology that much more pressing to solve than anywhere else in the world.

This is where Hamdi, Mohammad, Fatima and Fadl have interjected with their different solutions across the spectrum of learning. Abwaab's system change in tutoring and virtual learning to enable access and engagement so that the upcoming generation can learn in the way that suits them most rather than simply relying on personal tutors solves for generation alpha's individualities. Similarly, Classera has dramatically changed how schools and curriculum are managed and delivered in advance of the youth bulge, filling the growing infrastructure gap for managing the ever-increasing number of students and how their curriculum were being delivered.

Metaschool, meanwhile, has introduced a system change by teaching cutting-edge blockchain technology skills to emerging markets, enabling coders to compete in the global workforce and become participants in the industries of tomorrow. Finally, on the tertiary side, Nexford has instigated a complete system change around the tertiary education, shifting the focus from an in-person, per-course model to a completely virtual, highly adaptive, monthly subscription system, while teaching skills needed for the workforce and illustrating improved careers.

Across these founders, the impact is part of a far broader trend towards innovative, accessible, and practical education. By contributing to a shift in how education is delivered and perceived, they are influencing new and traditional educational institutions, and how they adapt and evolve. In MENA, these are solutions for the next generation – genuinely thinking about how to teach in the absence of school systems, and how to address the youth. The opportunity to continue to do so is immense and important.

The accumulated efforts of these pioneering founders may have led to many millions of students and hundreds of tutors, but it will be exciting to see how AI further accelerates learning across the region; how a revision of curricula will lead to qualifications that are more relevant; how virtual reality will increase educational access; and how employment prospects will be exponentially improved for those graduating school and university. This next generation is the future of the region and its economy, more so than anywhere else in the world. Investing in them and equipping them with the right tools will be crucial for sustaining regional growth.

CHAPTER 9

FEEDING THE NEXT GENERATION

الذي لا ينبع ينتهي

That which doesn't grow [seed], ceases [to be].

– ARABIC PROVERB

ALEPPO, SYRIA

EDWARD HAMOD – PART 1

"How many hostages do you have?" Edward's voice trembled; he sat down to understand the situation. His employees were like family to him, and they had given everything to help him build his business, including risking their lives and working throughout the war. How could they all be hostages now? He could imagine them, sitting on the factory floor, in the dark, with no electricity powering the area, no money for the diesel for the generators, and their lives being threatened.

Edward felt helpless – he had managed to leave Syria a month earlier, following his family out of the war, but his employees and staff were unable to follow suit. They had no option but to stay, and so were continuing to run the factories and produce food for the millions of people stuck in the country at war. They continued the work he had started many years ago. A month later, the rebels had stormed the company's facilities and threatened to kill everyone inside. "I spent the next month negotiating with the Free Syrian Army to release my employees. It was incredibly tough," he says, falling momentarily silent.

After hundreds of hours of tenuous negotiations, his employees were released, but millions of dollars' worth of raw materials and finished goods were lost. As his homeland slid further into the abyss, Edward witnessed the traumatic effects of food scarcity first-hand. The conflict would push 12.9 million Syrians into food insecurity (more than half of the population), with a further 2.6 million at risk of becoming food insecure.[122] The civil war disrupted agricultural production, displaced millions, and caused untold suffering. Before the war, Syria produced over 4 million tonnes of wheat a year. By September 2022, that figure had fallen to 1 million.[123]

Before the fighting started in 2011, Edward was busy running a multimillion-dollar food processing business in Aleppo. The country's fertile soils, rich in agricultural bounty, were the backbone of his enterprise, supplying commodities essential to the lives of millions across the region. For him and his family, life continued much as it had for decades, despite the undercurrent of political tension unfolding across the region. His working days were filled with the rhythmic hum of machinery and the aroma of freshly processed goods.

Initially focused on trading Syrian commodities and exporting them in their raw form, Al Manal Food Industries entered the food processing market in 2006. It opened lentil splitting and bulgur factories, sorting operations, grain terminals, and milling and wheat processing plants. From its 30,000-square-metre facility near Aleppo in the country's north-west, it exported food to Egypt, Iraq, Lebanon, Turkey, Europe, the United States, and Saudi Arabia, and traded with towns and cities across Syria. "It was a very successful and fulfilling business," reminisces Edward. "After the initial investment, it became self-sustainable and was profitable. Then suddenly, we had to leave everything behind."

When civil war broke out in March 2011, Syria was thrown into chaos. Along with many others, Edward took the painful decision to get his family out of the country before it was too late, while he stayed behind to salvage what he could from the business. "I stayed behind because I couldn't comprehend that everything we had built was going to be taken from us. 2012 and 2013 were the most difficult years of my life. I was young. I was grinding, making progress, investing, and I thought I had my life planned out. And then in the blink of an eye everything changes. You find yourself not knowing how to manage yourself, your family, your well-being, your parents, your business, because the rules of the game change in a second. It goes from having rules to having no rules at all." But eventually, and just in time so he could ultimately negotiate the release of others, he left.

After reuniting with his family in Beirut for a short period, Edward made the move to the UAE where he started a new business with a few partners out of an office in Dubai Multi Commodities Centre. "One day I got a call from my ex-operations manager, asking me to turn on Al Jazeera. And there I saw a guy sitting behind my desk, lecturing people on how to recruit freedom fighters. I was in shock." Edward was frozen in disbelief. The company's facilities had been turned into a training camp for the Free Syrian Army.

From the UAE, Edward again came face-to-face with the question of food security. Unlike Syria, which had been self-sufficient in wheat, vegetables, and fruit, the GCC was food scarce. Extreme heat, limited water resources, and poor-quality soil meant that barely one per cent of the UAE's land is currently suitable for agriculture. Of the three major sources of food supply – imports, local production, and food stocks – the UAE relied for 90 per cent of its needs on imports.[124] The country imported nearly 6 million tonnes of produce in 2015, with wheat and rice accounting for the largest share (39 per cent).

These figures have not much changed. Together, the countries of the GCC import about 85 per cent of their food, with rice imports comprising virtually all consumption. Approximately 93 per cent of cereals, approximately 62 per cent of meat, and 56 per cent of vegetables are also imported,[125] rendering the GCC vulnerable to disruptions in global supply chains.

Food Security
Food Imported (%)

OECD 30%   **GCC 85%**

Source: OECD, PwC (Most Recent Data)

The UAE's fragility was first hammered home by the 2007 global food price crisis, which exposed the country's susceptibility to volatile food prices and supply chain risks – events which disproportionately affected the poorest in the area. MENA's vulnerability was further highlighted in 2015 in a study by the Abu Dhabi Global Environmental Data Initiative (AGEDI) – which warned that a combination of climate change-related risks, including declining agricultural productivity in food-exporting countries, tightening world food markets, and recurrent food price spikes, could have adverse effects on the country. The conclusions were stark. Without the right preparation, the entire MENA region was vulnerable to severe disruptions in the supply of essential items such as cereals, vegetables, and meat, frequent food price increases, and the necessity for significant food subsidies.[126]

In response, the UAE government placed food security at the top of its agenda. Their initial focus was principally on acquiring agricultural land overseas, mainly in East Africa, but also Pakistan and Eastern Europe. In 2013, Abu Dhabi-based Al Dahra had already invested $400 million in Serbia, acquiring eight bankrupt agricultural firms and developing fodder plants. Now, following the report, it extended the programme to invest in Egypt, the US, Spain, and Australia. However, these strategies had risks.

In Egypt, the company was hit by a $43-a-tonne export tax, labour strikes and diesel shortages. A backlash against what some viewed as an aggressive 'land grab' from poorer African nations also ensued. Further risks were highlighted by the AGEDI study, which concluded many of the countries in which land-lease arrangements had been established were likely to experience the adverse impacts of climate change on agricultural productivity.[127] Rather than being shielded from food market volatility, the cost of agricultural production from such lands was likely to fluctuate, sometimes dramatically. It was clear a diversification of policies to address the single challenge of potential future food shortages was required.

Edward, who had never been a fan of land acquisition, was working for the National Feed and Flour Production & Marketing Company (later rebranded as Emirates Food Industries) at the time. He identified a clever shift in the country's approach to food security. Following the appointment of the UAE's first Minister of State for Food Security in 2017, the focus turned to developing sustainable agricultural practices, enhancing food production capabilities, and securing food supplies through strategic investments and international partnerships.

Edward knew nothing about foodtech, but during the tenure of the Minister of State for Food Security, the conversation around high-conversion proteins, plant-based diets, local production, and alternative sourcing was amplified. For the Minister, it wasn't just about growing food, it was about nutrition, strategic storage, tackling the GCC's chronic food waste, and innovation-driven food security.[128] All of which pointed to a new strategy to address the region's ultimate challenge: How could the country use technology to reach its food security targets?

"This is where the conversation around protein, around foodtech, around plant-based products started," says Edward. "Because at the end of the day, one of the biggest elements of food security is your protein. You can produce as much leafy greens as you want, you can produce as many tomatoes as you want, you can produce as many raspberries or blueberries, but these won't fill people up and won't give them the necessary proteins that they need to survive." Covid-19 only heightened these conversations, as food sourcing became a critical concern and the vulnerabilities of global supply chains were exposed.

Moreover, the uncomfortable reality that the region has a mix of dependency on imported food products and poor diet which has led to a rise in weight related diseases. "We are one of the highest consuming meat regions globally. We consume three or four times the global recommended meat intake per person and we have one of the highest rates of obesity, diabetes and cardiovascular disease in the world. Add to that the speed of population growth and the food waste numbers. Things have to change."

Food security was also a question of sustainability. Seventy-seven per cent of the world's agricultural land is used for livestock farming – either as pastureland or to produce feedstock such as corn and soya – yet livestock accounts for only 18 per cent of the world's calories and 37 per cent of the world's protein supply.[129]

The livestock industry is also responsible for approximately 12 per cent of global greenhouse gas emissions,[130] meaning it plays a significant role in contributing to climate change and environmental degradation. The primary culprit is cattle, which account for approximately 62 per cent of all livestock emissions.[131] In other words, a plant-based diet is much less resource-intensive than a meat-based one and better for the environment. This led to exploration into different ways huge demand for protein in the region could be satisfied efficiently, healthily, safely, and without compromising the consumer experience.

When Edward began researching alternative proteins in 2021, much of the hype was around cultivated meat, or cell-based agriculture. There was much discussion also around precision fermentation. However, he was disturbed by cellular agriculture, which, in his experience, was heavily dependent on "Hazmat suits, bioreactors, incubators, dark rooms, and flashing red lights".

The technology was also far from being commercially viable, while precision fermentation was in the early stages of research and development (R&D) – needing millions of investment dollars. While the theory was right, such 'replacement' meats – in practice – were too expensive to produce, and therefore to consume, adding elements into the food chain that, in his opinion, didn't belong there. Then there was the conventional plant-based sector. Edward knew the technology was there, because Beyond Meat and Impossible Foods were already producing popular plant-based, high protein meat alternatives in the US. Moreover, the category was experiencing double-digit growth in the GCC, with no regional marketing, education, awareness, or sector-wide promotional initiatives.

Significantly, this growth was being achieved with no product market fit. General products such as burgers, sausages, and nuggets were being imported, which did not necessarily appeal to the taste buds of local consumers. "Once we had a better understanding of what we were doing, we realised the need to improve what the market was offering at the time," he says. "We started first by benchmarking Beyond or Impossible, but then we realised that their products weren't really what we wanted to offer. We wanted to offer something better – from a nutrition perspective, from a health perspective, from a clean label perspective, and, most importantly, from a taste perspective. It was important – and I remind my team every day – that we remain a food company. Yes, we use technology but the consumer doesn't eat the technology, doesn't savour the technology, doesn't enjoy the technology. It's the taste they savour."

"It was just a matter of not reinventing the wheel, understanding the technology, and adapting it to our region. When we looked at the category of plant-based meat alternatives, we saw that the region's consumption per capita was less than a tenth of what it was in mature markets such as the US or Europe. This is when we saw the first opportunity. We also saw a young and educated population that was aware and informed. Health and ethics played an important role, much more than sustainability. So we thought, 'What if we use technology to produce a healthy, nutritious, and sustainable product locally, so we can bring the price down and cater to consumers' taste palates and culinary habits.' This was the idea behind Switch Foods."

At first, Edward worked independently, reaching out to experts in food engineering, food technology, and food science. He immersed himself in the world of plant-based tech, seeking to understand the biotechnology, food chemistry, and engineering needed to replicate the taste, texture, and nutritional profile of traditional Middle Eastern cuisine. Food scientists in the US and Canada were employed on a project or consultancy basis before everything was shifted to the UAE. Only in the domestic market could he develop products to suit the taste buds and demands of the local populace.

"Our initial round of fundraising was based on an idea and a business model that we thought made sense," remembers Edward. "But we didn't have an MVP yet. We didn't have a facility. We didn't know the equipment. So we struggled a lot before reaching our final formula. There was a steep learning curve as we invested significant time understanding the technology, and trying to transfer knowledge from the food scientists and consultants we collaborated with. But we had limited success because they didn't know our product. Even on the mince side, the only product they understood was the burger. So product development was very, very challenging. A lot of very dark days – because the product tasted horrible."

To achieve that taste and texture, existing food processing machinery had to be identified and then modified to produce the world's first plant-based kafta and the world's first plant-based kabab. Edward had spent the second half of 2021 learning as much as he could about the technology in Canada and the US, before collaborating with equipment manufacturers to develop a more delicate machine. After all, these were soft proteins, not meat. It was the taste, however, that caused him the most sleepless nights. Replicating two of the region's favourite dishes was an exasperating experience, thanks in no small part to the creative sensitivities of the chefs involved.

"Scientists have their own personality. It's all dollars and cents," says Edward. "It's all numbers – they either make sense or they don't. With chefs there's a lot of creativity, there's a lot of art, so telling a chef the product is not good is one of the worst things you can do. They get very personal, very defensive, very aggressive. So we found ourselves never being able to retain chefs because they would defend a product which I thought was not good enough. I tried to hire three or four full-time chefs – none of them worked."

Edward didn't know where to go from here – could they really make kabab from pea protein? It looked like it wasn't possible – everybody seemed to agree on how poor it all tasted and felt. Edward was also properly focused on the nutritional elements as well and getting both right, in an affordable manner for an emerging market seemed too difficult of a task. Surely if it had been possible, the large international companies would have already done it. The fact that they hadn't probably meant it wasn't possible. There would always be a compromise between taste, texture and cost. Edward didn't want an expensive, high-end product. He wanted a product that everybody could afford. But that tasted good and felt right. Who could help him? And if it was possible to make something affordable in this field, would it not have already been done by those before him?

DUBAI, UNITED ARAB EMIRATES

FAHIM AL QASIMI – PART 1

Fahim gasped for air. The light was dizzying and the seawater was in his eyes. He was struggling to see straight. That must have been one of his longest dives. Unintentionally. While carrying a 15kg turtle back up with him. Removing the plastic that was trapping the turtle had been painstakingly difficult and took longer than he had estimated. As he slowly got his bearings, he started to realise how badly injured the turtle was. It was the second one this year.

"Two turtles in nine months," he reflected as he came out of the water for air. Free-diving had always been a hobby of his, and he enjoyed spending time with friends in Sir Bu Nair, a remote island. But now, he started wondering "Why was I there at the right moment – at the right time?' I realised there was a problem that needed solving. So, I put my mind to it. Is it a coincidence that, as I get older, a lot of the things I'm dedicating my life to are all ocean-related? I don't think it's a coincidence."

While his rescue efforts had clearly sown the seed of an idea, it was a dinner that night with Sean Dennis and Ramie Murray which really triggered his thinking towards solutions. Not least since Ramie was the owner of Dibba Bay Oysters, a Fujairah-based gourmet oyster farm that produces some of the finest restaurant-grade oysters in the world. Sean and Ramie had been brainstorming ways to enhance efficiency in the seafood industry and wanted Fahim's take on it.

"At that time, as an active investor, one thing I noticed was that a lot of the start-ups I was being approached to invest in were copycat technology," says Fahim, who had experience as an angel investor and as a partner in a handful of small businesses. "It was stuff that had been done in the US or Europe and was being repeated in the UAE. We had such an inferiority complex in the country and couldn't come up with something original. But finally, this was something completely different. This was something that I wanted to sink my teeth into and would innovate from this region to the world." And Seafood Souq was created.

In our quest for food security, the oceans are often forgotten. Two-thirds of the Earth's surface is covered by water, and yet its significance is all too frequently overlooked. Biodiversity is declining, habitats are degrading, and sea temperatures are rising. Increasing levels of carbon dioxide are being absorbed by the oceans, leading to heightened acidity and irreversible damage to species vital to life, most notably corals. These vibrant ecosystems are indispensable, offering sustenance, income, and protection to 500 million people worldwide.[132] A sustainable approach to our oceans is therefore critical if we are to preserve the health of the world's marine-based economies and ensure our own survival.

The first 'meeting' between Fahim and Sean, the two co-founders, took place at Fahim's house, where they wrote 'fish' and 'money' on two blue and green Post-it notes and stuck them to the wall. The former symbolised the movement of seafood from supplier to consumer, while the latter represented the financial dynamics of the founders' start-up. They then veered into a conversational tangent. A few hours later, Fahim's wife entered the room, looked at the wall, and said: "You've been here for two hours and all you came up with was fish and money?"

They laugh now, but fish and money would become Seafood Souq's mantra.

The two partners came from contrasting backgrounds. Sean was a Hong Kong-born British expat with wanderlust who had spent years at the cutting edge of tech. He was also burnt out from his previous company and was working as an entrepreneur-in-residence at Dubai Future Foundation. Fahim was the half-German, half-Emirati head of international relations for Sharjah with a background in consultancy. Both, however, had spent their school years in the UAE, hanging out in similar circles and cultivating a love of the ocean.

It was only once the company had launched that the true scale of the problems facing the seafood industry became apparent. Eighty-five per cent of the world's marine fish stocks were either fully exploited or overfished,[133] one in five fish were being mislabelled, and 15 per cent of all seafood destined for human consumption was being wasted.[134] Ninety per cent of the world's large fish had been wiped out and trawling of the seabed released as much carbon dioxide as the entire aviation industry, contributing substantially to rising sea temperatures and the degradation of marine ecosystems.[135] An estimated 38 million metric tonnes of unwanted animals were also being caught and killed every year, including an estimated 300,000 small whales and dolphins, 250,000 endangered turtles, and 300,000 seabirds.[136]

Sean and Fahim also discovered that produce was being swapped, was going missing, or was being incorrectly dated. "If you asked yourself: 'Where has this piece of fish I'm eating come from?' Or if you went on a personal journey of trying to figure out what a piece of fish went through to get to your plate, you suddenly realise: 'Wow, nobody's looking at this! Everybody seems to know where their beef or chicken on their plate comes from, how it was raised, and even what it ate! But nobody can tell you the first thing about the fish on their plate.'" remarks Fahim. "And I think that was the one thing that struck us the most: the more we looked at what we were doing, the more we realised we were in a white space. Nobody was touching this."

At the very beginning, their focus was eliminating unnecessary steps in the supply chain and reducing waste. The more breakages, or parties, in the supply chain, the higher the price and the greater the wastage. As with all good business plans, they started with a question to answer: how could fish be delivered from the producer, via a single distributor, to the consumer in the business-to-business (B2B) sector in the most efficient way possible?

Their goal, therefore, was to create a marketplace and fulfil orders effectively and efficiently. When the company officially launched in the summer of 2019, a year of hard work had already gone into creating an ecosystem where both businesses and the planet could thrive. The founders had wanted to connect seafood buyers and sellers from across the world in a sustainable and mutually beneficial way, but when Covid-19 hit, 90 per cent of the company's business was in the UAE. Supply chain disruptions caused by the pandemic meant that changed almost overnight, and Seafood Souq became the largest king crab supplier, and the sole supplier of bass and bream in the UAE, leading to growth of 300 per cent in a single month.

In the meantime, in Oman, a staggering 45 per cent of all seafood was being wasted on the four-hour drive to Dubai, primarily due to an unmonitored cold chain with four or five breakages, where the seafood is not kept at the required low temperatures during transport. "That meant the oceans were being overfished to account for the fact that 45 per cent of what was being caught was being wasted," says Sean. "This meant prices went up, because each person at every step in the supply chain needs to be paid. There was a 107 per cent hike in price in that four-hour drive. That creates downward pressure on the fishermen. There was a time when the fishermen catching the tuna – grade A, beautiful yellowfin tuna – were being paid 75 cents per kilo because of the wastage and the inefficiencies that occurred. That wasn't even enough for them to pay for the gas to go out and catch the fish in their skiff or boat."

In response, Seafood Souq partnered with a charity called the International Pole and Line Fishing Foundation. Together, they trained fishermen on Oman's Masirah Island, transforming handline tuna into a grade A product suitable for global export. "The fishermen learnt how to catch the tuna perfectly, or as well as possible; how to treat it during the fifteen minutes after they'd taken it out of the water; ice it to maintain the grade A quality; and then bring it inshore to sell as Oman's first grade A, or sashimi quality, yellowfin tuna," says Sean. "That's good enough to eat raw at restaurants. It had never been done before. These fishermen now get $12 to $16 a kilo for the fillets, with minimal wastage along the supply chain. So they're getting paid more, they don't need to fish so much, and we've taken pressure off the fish stocks. For every ten tuna they caught before, they now catch one. So not only is there an environmental impact, but also a socio-economic impact, because they can feed their families and countries are now buying tuna from this area at this quality."

As their marketplace began to scale, Fahim and Sean kept encountering the same fundamental challenge: the opaqueness of their supply chain. It quickly became clear that to build their company, they had to accept that traceability was inherent to their business model. They couldn't get around it.

Traceability was incredibly difficult to solve, but had two primary benefits. First, it was a value add, allowing producers to charge more for a sustainable product with verifiable origin and quality. Second, it could help counter 'bad actors' who exist along the entire supply chain and exploit it with great financial reward for themselves. Those bad actors were fishing in restricted areas, using prohibited fishing methods such as gill netting, exceeding catch limits, or mislabelling seafood to deceive consumers about the species, origin, or quality of the product.

In all cases, such actors failed to comply with local or international regulations regarding fishing quotas, environmental protections, and food safety standards. In short, they were contributing significantly to the devastation of the world's oceans and it became clear to the founders that before you could achieve sustainability, establishing traceability was imperative. After searching for such a platform, it became clear that none existed.

Fahim and Sean pivoted. In addition to the marketplace, they set about creating a tech solution to build transparency through the full supply chain. But the seas and oceans are global. Fahim was focused on building a global, asset-light tech company anchored with the fundamental core of traceability. Sean, whose expertise was deeply rooted in operations, was eager to continue to improve the operational practices of different markets and scale operationally.

The lack of alignment on the future of the company created tension between the two friends. Whereas Sean could see Fahim's outlook, he was much more of an operational person and less interested in building the technology. Fahim, since the first dinner years ago, had wanted to build a new and innovative global tech company – and he could now see it happening within Seafood Souq – at the same time as the opportunity to create change in the industry most important to him.

The two co-founders could not decide where to take the company. What was next? Should they stay and build together with one of them compromising their vision? That would never transpire well. Should one of them leave? Which one of them? What would happen to their life-long friendship? What would happen to the company? How would they share this with the team? What would the fallout be? The questions in Fahim and Sean's minds were endless. No matter what the path they would choose would be, it felt like it would be the wrong decision and the end of Seafood Souq.

JEDDAH, SAUDI ARABIA
RYAN LEFERS – PART 1

Seven-year-old Ryan rushed out excitedly into the pouring rain in South Dakota. He wanted to feel it soak him and he started stomping his feet and splashing with the little puddles that were forming. His mother followed him, laughing, joyful, yet concerned all at the same time. The rains were definitely welcome after the drought they had been experiencing, but this looked more ominous. It could be a longer storm, a flood or hail. Their crops could be completely destroyed. Their farm, and the neighbour's farms, were all at risk. Last year's hail had completely obliterated everybody's crops. Ryan looked up at his mother. The smile had disappeared from her face as she looked out at the grey turned to green (a sign of hail) clouds. He stopped splashing in the puddles.

That moment never left Ryan. Decades later, his parents' and family's reliance on rain-fed agriculture, susceptible to drought, flooding, hail and changing weather patterns had built in him a sense of resilience and purpose. This took him to one of the toughest agricultural environments in the world: Saudi Arabia, to pursue his PhD at the King Abdullah University of Science and Technology (KAUST), where he would meet Mark Tester, a professor of plant science and a world-renowned scholar in plant salinity tolerance and Derya Baran, an expert in organic electronics, specifically semiconductors for solar cells and sensors.

Conducting research in Saudi Arabia, Ryan, Mark, and Derya quickly became friends and started comparing notes and experiences. All three wanted to apply their scientific research in practical contexts. "The things we had been doing on the research side were interesting and cool, but were they making an impact? And honestly, Mark and I had to conclude that the answer was no," admits Ryan. "Mark is one of the top one per cent of scientists in the world by citation, but in terms of non-academic impact, he and I both felt that was something we wanted to have – in terms of getting the research out of the university and into the hands of people who could benefit." They knew their research could change the world – if only it could be used well!

"For me, I was really good at things like math and science and I saw those as opportunities to contribute to agriculture on a wider scale," he says. "And so this whole thing around problem solving and feeding the world and using resources wisely was part of my upbringing. It was something I was passionate about in terms of making an impact for the long term."

How could they achieve this? They could either license their technologies, or start their own company. Ryan and Mark chose the latter. Initially, it was just a side project – continuing that way for about a year. Then Ryan began allocating more time and they eventually launched Red Sea Farms (now iyris) in 2018. Their purpose was driven by Ryan's childhood: the twin issues of heat and water scarcity. Their aim was to enhance agricultural productivity in arid and saline environments by leveraging saltwater greenhouse technology – the result of thousands of hours of research – how could they leverage it to build something meaningful?

Their original focus was using saltwater for cooling systems and breeding crops to be more tolerant of salinity. Due to their natural salt tolerance, tomatoes were the first crop to be trialled, with a subsequent emphasis on tomato rootstocks. Those rootstocks allowed any tomato – cherry, plum, or beefsteak – to be grafted for greater resilience. "Fresh crops like tomatoes or strawberries don't keep well, but they're highly nutritious, and if you're going to solve food security, it's not just about calories, it's also about nutrition," says Ryan. "So we really focused our efforts on what we saw as highly nutritious fresh crops, and those had to be grown in a controlled environment for year-round production because of the high summer heat."

Seed investment of $1.9 million was secured in 2019, allowing the founders to build a 2,000-square-metre pilot facility at KAUST. Once built, the greenhouses reduced water and carbon footprints by substituting 80 to 90 per cent of the freshwater used in cooling with saltwater. Tomatoes were grown with up to 10 per cent diluted seawater, making the crop exceptionally sweet, with higher levels of antioxidants. This fresh agricultural produce was sold under the Red Sea Farms label, enabling them to run proof-of-concept facilities while refining

moment for Ryan! They had found a way to reduce water in indoor farming by up to 90 per cent and were trialling with a local retailer on campus. Given that water was one of the largest risk factors of indoor farming, this was a game-changer in making indoor farming profitable and sustainable. It was proof that their research could not only be commercialised, but also used to improve the outlook of food security.

Derya, meanwhile, had created a company called iyris, whose original technology was a transparent photovoltaic cell that collected a spectrum of solar radiation not traditionally used to create energy. That spectrum of near infrared radiation took heat and converted it into electricity.

"One of the first things I said to Derya was: 'This is amazing. If you can just block the heat for us in greenhouses, that's 90 per cent of the battle. We're going to save so much energy on cooling, we're going to save so much water on irrigation, the plants are going to be happier, and they're going to grow for longer,'" he recalls. The team immediately set off to work, eventually finding a way to block heat at a relatively low cost. SecondSky was born.

Although Derya had made the original discoveries in the lab, it was Daniel who focused on the productisation, transforming the findings into a master batch additive scalable with third-party manufacturers. "They both played a really critical role and I can't understate the importance each of them has played – and continues to play – both at the foundational, discovery level, and then at the really difficult productisation level," says Ryan.

Ryan saw their technology's ability to block heat as a game changer and started to see synergies between the two companies. The more he considered the synergies, the clearer the idea became: the companies should merge and become a leading technology solution provider for indoor farming. Ryan started to think through what could be possible, how this could all be built, the impact on the environment, on food security, on the world. He was getting ahead of himself. He would first have to see if Derya and Mark thought it was a good idea. Would they be willing to join forces? H was so impressed with what they had built that he was ner What did they think of what he and Mark had done? Did a especially so early, make sense? Ryan believed that they well together and build something meaningful if they joined forces. Ryan started preparing his pitch in his head.

*****

ALEPPO, SYRIA
EDWARD HAMOD – PART 2

Edward decided to hire the world. "We moved to a project-based model, where we'd go to different chefs from different regions, hire them on a consultancy basis for a specific duration for a specific product, and work with them on that front. All while running consumer tasting through friends, family, acquaintances, and events."

By the end of 2022, the team had expanded to ten. The food science team concentrated on the nutritional aspects of the company's initial product line, prioritising protein content and the complete amino acid profile when developing their formula. Meanwhile, the culinary team focused on taste, texture, and consumer experience. The goal was to avoid creating a product that was nutritionally beneficial but lacking flavour. Edward wanted a clean label with all-natural ingredients: no synthetic products, no preservatives, and an allergen-free, non-GMO product. By the time they were ready to go to market, their burger had nine ingredients – a sharp contrast with the eighteen to twenty in other products.

Everything was running in parallel. The team was busy constructing a facility in Khalifa Economic Zones Abu Dhabi (KEZAD), developing products, collaborating with the culinary team, modifying equipment, and preparing for production. When the company launched in April 2023, it did so with a product line comprising minced meat, kabab, kafta, a burger, and, by a quirk of fate, soujuk sausage. Barely eighteen months separated the company's incorporation and inauguration of its KEZAD facility, bolstered by the region's emphasis on food security, and the need for food independence. By then, Switch had grown to twenty full-time employees and Edward had forged a company built on three pillars: taste, health and nutrition, and sustainability.

Since then, Switch has expanded into Oman, Kuwait, Lebanon, and Qatar. Monthly volumes are increasing, and the company holds a leading market share position, ranking either first or second across all outlets. It has also expanded into food service, supported by local and regional collaborations with major food groups. "From day one, we didn't want to build one gigantic facility. We knew we would build smaller satellite production facilities across every major market we wanted to serve," says Edward. That includes Saudi Arabia and Egypt, where a more price competitive product range is to be launched.

As Edward reflects nostalgically on his first company, which produced an exceptionally valuable commodity – nourishment – and oversaw one of the largest food organisations in the country, he shares, "All that blood, sweat, and tears were taken way. But that created the Ed you see in front of you today – resilient, driven, and confident. You reach a point where your computers have been stolen, you don't have access to your finances, you don't know your receivables from your payables, and your bank accounts have been frozen because you have an address in Syria. All over the world, Syrians were treated unfairly, even people like us who were never involved in any conflict. We had nothing to do with politics, we were just a small family that had made an honest living for generations. But it taught us a lot. It taught us how to be resilient, how to manage crises, how to deal with different risks, even if those risks were never taught to us in school. It was a very long three years but it made me the person I am today.'"

DUBAI, UNITED ARAB EMIRATES
FAHIM AL QASIMI – PART 2

Fahim and Sean stood nervously in front of the Seafood Souq team with some important news to share. Sean looked around the room. He could see that the team he had helped build – Scott Chambers as COO, Osama Al Muqbel as CTO, and Tariq Alimohamed as CFO – was now equipped to elevate the technology to new heights. It was a moment of transition, one Sean embraced with confidence, knowing he was leaving the company's future in capable hands. Fahim and the team took a moment to reflect on Sean's departure. It was an incredibly sad moment; and yet, there was no time to waste.

Launching a new project in South Africa, Seafood Souq began developing digital logbooks for pole and line fisheries, creating traceability at the very beginning of a catch's journey from the sea to the plate. That solution evolved into (Seafood Souq Trace) SFS Trace, an automated algorithm that provides source-to-delivery tracking by pulling data at every stage of the supply chain.

"By integrating directly with the trawler, we can monitor the fishing practices that are being used, we can track the boat, make sure it's fishing within its quota and within its area. We can monitor bycatch, ensure the proper lines are being used, record precisely when the fish left the water, and track its journey at every source." Traceability tools for fisheries, processors, distributors, hotels, supermarkets, and restaurants have since followed, allowing SFS Trade to align with the Global Dialogue on Seafood Traceability, an international initiative promoting global seafood traceability standards.

As the team went global, rather than concentrate solely on established markets, they also focused on emerging source markets, which buyers typically had limited access to: markets such as Oman, with its abundance of fish stocks, and Senegal, with its 500 kilometres of Atlantic coastline. This emphasis became a unique selling point, underscoring the company's commitment to environmental protection and developing a sustainable blue economy. Sean and Fahim wanted to alleviate pressure on fish stocks in established markets; and reduce wastage in regions plagued by inefficient practices and inadequate cold chain management.

In 2022, an estimated 62 million people were involved in fishing and aquaculture worldwide.[137] Of those, 54 per cent were engaged in fisheries and 36 per cent in aquaculture, although a significant proportion were artisanal or small-scale operations, such as in Oman and Senegal. In many lower and middle-income countries, the fish these artisanal fishermen caught were, and are, the primary – or only – source of protein and essential nutrients, including omega-3 polyunsaturated fatty acids. As such, they play an essential role in ensuring food security and nutrition for coastal communities.

"We've cared about the ocean for a long time," says Fahim. "We've done what we've done because we care and we were in the right place at the right time. Just as we were maturing into a business model that was validated, the world woke up to the fact that the oceans matter. With us building traceability into the supply chain, we're now building the sustainable supply chains of the future," says Fahim. "By building traceability into it, by building resilience into it. Did we think we were going to do this from the Middle East to the world four-and-a-half years ago? No. Over the last year-and-a-half? One hundred per cent."

Seafood Souq's team is now twenty-two people working across thirty-five markets in five continents, producing data insights on 168 countries and contributing significantly to transparency in the blue economy. Today, Seafood Souq is building on the base it had built over the past five years to create a comprehensive ecosystem with a suite of solutions for stakeholders across the seafood supply chain, enabling traceability, sourcing, and transparency. The company has delivered over 100 million plates of traceable seafood, which helped enhance food security as well as provide traceability audits for hotel groups.

Many years ago, after coming up from that dive and saving a turtle named Farah, Fahim could not have imagined what would transpire. As it happened, his kindness would attract widespread media attention. A photo of Fahim with the turtle before releasing it back into the sea captured the public imagination, threw Fahim into the media, and enabled the launch of Seafood Souq – a chance encounter that changed lives, both of people and the seas.

JEDDAH, SAUDI ARABIA
RYAN LEFERS – PART 2

Initially, the two companies – Red Sea Farms and iyris – worked together unofficially, but after about a year-and-a-half, they merged, transitioning to a pure-play technology company in 2023. By developing agri-climate tech solutions enhancing the sustainability and efficiency of farming in arid climates, iyris would help growers increase crop yields, reduce input costs and risk, and extend growing seasons in some of the most difficult farming environments globally.

The company had a strong direction and focus, which did not include the assets of indoor farming that had been built and used for testing early products. As a result, Red Sea Farms' controlled environment agriculture facilities were transferred to Pure Harvest Smart Farms in late 2023. The focus now was on developing technologies that could make food security far more achievable.

Bringing SecondSky – iyris' flagship product – to commercial maturity would not be easy. First, there was the product challenge itself. A patented material science innovation, the solution harnesses patented nanoparticle additives – strategically engineered to enhance light transmission while mitigating the harmful effects of near-infrared radiation (heat). Because SecondSky is a chemical product, getting the mix right was critical. Getting technologies out of the lab, building early-stage prototypes, and testing them had been an occasionally frustrating experience. But the team was adamant that it would work.

"We were going to world-class manufacturers who produce covers for greenhouses on an immense scale and were asking them to take an additive from a company they had never heard of," laughs Ryan. The potential to save energy and water consumption was so tempting, so some took the risk, and they proved that the technology worked.

SecondSky reduced energy use by over 40 per cent and water consumption by 30 per cent. The amount of heat allowed in can also be adjusted, with a low integration blocking less heat and a high integration blocking more heat, while continuing to allow for the needed light to enter. This was a game-changer since produce could be grown at lower costs and in hotter climates than ever historically possible.

The technology ensures both optimal growing conditions for crops, and promotes sustainable farming practices by conserving resources and improving crop resilience. In total, iyris' platform of proprietary technologies can reduce energy and water consumption and have been installed across the world.

However, the team didn't stop there. A successful Series A round brought in a further $16 million in May 2024, allowing the company to accelerate sales and delivery of SecondSky. It also enabled the founders to continue developing further heat blocking technology and resilient plant genetics. The latter includes the development of plant genetics via a novel hybridisation process, which has the potential to breed resiliency to salinity, heat, and drought across a broad range of crops.

"As the climate is changing and we see more extreme events globally, and as humans need to tap into areas of the planet where we weren't otherwise growing food, the need is there to find crops that are more salt tolerant, either because of salty soils or salty water for irrigation," explains Ryan. "Salt is a big challenge and it's directly linked to heat and to climate change, so it's a big part of climate mitigation and climate adaptation."

"It's not a question of if, but when and how agriculture has to change," says Ryan. "We know this has to happen. All we're trying to do is enable farmers. We're trying to give them another tool in their tool chest that they can use to adapt to the changing climate and feed people. At the end of the day, farmers are there to produce a crop and whatever they can find to support them in that, they're going to adopt it, as long as it also contributes to their bottom line. That's where we come in. I hope ten years from now, as we look back, we're going to see that we've made a huge shift in the industry."

* * * * *

Food security is clearly not just a MENA concern but a global one. In 2022, 2.4 billion people – nearly a third of the world's population did not have consistent access to food, including an estimated 900 million individuals who face severe food insecurity.[138] Conflict continues to be a major contributor, but dwindling natural resources, deforestation, global warming, and surging populations, especially in the Global South, are all exacerbating the problem. The World Bank has predicted food production will have to increase by 70 per cent (on 2009 levels) to feed a projected global population of 9.8 billion by 2050.[139]

At the same time, climate change could cut crop yields by over 25 per cent, with extreme weather events devastating the livelihoods of communities across the globe, particularly in sub-Saharan Africa and parts of Asia.

In the MENA region, these issues are compounded by the harsh environment. As temperatures rise and annual rainfall decreases, the region's fragile landscape faces potentially devastating pressure. Five Middle East nations – Bahrain, Kuwait, Lebanon, Oman and Qatar – are among the world's six most water-stressed countries,[140] and even prior to the climate crisis, Kuwait was one of the hottest places on Earth. In 2016, a record high of 53.9°C was recorded in Mitribah, a weather station in the country's north-west, and an identical temperature was documented in Iraq. The latter faces a perfect storm of soaring temperatures, diminishing rainfall, intensified droughts, frequent dust storms, and flooding.[141]

It is a similarly sombre story in the once-fertile lands of Egypt, Iraq, Lebanon, and Syria, elevating food security concerns to critical levels. Even before the climate crisis, Egypt relied on just three per cent of its territory for agriculture, placing a considerable burden on the land available for cultivation. Such a high percentage makes Egypt susceptible to deteriorating climatic conditions. Egypt's economy has diversified considerably over the past few decades but agriculture still provides the livelihoods for 57 per cent of the population and directly employs 26 per cent of the labour force.[142]

In Saudi Arabia, where approximately 1.5 per cent of the country's landmass is classified as arable land, if no climate change action is taken, the Kingdom could witness an 88 per cent increase in the frequency of agricultural drought by 2050.

Alternative farming solutions are essential. Biotechnology is being used to enhance nutrient value, increase crop yields, and minimise the carbon footprint of crop production. Meanwhile, controlled environment agriculture is helping to cut the consumption of energy and water, while enhancing the yield and quality of crops such as lettuce, tomatoes, and kale. The use of greenhouses, hydroponics, artificial lighting, and automated climate control systems is enabling controlled environment agriculturists to use up to 95 per cent less water than traditional farming, bringing the region a tentative step closer to agricultural salvation.

As these founders tackled this tremendous issue, it is incredible to witness how both Fahim and Ryan moved away from capex-heavy models in order to build global technology platforms in order to scale beyond the region. The founders' intense desire to reshape the world of agriculture and food, to commercialise great research, and to build global companies that could improve the world's condition never ceases to astound. Indeed, now both iyris and Seafood Souq generate substantial revenues outside the MENA region, and are regarded some of the most innovative companies in their fields.

Whether it was tracing seafood, innovating in the field of plant protein, or making controlled environment agriculture more affordable and sustainable, these three founders all set out with one goal in mind – to improve how our food is grown or caught. Irrespective of where they grew up, their knack for spotting challenges in the region and tackling them with creative solutions has kept them ahead of the curve, both in terms of innovation and commercial success.

iyris' SecondSky, and its work on resilient plant genetics, enable sustainable farming in harsh environments, conserve water, and heighten crop resilience. Fahim and Sean's focus on traceability and the development of a sustainable blue economy are enhancing transparency, supporting the health of marine ecosystems, and driving more responsible and environmentally friendly practices.

Meanwhile, Edward's culturally relevant focus on producing protein-rich food locally and more efficiently and his prioritisation of sustainable practices, is helping to address the crisis of food insecurity. Whereas plant-based protein is regarded as a high-end vegan-friendly option in most markets, in the MENA region,

Edward's solution is created and priced in a manner that genuinely addresses the challenge of nutrition.

Their unique approaches in helping to solve the enormity of the region's food security challenge is a key learning for entrepreneurs everywhere. They are successful because what they have achieved had never been done before. Their innovations have resulted in the creation of valuable products, and the building of intriguing companies with significant impacts on a global scale. Importantly, all began with something they were deeply passionate about.

Each advance represents, *inshallah*, a significant step forward in their respective fields, illustrating the diverse ways start-ups can drive meaningful change. Passionately obsessed with food, these little innovations have allowed our founders to create standout products while transforming their vision into impactful realities.

As the region continues to grapple with issues of food security, sustainability, and climate change, there is an increasing imperative need to invest in technologies and practices ensuring accessibility to food. This includes exploring innovative food solutions that provide necessary proteins and nutrition for its rapidly growing population. Addressing these needs supports regional self-sufficiency and contributes to the MENA region's overall health and stability. The region's challenging circumstances, including limited arable land and water scarcity, have made it a hotbed for innovation in food and agricultural technology. These conditions drive entrepreneurs and researchers to pioneer unique solutions, making the region one to watch for future breakthroughs and opportunities in sustainable food practices.

CHAPTER 10

RESHAPING THE GLOBAL SUPPLY CHAIN

الحركة بركة

Movement brings blessings.

– ARABIC PROVERB

DUBAI, UNITED ARAB EMIRATES

FAHMI AL SHAWWA – PART 1

His fortieth birthday party behind him, Fahmi knew he was at a crossroad. There had to be more to life. There was no motivation and it felt unfulfilling to simply go out there, work and manage or run companies. He exited his convenience store business after seven years, and was searching for something different. As he considered one opportunity after another, he realised that nothing was sparking his interest.

"So I took a year off work and life, and this German friend of mine, who was selling these 3D printers, said come and join me as a consultant. I had just turned forty. I just wanted something completely different. This sounded out there! So yeah, maybe it was a moment of reinvention or simply just mid-life crisis.

But 3D printers in 2015? What were they going to print? Fahmi leaned into his entrepreneurial mindset – he had already started and sold two companies, one restaurant business and one convenience store business. Whereas those couldn't be more different than 3D printing, the core lessons of entrepreneurship remained the same.

Born in Kuwait to Palestinian parents from Gaza, Fahmi's approach to life was about continuously exploring new avenues until something clicked. This 3D printing project had lit up his curiosity – and for someone in search of new purpose, this was exciting and inspiring! Once he had grasped the potential of the 3D printer, he became a man possessed. "To be honest, it got me energised. You're learning something new, you're thinking, and the challenge was interesting." It was certainly a more productive way of dealing with a mid-life crisis than buying a large new motorcycle.

Fahmi threw himself headlong into the world of 3D printing. He had no engineering experience and knew nothing about additive manufacturing, so he spent a year intensively studying the technology. He took courses at MIT, Singularity University, and London Business School, and visited every 3D printing facility he could find. He even flew to Ogden, Utah, where one of the world's largest 3D printing companies at the time had its headquarters – even though he didn't know where Ogden was.

Equally, cementing his role as one of life's great pioneers, he only had a vague idea of how he was going to use the technology. So he brought in a handful of close friends. "I told them: 'Listen, we're going to set up this thing. Honestly, there's no business plan. I don't know what we're going to do. I'll put up half the capital, you put up the other half, and I'll set it up. Give me a year, we'll figure out the business model." They were all just as excited, and decided to gamble on his enthusiasm and Immensa was formed.

His next step was acquiring a facility in Dubai Production City; purchasing an industrial printer for €350,000 and hiring three graduate engineers. It was October 2016. In February the following year, the company entered a competition run by the UAE government called Drones for Good. Fahmi and his team took an off-the-shelf drone, redesigned it, and developed a model that could enhance safety, efficiency, and data analysis during the inspection of construction sites. The $1 million prize money helped the company sustain itself while Fahmi sought a practical application for the technology.

In the beginning, they tried to mimic Europe and the US by catering to the aviation and medical industries, which had both embraced 3D printing's ability to create complex, customised, and lightweight components efficiently. The problem was that the GCC didn't have an aviation industry. It didn't have medical research facilities either. Immensa soon faced serious difficulties. It had no sustainable business model, the UAE was facing negative economic headwinds, and Fahmi and his loyal friends had invested a significant amount of money in a company that was clearly failing. Then, out of the blue, one of the region's largest contractors reached out. It needed spare parts for cranes and wondered if Immensa could help. It was the company's first strategic breakthrough.

"They said, 'Can you guys do this?' The four of us took the parts, designed them and made them independently. That was our first 'aha' moment. Of the twelve parts, nine were cheaper to 3D print than to buy," says Fahmi. 3D printing was considered expensive, especially in Europe and the US, where producing a spare part within the same country or state was far more cost-effective than 3D printing and shipping it. Why would anybody take the risk on a new technology and 3D print something that they could simply manufacture in-country for less money using proven and conventional manufacturing methods? They wouldn't if they had onshore or nearshore manufacturing.

The UAE, however, did not have significant or sophisticated in-country manufacturing in the same manner as other countries. The sector accounted for approximately 8 per cent of the country's GDP by 2017, compared with 28 per cent in China and 14 per cent in India.[143] So the options buyers had were different: either import from another country, or take a risk with a new technology in-country.

In recent years, there has been a notable shift in how supply chains are conceptualised. Traditionally, they were viewed as linear processes, with raw materials moving from suppliers to manufacturers, to distributors, and finally to retailers and consumers. However, with the advent of digital technologies and a growing emphasis on sustainability, companies now increasingly see supply chains as interconnected networks. Metaphors of raw materials travelling downstream from source to consumer are no longer valid. Supply chains are now multi-faceted and multi-directional, more akin to a spider's web of inter-dependence. What this new flow of goods has also created is the understanding of the increasing emphasis on the benefits of sourcing from within a consumer's own community, which encompasses everything from food to the production of goods. Advances in material science and the rise of additive manufacturing (the fabrication of objects layer-by-layer) have radically altered supply chains, allowing for local fabrication and a reduced need for long-distance shipping and international air freight. Such a localised production model challenges our traditional dependency on global trade networks.

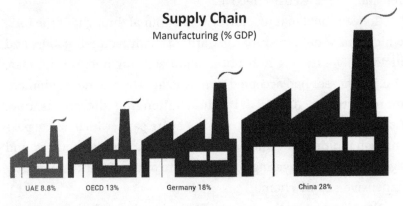

Supply Chain
Manufacturing (% GDP)

UAE 8.8%   OECD 13%   Germany 18%   China 28%

Source: World Bank (2022)

The environmental implications of this shift are potentially profound. When production is brought closer to the end consumer, it generates more than time, labour, and material savings – it leads to shorter transit times, the reduced need for extensive inventory storage, and less transport-related pollution. By reimagining manufacturing, we have an opportunity to reduce our carbon footprint significantly. The future of supply chains may not rest solely on improved transportation but on a profound shift in how and where goods are made. Fahmi firmly believes that, sooner than we imagine, companies and individuals won't be shipping physical products globally but will instead transmit digital files to produce parts locally.

"In other markets around the world, such as the US, you already have an industrial base," says Fahmi with the authority of a true believer in the new technology. "The mindset needed to change from conventional manufacturing to additive is therefore a challenge. They have no incentive to change because it's available, it's local, and their manufacturing capabilities are a couple of hours away. So you really have to work three times as hard to convince them to try a new technology. Plus, there is pushback because this new model will result in a lot of unemployment in conventional manufacturing. In the UAE, companies were importing the parts and we were telling them they could source it down the street. So it was a much easier sell and far more cost-effective."

Conventional manufacturing was minimal throughout the UAE, which was a net buyer, particularly of manufactured goods, and historically a trading hub, not a manufacturing hub. For decades, UAE businesses had accepted terms dictated by original equipment manufacturers (OEMs) without challenging the status quo. Companies often faced high costs for spare parts, which had to pass through multiple intermediaries such as couriers, distributors, and agents. This cost layering contributed to an inefficient and overtly expensive supply chain.

Now, Fahmi saw the opportunity and business model.

It coincided with the UAE prioritising the development of manufacturing capabilities under Operation 300bn, a government initiative to increase the industrial sector's annual contribution to GDP from AED 133 billion ($36 billion) in 2021 to AED 300 billion ($82 billion) by 2031.[144] Achieving that objective would require more than just building factories; it meant investment in AI, automation, and additive manufacturing, so companies can bypass outdated legacy systems and embrace cutting-edge digital solutions for their supply chains.

Immensa's first big contract was with Dubai Metro, providing the solution to a recurring issue: a small plastic component within the ticket machines was breaking due to regular wear and tear. The manufacturer of the ticket machines refused to sell the plastic component to Dubai Metro, on the basis they would make more money by selling them the entire mechanism. The net result was that Immensa was commissioned to produce the component on demand. Their solution was cheap and effective. Immensa now had a high-profile client they could discuss to provide confidence to other potential customers.

In the summer of 2018, Fahmi had two lucky breaks. First, the Kuwait National Petroleum Company (KNPC) requested an impeller (a rotor used to increase the pressure and flow of fluid) to be 3D printed as part of its research into emerging technologies. Second, a global consortium of leading energy companies began to develop guidelines for the 3D printing of components used in the energy sector. Immensa participated in both, producing the very first titanium 3D printed impeller for KNPC.

The project was so successful that Immensa was asked to contribute to the development of industry standards. This put them at the heart of future developments, in a key industry they could develop products for. It also gave them enormous credibility with future clients. That programme lasted two years and resulted in global standards and certification criteria for 3D printed parts in the energy and maritime industries.

"We participated in all these initiatives, albeit as junior participants who observed more than contributed value, to be honest," admits Fahmi. "You're sitting there and you're listening to all these great minds talking about the digital supply chain and the importance of producing parts on demand using new technologies. That gave us the cue to say: 'Okay, this is where we want to go.' So by 2019, we were positioned. We understood where the energy industry was going, we'd done a couple of projects that nobody had done, and we started knocking on the doors of all these companies, whether oil, renewable, or clean energy."

The energy sector was saddled with a hugely complicated supply chain. Complexity was further heightened by the need to customise equipment to suit specific environments. Even more crucial was that every minute of plant downtime could mean millions of dollars in losses. The spare parts market alone was valued at $90 billion a year. Of that, an estimated $10 billion could be realistically produced using digital supply chain technologies. It was the push Immensa needed to scale up.

Sitting at the intersection of energy and additive manufacturing, the company began building its capacity, identifying first the need to scan large numbers of parts. Immensa embarked on a multi-year project to develop its own proprietary scanning technology. It designed, developed, and manufactured an automated industrial scanner that allowed it to significantly enhance its digitisation process.

Fahmi was excited. After five years of experimenting, they could finally see the business opportunity. They had a product. They had proof of concept. They were leading the charge in their space. Now, all he had to do was raise money to build to grow.

Then came Covid-19. It was going to be impossible to fundraise in this environment. Fahmi was starting to understand that maybe this company was just not meant to be. How would he explain to his team and his investors that they had run out of money and that given the pandemic, people were not investing in new inventive technologies? Investors had become risk-averse. Nobody needed his technology. The world was shutting down. How was Immensa going to survive? They had just enough money in the bank to lay off the team and pay severance.

AMMAN, JORDAN
CHARIF MZAYEK – PART 1

The ringing of the school bell announcing the end of the day finally arrived! Charif grabbed his books and raced down the old and uneven streets of Amman, crossing roads without waiting for the cars to stop, as he knew they never would if he waited. Without so much as a single pause or looking back, the 12-year-old boy finally arrived, panting and breathless. As he did every day, he opened the door to the flower shop and greeted his parents. He loved helping them in their business every afternoon. It was the highlight of the day, the weekend, and every holiday.

Born in Beirut to Palestinian and Syrian parents, Charif's family moved to Amman at the beginning of the Lebanese Civil War in 1975. In order to make ends meet, the family opened their first flower shop in Jabal Amman. "The flower shop proved so successful that they expanded and had several shops. As kids, my siblings and I grew up working in the store at weekends, afternoons and during the holidays. We all had a strong emotional attachment to that first shop and we spent a lot of time there, helping our parents and doing our part." Charif's entrepreneurial spirit blossomed in the flower shop. And then in the multiple flower shops.

The flower shops were such a success that Charif was able to go to university in Germany and the US, graduating with degrees in audio engineering and film production. But his heart was still in the flower shops and with his family – so rather than pursuing building his career overseas, he returned to Amman to work in the flower shops – just for a year or two. Or so he thought.

However, frustrated with the quality and selection of the flowers they were selling, he soon began experimenting with hydroculture growing techniques, which enabled the company to reduce water consumption, optimise fertiliser use, and expand its network of farms across Jordan. Fascinated by what he was discovering, and driven by a desire to improve efficiency, Charif began to look more closely at key issues affecting the business and their growers – from water use to the most eco-friendly ways to use pesticides.

"At that time, we were the main retailers, then we were the main growers, and had established an agribusiness that began connecting breeders and providers of planting material to growers across the Middle East," says Charif, with evident delight. "That started expanding and became a much larger business. We went from the Middle East to India and Central Asia, working very closely with flower growers, and then expanded the business into providing floral solutions to five-star hotels and high-end events." With his siblings, who had joined the company a few years after him, he grew the business into a successful regional operation, extending across the GCC and Turkey, with projects in the Seychelles and the Maldives.

Whereas the expansion of the family business should have felt like a magnificent success, it also gave Charif a holistic view of the floral industry, and what he saw bothered him. Plant breeders were predominantly based in Europe, growers were scattered across the world, freight forwarders were operating on a global level, and local businesses were beset by a multitude of challenges including limited choice, lengthy purchasing processes, and dependence on an antiquated system of van-based sales. The result of this system was that growers were underpaid, end customers paid too much, and the ultimate selection and lifetime of the end product was too limited and too short. Everybody was settling for a compromised position.

Charif had an idea and decided to experiment with the family business, piloting a scheme that connected the company's production in Jordan with the French market. It was a non-digital solution with speed and efficiency at its heart. "That experiment taught us a lot of lessons and highlighted a lot of the challenges that needed to be solved. But it didn't work out," admits Charif. "We were victims of our own success. We didn't have the supplies to match the demand and we didn't have the production base (that we have now in Kenya and in South America). But that experiment was proof that there were indeed challenges in the sector and they needed to be addressed."

He proved that he was onto something and his idea made sense. The conviction had him imagining a new world: one with a more streamlined and connected marketplace; where processing and delivery times were cut by 50 per cent, costs were lowered for the buyer, the grower captured more value, and the highest levels of quality and service were ensured. But the family business was strong and provided an income stream for multiple generations of family members. It made no sense to risk the family's livelihood for his 'idea'.

But sometimes the best ideas require sacrifices. With a heavy heart and creative mind, Charif decided to share with his family that he was going to leave the business he had helped build since he was a young boy to try something radical. "It was one of the toughest decisions of my life. To leave what I know and venture into something I believe. To leave the family legacy I was building with my siblings and do something by myself. And then, what was harder was to actually share that news with them." In a bittersweet moment, Charif stepped down as the CEO of the family business.

In 2016, Floranow was born, with the ultimate and simple goal of creating the fastest possible connection between sellers and buyers in the flowers industry. "From the first day, we built logistics into the DNA of the company," says Charif. A buyer in Abu Dhabi, for instance, could order flowers from the Netherlands, Kenya, Colombia, and South Africa, with a minimum order of a single bunch of flowers per seller. The company would then aggregate those orders (alongside the orders of other buyers) at fulfilment centres and carry out the last-mile delivery.

Floranow began with two exporters in the Netherlands and five clients in the UAE. The very first order – for a single bunch of roses – was from a client in Ras Al Khaimah (a market traditionally underserved in one of the Emirates). "We wanted to validate the concept because the market was competitive, crowded, and very traditional," explains Charif. "The first feedback we received was that nobody was interested in having another wholesaler in the market. We were trying to say we are not a traditional wholesaler. We are an enabler of the industry. We bring about efficiencies by removing the middle people and we control a very efficient, quality-obsessed logistics solution."

The competitive advantages were clear. Flowers could be ordered from exporters or directly from growers, placing an unlimited offering at the fingertips of buyers. Because the product was shipped directly from the source, it remained fresh in the cold chain. By removing middlemen, cost was also reduced. The company introduced a transparent set of references. Roses, for example, have distinct characteristics in color, fragrance, shape, and growth habit. All this information was provided. Specifications relating to stem length, cut stage, and bloom size further enabled buyers to purchase products best matching their needs. "We democratised the buying decision. It's no longer a wholesaler sitting and deciding what works for them – we have moved the decision of what to buy to the buyer, and empowered them with choice – they could choose which type of rose, stem, shape, fragrance now – not just depend on what the wholesaler had selected. And we empowered the grower – they could sell directly and could charge what the market was willing to pay, not just what the wholesaler offered," Charif concludes.

But Charif wasn't happy to stop here. The next challenge was clear to him. If Amazon could deliver non-perishable products the next day, why couldn't the floral industry achieve the same? A discussion with the packers, logistics providers, and airlines ensued before Floranow piloted next-day delivery to the UAE. It took two months to calibrate, but solutions were found. "In the early stages, there was a lot of pushback," remembers Charif. "We were challenging every single player. We were challenging growers to process, pack, and have their shipments ready three times faster than they would with traditional models. We were pushing the airlines, we were pushing the freight forwarders, we were pushing our tech partner at the time, because we didn't have the tech in house. They were ridiculously slow. So we were hitting a wall every time we tried to do something. But we finally managed to make it happen."

On the growers' side, Floranow provided direct access to many new growers. In Kenya, the company improved the livelihoods of growers by connecting them to a network of buyers, while also taking care of logistics and guaranteeing payment – a major issue in the industry. There were doubters of course.

And those doubters often creeped into Charif's mind. Especially in early 2020 when the world went into a pandemic lockdown. Suddenly, nobody had any more need for flowers; there were no celebrations or events for which people needed flowers. Tourism had come to a grinding halt, meaning hotels, once a very large customer, no longer needed to decorate their lobbies or rooms. Florists were closed. There was no business.

On the other hand, Floranow had over 100 employees, all depending on their salaries to support their families. Charif knew what that meant. He could not bring himself to downsize; and yet they were running out of funding. Despite his instincts, he had raised money from venture capital firms in order to build Floranow – the tech had demanded that capital and he had taken it and was building out his vision and dream. Now, in hindsight, he was wondering if that was the right decision. What was he going to tell his board? How was he going to survive this lockdown? Would the business survive? With zero revenues and a couple of months away from no funding in the bank, Charif was considering what options he really had.

ABU DHABI, UNITED ARAB EMIRATES
AZAM PASHA – PART 1

"Dheere bolo. Dheere bolo." Speak slowly. Speak slowly, urged Azam. Standing in the fields in the scorching Indian heat amongst these thousands of farmers, Azam was far away from his comfortable consulting life in the UAE. He was desperately trying to take notes while the farmer was excitedly explaining to him how their post-harvesting sales process worked. Why he had no say in how much he sold his produce for, and why, no matter how hard he worked, there was never enough money.

He remembered his time in Tajikistan, where he had worked with cotton farmers to enhance crop quality, expanding their reach to global markets and developing innovative processes for crop trading and financing. But that was not enough. It was in Central Asia that he first identified the challenges facing small producers and the inequalities they faced. "Initially, I thought this issue was isolated to one region. However, my work in other countries confirmed the same pattern. In the UAE, SMEs face similar challenges with low margins despite being downstream. The same problem exists everywhere including in developed economies.

Clearly, something was fundamentally wrong. Despite adding the most value throughout the value chain, farmers earn the least," he concluded ruefully.

Though Azam's heart was in farming, his head was firmly in business, and he quickly recognised something in the industry was very wrong.

Azam identified the core issue affecting farmers was their inability to access international markets where the prices are higher than the domestic market – making it nearly impossible for them to secure better margins. Farmers were being told how much they would be paid for their produce, but with little or no room to negotiate. These aggregators who would buy the produce would combine and sort it and sell it to a middleman. Who would sell it to another middleman. Who would export it via a middleman. Then, another middleman would import it on the other side. This middleman would sell it to another middleman. Then to a wholesaler. Then to the retailer. Then to the consumer. Azam thought hard about these middlemen who controlled the pricing. What value did they bring to the equation? The only value Azam could come to think they were bringing was an element of trust. They knew both parties on either side of them, and both parties trusted them to execute at the lowest possible risk.

"Could there not be a better way to create this value and eliminate them, giving the farmers the ability to quote their own price?" Azam asked Rohit Majhi over dinner one day. "Both of us had a deep understanding of export-import processes," says Azam reflectively. "We understood trade and supply chains and when we started discussing our ideas we knew we wanted to make a difference to the SME segment, which I had worked with extensively. There were a lot of issues – the risks in these trades were difficult to address by conventional means and we thought we were at a point where technology could help us address those complexities."

Azam and Rohit decided to join forces and see if and how they could tackle this problem. Even though there were close to half a billion small and medium agri-enterprises worldwide, the vast majority of international trade was driven by large enterprises, with

SMEs accounting for less than a third. Low participation was due to several factors, not least the risks and complexities associated with importing and exporting goods, and access to finance. In terms of risk, the SMEs are unable to acquire tools to mitigate risks in complex international trade, while from perspective of finance, long working capital transactions (often extending to 120 days) meant that without access to finance, exporters could not ship their produce and hence loose the opportunity to realise better prices. Azam and Rohit's focus would be SME agri-producers based anywhere exporting to the UAE market helping to address the country's food security concerns.

Their solution lay in providing a risk management platform, enabled by blockchain and smart contracts, empowering small food and agri-businesses to directly access cross-border trade. Their desire to empower these farmers and "drive social change, making a real, tangible difference" was apparent.

It took eighteen months to get their first MVP up and running, with the founders opting for a demand aggregation model, which meant consolidating the purchasing needs of multiple buyers to achieve better pricing, improved terms, and continuous food supplies. That meant identifying technology-based solutions that could mitigate risk and lead to faster transactions in the perishable food space, while enabling trust.

"For us, that was a critical space because our passion and ambition was to help the small agri producer, which is driven by perishability and where funding is low. Most of these small businesses have to use their own money to be able to produce the product, and then export it and wait to be paid." Sometimes the waiting could be for months, and not fully.

On the risk side, they began to define the dangers involved. For the seller, there was a danger they wouldn't get paid. For the buyer, it was whether farmers or exporters could guarantee supply. It was Maalexi's role to mitigate these two core risks – requiring evaluation of the 'value at risk' (amount of money that could be lost) and 'probability of default' (likelihood of a default event happening). Maalexi had to be a trust centre.

This led to the development of an advanced blockchain platform utilising smart contracts as the foundation of trust, providing users with comprehensive visibility at crucial risk points through a transaction. It also integrated AI to offer access to critical data to help prevent defaults and resolve disputes, and continuously identify and develop risk mitigation tools to make the food and agri supply chain more efficient, and predictable for all the stakeholders.

To deliver these capabilities seamlessly, Maalexi created a closed-loop system where buyers and sellers are verified as they enter the platform. It then developed proprietary procurement risk analysis models to process data to determine buyer and inventory limits, pricing based on underlying risks, and the advance payments counterparties need to provide for transactions on its platform. These models, which include a unique scoring system based on both financial and non-financial information, allows the company to effectively evaluate and engage with buyers, and purchase food inventory that Maalexi holds in its warehouses in the UAE.

The company's rating models uses eighty-six variables for buyer scoring, and twenty-five variables for inventory scoring, incorporating financial and non-financial data, plus continuous transactional data from customers already on the platform. This data includes payment and performance metrics. Once processed, ratings convert into a score for each buyer and for the inventory which is purchased by Maalexi, determining their buyer and inventory procurement limits and pricing on the platform.

Once a purchase decision is made, Maalexi issues a digital contract outlining the agreed quality, quantity, weight, delivery, and payment terms. The platform then initiates an inspection process, where inspectors evaluate the product against the contract's specifications using pre-populated forms. A discrepancy report is then generated, highlighting differences between contracted and delivered goods. AI technology has accelerated report generation from two to three days, down to just fifty-five minutes – crucial for the sale of perishable goods – and providing rapid visibility and acceptance options for buyers. This report is given to the buyer, who can digitally accept the quality, quantity, and weight, which then activates a smart contract.

"Everything we have done on our platform we have done ourselves, from coding to process engineering," says Azam proudly. "Everything is in-house. There was no standard tool we could buy because this is a solution that has been built specifically for the purpose of addressing a problem in our domain. We wanted to create value for small businesses. We have seen how big companies work, but it's SMEs which aren't able to survive. Can we make them sustainable? Can we make them better? Can we truly assist them, including agricultural producers, in improving their post-harvest processes for bringing their products to our platform? Bridging these gaps is a lengthy process, not a short one."

Because the sector was disorganised and not used to contracts and inspections, it took the founders three months to onboard their first buyer. By the end of the first financial year, they had ten buyers, rising to 100 in 2024. With the initial ten customers, the founders could fine-tune the company's MVP, creating a comprehensive platform covering the full transaction journey, from onboarding buyers and sellers to managing contracts to end-point order delivery.

But the users, delighted with the solution, asked for more. One after the other, they would approach Azam with an increasing number of problems. However, there was one that came up repeatedly: they needed a loan. A small loan. But a loan, nonetheless. They had no access to risk mitigation and financial services, and they were unable to buy what they needed in order to grow the food. Or there was a storm and their crop was gone, and sometimes when they had a solution, they needed the funding to make the solution happen.

Had Azam solved one problem only to discover, or create, another one? As he was empowering these farmers by eliminating the middlemen, were they suddenly more eager and able to see the light at the end of the tunnel, but were facing another stumbling block? Could he help them overcome this one too? But Maalexi was not a financial services company. What did he know about facilitating loans? Was it even possible? Did they have any collateral?

But wasn't the entire point of Maalexi to work with this underserved community? Azam felt torn: stick to his business model and continue to scale quickly yet safely but maybe hit a ceiling soon? Or help the community in new forms that he wasn't comfortable with?

SINGAPORE / DUBAI, UNITED ARAB EMIRATES
CONSTANTIN ROBERTZ – PART 1

The overwhelming heat and humidity in Singapore was a stark contrast to Constantin's home in Germany. Yet, in Singapore he found himself; building out the online fashion marketplace Zalora. Shuttling between Malaysia, the Philippines, and Indonesia, Constantin continued to be blown away by the size and growth rate in the market. However, it quickly became clear how much regional brands were struggling to scale due to inefficiencies. As he tried to encourage brands to come onto the Zalora platform, he was realising how much time and resources they were allocating to logistics management, hindering a company's ability to develop its brand and increase sales.

A German national, he had previously worked for Rocket Internet, where he had internationalised e-commerce platforms in emerging markets. He was struck by how brands struggled to scale their e-commerce and omnichannel businesses. Cross-border shipping, delivery lead times, and cultural nuances were hindering the smooth and efficient flow of goods across the world. Somehow, here he was again – witnessing the same challenges for each brand every day.

The solution, however, was far from obvious. So he and two friends, Jannis Dargel, with whom he worked at Zalora, and Shrey Jain, who had spent a significant part of his career optimising last-mile passenger transportation at Grab, started brainstorming.

How could you build a logistics company without building a logistics company? How do you build a logistics simplifier? Was logistics like every other industry in that once there were so many providers, in this case 3PLs (third party logistics providers), then they became a commodity, and a platform had to sit on top of them to simplify and streamline them? As 3PL services became increasingly commoditised, businesses sought alternative solutions to their logistical needs – could this lead to the emergence of fourth-party logistics (4PL)?

What if they created something new to do this – a technology-led logistics orchestration platform? What if they created a cloud supply? Essentially an external service provider that manages an entire supply chain on a company's behalf, the 4PL model provides an essential layer on top of these commoditised services, offering comprehensive management and integration of multiple logistics providers, as brands scale their operations globally – taking away that pain.

The strategic development of 4PL services is prominently centred in hubs such as Singapore and the UAE, both of which have emerged as critical nodes within the Global South. These regions serve as pivotal points in the global supply chain and reflect the burgeoning consumer markets driving this growth. The Global South, after all, has emerged as the world's fastest-growing economic zone. Driven by a young and expanding population, digital transformation, and geopolitical shifts, both brands and consumers are flocking to this dynamic part of the world. As Constantin was discovering first-hand.

Together, in 2020, Constantin and his friends founded Locad: a plug and play logistics solution where a cloud-based platform would act as an asset-light integrator within the supply chain space. In this way, any retailer could, through one platform, distribute their products in many countries without having to identify and manage many different 3PLs.

The goal was to develop a system that companies could leverage for smooth, efficient, and timely products delivery – a logistics engine offering robust infrastructure, a distributed fulfilment network of warehouses, and a fully digital logistics platform. AI and machine learning would also assist companies in forecasting sales and inventory movements, ultimately serving as the backend engine for a commerce business via a cloud service.

Architecturally, that meant building an operating system (OS) with three components: a merchant OS, a warehouse tech stack, and a connectivity tech stack. "In the supply chain you have both digital products, which is your tech stack, and that's all about the APIs and the data flowing and the intelligence layer that is plugged in," explains Constantin. "But you also have an intensely physical layer, which is the physical movement of goods. Both need to be very closely in sync; you're effectively building two companies at the same time – the software company and the physical logistics company."

That was a challenge and ultimately an advantage, allowing Locad to offer cutting-edge software solutions whilst simultaneously providing Infrastructure as a Service (IaaS), delivering comprehensive support to brands beyond just software.

The founders began by building the merchant OS, encompassing everything from placing inventory across different fulfilment centres to order forecasts, analytics, and monitoring order fulfilment. "If you are an e-commerce manager or a supply chain manager of a consumer goods company, this is the cockpit you want to look at every day to see how your supply chain is doing," says Constantin. "Then you have the warehouse tech stack, which is all about empowering warehouse operations through technology, minimising errors, and maximising efficiency. Everything in a warehouse is driven by what the system tells humans to do, in terms of picking, packing, and ensuring it's impossible to send out the wrong items."

Finally, the connectivity stack plugs a brand's supply chain into the ecosystem around them, including marketplaces such as Amazon and e-commerce platforms like Shopify. It also provides a transport connectivity layer, allowing brands to connect to any external system they wish, such as last-mile delivery firms like EMX.

"We were looking at how to build this out one brick at the time while still providing a comprehensive offering, which we did by focusing initially, and solely, on e-commerce, initially in one market and on certain channels. We first focused on the merchant stack that connects the warehouse with the sales channels and manages inventory and orders for the merchant. And we built out from there, going deeper into the warehouse operations with the tech, and then integrating deeper with the rest of the ecosystem, such as last mile transport carriers, more and more sales channels, and the whole data analytics layer that ultimately brings smartness into the digital supply chain."

Locad began its operations in the Asia Pacific (APAC) region, leveraging its robust e-commerce growth and diverse market dynamics. APAC's rapidly expanding online retail sector, coupled with its complex logistics landscape, were an ideal environment for Locad's integrated software and infrastructure solutions. By establishing a presence in key markets such as Singapore, the Philippines, and Australia, Locad could offer localised support and tailor its services to meet the specific needs of businesses in these countries.

This strategic focus enabled Locad to effectively manage inventory placement, optimise supply chain operations, and streamline fulfilment processes across a geographically diverse and economically vibrant region. It opened warehousing spaces in six countries – Singapore, Indonesia, the Philippines, Thailand, Hong Kong, and Australia – and built relationships with a broad range of logistics companies, such as shipping partners and last-mile fulfilment agents.

However, a third-time founder, Constantin had been in the industry long enough to know ideas and companies are easily emulated, and whereas he had a first-mover advantage in South-East Asia, the same would not be true in other markets if he didn't move quickly. Very quickly. So he started to eye the other logistics hub in the Global South: Dubai.

As Constantin started looking at the numbers and opportunities in the GCC and broader MENA region, it became clear that Locad would have to expand immediately. But how would he do that? The company was still young, and growing incredibly quickly in South-East Asia. His founders could see how important it would be to cement their market position and growth in their existing market. Wouldn't a new market so far away distract them? How could they manage that growth? Besides, they knew very little about the GCC – where would they start?

* * * * *

DUBAI, UNITED ARAB EMIRATES
FAHMI AL SHAWWA – PART 2

With his eyes closed, sitting in the dentist's chair in the midst of the pandemic, Fahmi started preparing and playing out the speech he was going to give to his team the next day in his mind to share the news. There was going to be no easy way to do it. The dentist's rant interrupted his thoughts, "Can you believe they have increased the costs of these visors by twelve times in the last two weeks? And we can't even get them – everybody is out of stock. It's absolutely terrible because we are not allowed to work without them." Fahmi opened his eyes. "Let me see it." He said, and inspected the visor, "You know what? I'm going to make you ten or fifteen of these and send them to you." Within two weeks Fahmi had an order for 500 visors.

Then the Dubai Health Authority called him. "I remember the call vividly," he recalls. "They said: 'We will buy everything you can produce'. We had the capacity to produce no more than 150 a day. I went back to the team and said: 'Guys, we have to do 50,000 a week'. We went and bought 100 printers and had to hire people off the street in lockdown. We received a permit from the government and we were producing thousands of visors. We reached revenues of $2 million. That was a record year for us."

The ending of 2020 proved to be very different than the beginning. After the most intense year of his life, and about to take some time off with his family and celebrate New Year's on 2020, and still in the throes of Covid-19, Fahmi had just checked into a hotel in Ras Al Khaimah, the UAE's northernmost emirate, when he received a call from the Abu Dhabi National Oil Company (ADNOC). They needed a spare part for one of their refineries – and they needed it within ten days. "By 2pm, I was in the car driving to Abu Dhabi. They gave me all the permits [needed to cross different Emirates during Covid-19], I picked up the metal part, went to the office, dropped it off, and drove back to Ras Al Khaimah to celebrate the New Year. We had the part digitised, analysed, dissected, designed, printed, and sent back to them within ten days. And that was it. We didn't hear from ADNOC again until April."

Then, suddenly, Fahmi received a text message from an acquaintance asking if he'd seen a tweet by His Excellency Sultan Al Jaber, the UAE's minister of industry and advanced technology. "I opened Twitter and Dr. Sultan Al Jaber was there with a metal 3D printed impeller, indicating this is the future of ADNOC. Spare parts on demand, produced in the UAE. My heart stopped. This just opened the whole door for us."

Immensa began to expand at a rate it struggled to keep pace with. It took over the adjacent facility in Dubai Production City, doubling in size to 16,000 square feet, and then expanding to 25,000 square feet. It had found its niche transforming the world's spare parts supply chain.

By transitioning to digital warehousing and on-demand manufacturing in a way that was sustainable, efficient, and financially viable. In the world Immensa had created, there was no need for the 'just-in-case' manufacturing, import, or warehousing of physical spare parts, Immensa was building a world of "Real Time" production and procurement.

"The future is now in regards to digital supply chains," says Fahmi. "Of course, there's digitisation and additive manufacturing and localised production, but the underlying business that Immensa is completely reinventing (or disrupting) is logistics. By moving supply chain from the current lethargic movement of parts across the world using ships, trains and planes, we are moving data around the world and recreating the physical parts from the digital assets. We will look back in six to seven years and find it ridiculous that people actually shipped physical parts from one country to the other – it will seem just as absurd to a teenager today as the fact that we used to order CDs to listen to music or visit Blockbuster to rent a movie. With the convergence of material science, computing power speed, and digital connectivity, digital assets and parts on demand are becoming more of a reality. Geopolitics coupled with de-globalisation and environmental challenges are only expediting the adoption of digital supply chain. No more shipping a part from China to the UAE – you send a file and produce it locally."

"We are transforming industries to a place where they can ship bytes, not bits."

Rather than manufacture billions of dollars of spare parts using raw materials in a foreign country, have these parts shipped to the country needed, with all the impact that has on the environment, and keep these parts in a spare part warehouse in case they are needed, draining a company's working capital, the industry could start moving to a new model: keep 3D blueprints of these spare parts (dubbed Digital Assets) in a digital warehouse, and 3D print them locally as needed and immediately. The result: reducing inventory and warehousing costs, shortening lead times, cutting waste, and ultimately freeing up working capital.

When Immensa launched in 2016, the materials Fahmi could work with were limited. They included polylactic acid, a biodegradable plastic made from renewable sources such as corn starch, sugarcane, and other plant materials, and carbon fibre reinforced plastics. Material science has since advanced to such a degree that hundreds of plastics, metals, resins, and composites can be printed, although Immensa's concentration on the energy sector has seen it focus on specialty metals such as titanium, nickel-chromium superalloys, and stainless steel.

Perhaps more importantly, innovation is integral to its operations, reflecting a deep-seated commitment to pushing boundaries and leading in their field. Today, Immensa is the world's leading digitisation and advanced manufacturing company for the energy sector. Such is the demand – the company has expanded into Saudi Arabia, employs 110 people, and began working directly with OEMs.

"We don't stop innovating. We are now launching a handheld scanner (the size of a mobile phone) that is the first of its kind, with patents registered for both hardware and software. This device eliminates the need for engineers or technicians to travel to capture and scan parts. You can send this $800 device anywhere in the world, and anyone can use it to upload a scan to our platform within minutes, providing an automatic assessment, price, and data for digitisation. Everything developed by the Immensa team arose from necessity rather than vision, to be honest. We started off wanting to produce spare parts using 3D printers, but as we progressed, we encountered challenges and obstacles. When we couldn't find existing solutions, we were forced to develop them ourselves. We never intended to become a full-fledged technology company with our own software solutions and a universal digital inventory platform."

Though he recites the successes with obvious pride, there is also an endearing modesty to his story. "We don't claim credit for being visionaries or geniuses; our processes were formulated over years of taking on projects and 'doing'. The specific guidelines were devised when we tackled a large-scale digitisation project that initially seemed beyond our capabilities. The team worked through Christmas to develop a process ensuring quality, unification, efficiency, and accuracy in digitisation. This became the foundation for what will soon become global standards.

Ironically, we found ourselves diving deep into AI and machine learning, developing our own assessment software to handle large-scale projects. Immensa's AI-driven software enabled rapid scanning and assessment of vast numbers of parts, a capability that sparked the need for advanced scanning technology and massive data processing. In response, we developed the IMMENSA360 software platform, integrating AI and machine learning to manage, analyse, and interpret data from these scans with precision and speed. To gain credibility and trust with end users, we also established comprehensive guidelines and standards for our processes. This evolution was far beyond our initial vision – Immensa had simply set out to 3D print parts.

Instead, the company is a leading software company in the additive manufacturing field, and will soon boast digital assets for over 1 million spare parts – a game changer in the land of parts. As Fahmi reflects, he was so glad that his midlife crisis had enabled him to build such a company rather than buy the quintessential red sports car.

AMMAN, JORDAN
CHARIF MZAYEK – PART 2

Preparing for the board meeting with his investors, Charif rehearsed his lines over and over. The survival of the business depended on the support and action plan they could come up with together. An hour later, they surprised him with their confidence in his ability to turn the company around despite having no revenues, to streamline and come up with a creative solution, and to fund the gap he had until this could all be done.

Charif was elated. He could continue to build his company and work with the growers. In the meantime, he had to address the lack of demand and the heavy cost base. Charif got to work identifying new parts of the world for demand, working with growers, and reducing headcount as little as possible. Floranow became financially sustainable as a profitable company, albeit smaller than before. From there, Charif started to grow again, remaining profitable while innovating and changing the landscape globally.

Today, the company's seller base is global. It is also working to empower small-scale growers in Lebanon, Jordan, KSA, and India. "The minute we are able to extend our model to local growers, I think we're going to be able to start measuring the impact of Floranow on a different type of grower." The company employs 180 people, is present in seven cities across Saudi Arabia, as well as the UAE and Kuwait, and has buyers in twenty cities around the world. It has teams in Kenya and Dubai, a tech team in Jordan, and sales and operations are spread between UAE, Saudi Arabia, and Kuwait.

"Our focus in the next couple of years is on two main goals," explains Charif. "One is what we call GCC dominance. We really want to be the number one player and we want to be the enabler of the industry. We acquired a company in Saudi Arabia and have integrated well, becoming a leader in that market. However, the second, and more important goal is to really find a way to unlock the entire potential that international trade offers. Because what do we have today? We have a large network of growers sitting all over the world, so the global aspect of the supply side is already there.

We have the volumes, we have the scale, we have the relationships, and all of these growers are connected to us. We have the logistics sorted out. So now it's a matter of finding and scaling that business globally because theoretically, we can connect any potential buyer with any potential seller, as long as the logistics are feasible."

By streamlining distribution, the company has allowed growers to retain a larger share of their revenue, improving their livelihoods, and incentivising higher quality flowers production and adoption of sustainable growing practices. Meanwhile, buyer choice has been broadened considerably, providing a wider selection of products that are fresher, and superior quality.

Over much laughter and joy, sitting around the lunch table with his siblings, Charif often reflects how difficult it was to take the decision to leave the family business, and how strong his conviction was that there could be a better way to do things, to innovate globally, and build a new business. Looking down at his grandchild, he wonders if he had, indeed, improved the world for the next generation – even in a small way.

ABU DHABI, UNITED ARAB EMIRATES
AZAM PASHA – PART 2

Azam and Rohit spent many days revisiting their original project plan and ultimate business goals. Now that they had spent thousands of hours with the SME buyers and farmers, they could see the needs more clearly, and understand that solving one part of the equation would open a Pandora's box to the other parts. In a good way.

Although the average transaction size is relatively modest at $15,000, each buyer typically completes seven to eight transactions per year. In its first year (2023), Maalexi executed nearly 800 transactions on its platform. By 2024, the number of transactions were projected to exceed 1,000, along with a quadrupling in the average transaction value per buyer.

"Our impact to the farmer is only a spillover impact at this point in time. It's too early for us to be able to deliver true impact on the seller side. It will be only possible as we evolve and become bigger.

Presently, we buy the product from SME agri exporters, so impact is delivered there. But as we evolve, we will move to the next stage, working with small producer organisations in India, which have the capacity to export but don't have the ability to do so. Those will be the guys we go to in the next stage of our development. And then finally it will be the agri producer – the small farm sizes where farmers could give the product to us. But for that, we need warehousing in these origin markets."

When Azam pointed out how smallholder farmers in regions like Africa and Latin America often receive minimal margins for their work, he hadn't yet grasped the full potential Maalexi would achieve on a global scale. What began as a keen observation is now evolving into something far greater than anyone, including Azam, could have imagined. The platform is poised to double its transactions each year while intensifying efforts to empower even more smallholder farmers across the globe. *Inshallah*, the founders hope that small scale farmers will finally get the reward they deserve.

SINGAPORE / DUBAI, UNITED ARAB EMIRATES
CONSTANTIN ROBERTZ – PART 2

"Wow." thought Constantin, "Dubai and Singapore have so much in common – including the hot and humid weather." Within a few days and a marathon of business meetings, Constantin and his co-founders were convinced. They would expand immediately, setting up a significant presence and entering the MENA market as a second headquarters for growth and expansion.

On the immediate growth and global domination plans; Constantin laughs, "Yeah, I think it's ultimately a journey with ups and downs but it's the love of building something which keeps you going," he says. "It's building that international, connected supply chain network where, with every additional region we unlock, it becomes a more powerful tool for our brands. It's something that motivates me a lot."

Today, Locad operates in eight markets, including the GCC, and has 120 employees servicing 250 brands, from Reckitt Benckiser and

Crocs to Havaianas and Levi's. The company's machine learning models are helping forecast sales and inventory movements (what should be reordered, where it should be placed, optimal stock levels that optimise shelf availability etc.). The founders are also working with generative AI to create a co-pilot for merchants that synthesises data and insights, providing a natural language interface to communicate with Locad.

"We see ourselves as a platform and as an engine to enable the growth of brands and merchants on our platform. A big part of that is around cross-border connectivity and helping brands tap into new markets. In a way, we democratise the supply chain infrastructure that gives you distribution. In the past, only the biggest brands in the world were able to build global brands, because distribution and supply chain were big barriers to entry, involving a lot of capex and so on. And we believe that with Locad's logistics engine and cloud supply chain, we can significantly reduce the barriers for a brand to enter a new market and to scale in a new market. So as such, we do have ultimately a global outlook on things."

* * * * *

Geography has been central to MENA's importance, dating back to the ancient Silk Road. Although historians disagree on the details, there is consensus that the great trade route wound its way from China to the Mediterranean through bustling cities like Baghdad, Damascus, and Aleppo. From there, the Ottoman Empire linked it to Europe and Asia. The opening of the Suez Canal in 1869 further cemented the region's central role as a trade hub, dramatically altering the course of international trade. Today, the GCC continues this legacy, strategically positioned as a bridge between East and West, ensuring the MENA region remains a cornerstone of global supply chains.

In recent years, however, there has been a notable shift in how supply chains function. Traditionally, they were viewed as linear with raw materials moving from suppliers to manufacturers and finally to retailers and consumers. With the advent of digital technologies and a growing emphasis on sustainability, companies now increasingly interact with supply chains as interconnected networks. That in turn has led to an increasing focus on sourcing locally. Advances in material science and the rise of additive manufacturing driven by companies like Immensa, have radically altered supply chains, allowing for local fabrication and a reduced need for long-distance shipping and international air freight.

The environmental implications of this shift are profound. When production is brought closer to the end consumer, it generates more than time, labour, and material savings – it leads to shorter transit times, the reduced need for extensive inventory storage, and less transport-related pollution. By reimagining manufacturing, we have an opportunity to reduce our carbon footprint significantly. The future of supply chains may, therefore, lie in better transportation methods and a fundamental rethinking of how and where we produce goods – that is, the very beginning of supply chains.

Supply chains worldwide face ongoing disruptions, but the founders have tackled the challenges of this global landscape with innovation and unwavering determination. Starting with the beginning of supply chains and manufacturing, Immensa illustrated that the shortage in manufacturing capabilities onshore or nearshore could ultimately lead to becoming a huge advantage for providing a new additive manufacturing, 3D printing, solution. Had there been sufficient manufacturing capabilities in the home-countries, the acute needs of the products would have been met, and there would have been no need to venture into risky territory with new technologies and solutions. The lack of industry incumbents and the acute need of the time encouraged potential clients to take the risk and use the product, enabling the development of the company and then the leapfrog to new solutions, proving the idea and technology could work – and then scale globally.

Similarly, within logistics and supply chains, Floranow has made it easier to track and understand the journey of a buyer's purchases by streamlining an inefficient system and shedding light on often opaque and convoluted processes. This clarity has fostered greater trust and collaboration between growers and buyers, proving technology was now able to address some of the region's fundamental challenges that were ordinary in the old way of doing business. Floranow's impact goes beyond the MENA region, positioning the region in both the global floral and tech ecosystems through its solution.

Meanwhile, the scarcity of arable land and freshwater across the GCC translates to the Arabian Peninsula continuing to import almost 85 per cent of consumed food. Marrying the needs of smallholders with those of buyers in countries where food security is a pressing concern presents a mutually beneficial opportunity. Marketplaces and supply chain platforms that connect farmers and food producers to local or regional buyers – while simultaneously providing financial services, managing risk, and promoting transparency – can transform cross-border trade, improve the lives of small-scale farmers worldwide and enhance food security. What Maalexi was able to do is a clear illustration of the region's potential to leapfrog to more advanced ways of operating in a specific sector, leveraging the lack of infrastructure in the world of small-holder farmers by building their own solutions from scratch to cater to their specific needs.

In pursuit of supply chain efficiency, companies globally have sought to minimise costs while maximising service and maintaining quality. This led to the outsourcing of logistics to third parties (3PL), which, over time, became commoditised. To reduce costs, companies sourced inputs from various regions around the world, ultimately creating fragmented, intermediated, and globally distributed supply chains.

A 'just-in-time' philosophy reigned supreme to carefully align every stakeholder along the supply chain to customer demand. While this achieved desired results in cost efficiency, it meant a company's demand planning and management were ill-equipped for any shutdown of the world. As such, the vulnerabilities of globalised supply chains were dramatically revealed to the world during the pandemic, although their existence and consequences preceded it, and the creation of a 4PL platform to streamline the 3PL commodities was possible.

Whether Immensa disrupting global logistics by addressing the first step, manufacturing with 3D printing in Dubai, Constantin pioneering a new 4PL model by aggregating third-party logistics providers, Charif eliminating intermediaries to directly link Kenyan flower growers with wholesalers, or Azam leveraging blockchain to connect farmers to a global food demand network – each founder embraced the belief that no challenge is insurmountable, and that just because it hadn't been done before, it didn't mean it wasn't possible.

What began as solutions to local challenges have now turned into innovations with a global footprint, proving the region is not merely catching up with the world, but actively leading the charge in reshaping global supply chains. These founders have demonstrated how local ingenuity can address complex supply chain issues, and in doing so, they've positioned the MENA region at the forefront of global change, illustrating how the lack of industry incumbents, or alternatives, enabled them to succeed. It demonstrates that founders can dream and innovate from anywhere, proving the region is a hub for emulation and also a cradle of groundbreaking innovation and global achievements.

SECTION III

AS WE LOOK TOWARD the next decade, the MENA region stands at the cusp of a technological renaissance, driven by AI, crypto, and energy innovations. These industries are not just shaping the future of the region; they are positioning MENA to lead on the global stage.

The innovations and technologies created by founders across fintech, healthtech, edtech, agritech and supply chain tech enabled the MENA region to 'catch up' to where the rest of the world was, and then to leapfrog and create new solutions using the best global technologies to fill gaps where there was a lack of infrastructure. The region is now all caught-up, adding innovation to the world, and looking to create and lead the future.

Artificial Intelligence is already transforming industries across the region, from healthcare and finance to logistics and retail. Through its National AI Strategy 2031, the UAE aims to leverage AI to enhance government services, improve healthcare, and transform education. The impact will be significant – AI is expected to contribute AED 353 billion to the region's GDP by 2030, positioning MENA as a major player in the global AI race. The energy and innovation behind this ambition come from the region's young, tech-savvy population, eager to push the boundaries of what AI can achieve in solving real-world problems.

Crypto and blockchain technology are revolutionising finance in MENA, providing greater financial inclusion and faster, cheaper cross-border transactions. Countries including the UAE and Bahrain are emerging as crypto hubs, with the UAE's Dubai Blockchain Strategy aiming to make Dubai the first city fully powered by blockchain by 2025. The region's interest in digital assets is reflected in the fact that MENA has the fastest-growing blockchain adoption rate globally, with over 70 per cent of companies in the region expected to use blockchain technology by 2025. Additionally, the UAE government allows the use of USDC to pay for residency visas, illustrating the full acceptance of the technology.

Energy is another transformative sector in MENA, where vast renewable resources are beginning to reshape the global energy mix. With ambitious plans to diversify away from oil dependency, MENA countries are leading the way in solar and wind energy, positioning the region as a key player in the global energy transition.

In these three sectors – AI, crypto, and energy – MENA isn't just catching up with the world. It is rapidly closing the gap and is poised to redefine the future of global economies with technologies that will drive innovation, sustainability, and inclusion across the globe.

CHAPTER 11

EMBRACING ARTIFICIAL INTELLIGENCE

الغاية غير المخطط لها مجرد حلم

A goal without a plan is just a dream.

– ARABIC PROVERB

GLOBAL/BEIRUT, LEBANON

MAY HABIB

It was a humid dawn in the UAE in 2012, the kind of morning where the heat rises before the sun. May Habib was gripping the steering wheel of her car, eyes fixed on the empty highway stretching between Abu Dhabi and Dubai. She was on her way to meet a stranger – a potential co-founder who might just hold the missing piece to her vision. "I must be crazy," she muttered, glancing at the clock. It read 4:30 AM. Her roommate had said as much the night before. But May wasn't turning back. The meeting was at 6:00 AM sharp, at a JBR café. She didn't even hesitate when she'd gotten the text: 'See you there.'

Waseem AlShikh turned out to be everything May had hoped for – and more. "When I met him, I knew he got it," she says now, reflecting on that fateful breakfast. "We were speaking the same language, not just technically, but philosophically. It wasn't just about building something cool; it was about solving a real problem for people."

The irony was not lost on her. Having escaped the war in her home village in Lebanon when she was five, May's family had immigrated to Canada speaking only Arabic. Struggling to learn the languages of school and friends, she had encountered the problem of language barriers acutely as a child, and it had stayed with her over the years. Now, many years later, she was determined to use technology to solve it.

Together, May and Waseem launched Qordoba, a bold experiment to marry human translators with cutting-edge statistical machine translation. "We were trying to solve something massive," May recalls. "The idea was to align human-translated data with AI to create a bridge between languages." The stakes were high, and the hours were gruelling. Then, in late 2018, something shifted. Transformers – the groundbreaking AI model – burst onto the scene. Suddenly, they weren't just tweaking algorithms for better translation; they were staring at the potential for something transformative.

"We were adding generative features into a localisation platform, and it felt... wrong," May says. "Waseem and I fought constantly that year. Not because we were failing, but because we were *too* passionate about where the technology could go. We had raised money for one thing, but our hearts were pulling us in a completely different direction."

The breaking point came one late afternoon in 2019. In the breastfeeding room at her office, cradling her six-month-old son, the door burst open. There was Waseem, pacing, eyes ablaze, seemingly oblivious to the bonding and feeding taking place. "You have to make a decision," he said, his voice trembling with urgency. "Now?" May asked, blinking at him in disbelief. "Here?" "Yes, now!" Waseem shot back. "Who are we? What are we building? Are we going to stay tethered to the past, or are we going to chase what we know is right?"

May sat there with her son, quiet in her arms, staring at her co-founder. It was a moment of pure chaos – and pure clarity. "I realised then that we couldn't keep doing both. We had to commit, even if it meant starting over."

And so they did.

Laying off two-thirds of their team was agonising. "I had to keep a brave face, but inside, I was terrified," May admits. "We went from a company of dozens to just nineteen people, a founding group who believed in this new vision as much as we did. It was raw, painful – but it was also liberating."

The pivot wasn't just a business decision; it was a leap of faith. They founded Writer in 2020, built on the promise of generative AI. "We started small," May says. "The idea was just to improve AI-assisted writing, to go beyond the old rule-based engines that required armies of linguists. But the ambition grew – and fast."

Writer became a full-stack generative AI platform, designed for businesses that wanted more than just flashy tech. "Our customers told us what they needed: end-to-end solutions, real value, and AI they could trust," May says. "So, we built everything – the large language models, the retrieval systems, and on top of that, a studio where businesses could create their own AI assistants."

Looking back, May marvels at the journey. "Transformers gave us the tools to dream bigger," she says. "We went from editing language to creating it, and now, natural language is how you build software. That's the big idea. AI isn't just automating tasks – it's opening up new worlds of creativity and progress."

From her childhood in rural Lebanon to her company's latest $1.9 billion valuation, May's journey is proof that the toughest decisions often lead to the greatest breakthroughs. "There are easier ways to make money than this," she admits. "But this? This is about building something that matters."

DUBAI, UNITED ARAB EMIRATES
DINA ALSAMHAN

Meanwhile, Dina Alsamhan and her two co-founders, Morteza Ibrahimi and Ahmad Khwileh – with decades of experience at Google and DeepMind – are building something truly transformative for the e-commerce space. Their company, qeen.ai, is set to revolutionise the e-commerce space by harnessing the power of AI to enable completely new ways for businesses of all sizes to operate and sell online, solving long-standing challenges and improving customer experiences. "The rapid adoption of AI tools like ChatGPT is having a profound impact on the way people shop and interact online, and businesses will need to step-change their operations to keep up. We are reimagining and defining this step-change."

Qeen.ai is developing an AI-first e-commerce operating system (OS) that autonomously executes tasks and optimises their outcome based on observed user behaviour. At the core of this OS are domain-expert AI agents that merchants can interact with to carry out functions like content creation, sales and marketing operations, customer service, etc. "Any function where the human touch isn't critical is a great candidate for intelligent automation, no matter how complex it is" explains Dina.

Dina, who is from Kuwait and has worked in the Middle East for over a decade, sees immense potential in the region's AI landscape and its unique ability to catalyse innovation. "When there is an acute belief in something and a critical mass of investment behind it, progress happens rapidly" Dina says, noting how the proactive approach to AI of the leadership in the GCC sets the region apart. This belief, backed by investment and support for innovation, creates a virtuous cycle of AI adoption by society and businesses, as well as innovative start-ups that nurture and accelerate this adoption. Dina and her team aim to position qeen.ai as "the go-to AI-powered OS for e-commerce" with an initial focus on the Middle East. This region serves as an ideal launchpad due to its rapidly growing e-commerce sector and the lack of technologically advanced solutions that address its unique challenges and cultural nuances.

The incredible talent in the region is markedly different to when the Originals founded their companies. Reflecting on their team's growth, Dina notes, "If you motivate and incentivise talent correctly, they will come," a belief that's proven true as qeen.ai has attracted both local and international talent to help drive its unique and ambitious vision. "We have full conviction that what we're building is going to transform e-commerce beyond what we even imagine today," she says, showcasing her confidence in qeen.ai's potential to play a pivotal role in reshaping the future of e-commerce, starting from the Middle East and reaching far beyond.

RIYADH, SAUDI ARABIA
NOUR TAHER AND OMAR MANSOUR

As the different technologies evolve, the Arabic-first AI models currently being built by Nour Taher and Omar Mansour address the issue of the more than two dozen dialects across the region. The concept of curating labelled dialectal datasets and building data infrastructures that capture a wide range of Arabic dialects – and then developing call-centre solutions focused on converting the speech into actionable insights tailored to all the dialects – is a vision that could only come from a native Arabic speaker. Such a person understands that these dialects often function almost like separate languages rather than minor regional variations. Intella is currently collaborating with key clients to implement its advanced Speech-to-Text technology and text analytics models. This solution not only transcribes speech accurately across dialects but also analyses sentiment, tracks agent performance, and generates actionable insights to optimise call-centre operations and enhance overall customer service effectiveness.

The Arabic language, despite being one of the most widely used on the internet – with over 420 million speakers globally[145] – remains vastly under-represented in AI and web applications, with less than 1 per cent of web pages being in Arabic.[146] Those who recognise this gap have a unique opportunity to lead in developing AI solutions specifically tailored to Arabic speakers' needs. The potential for growth in this area is immense, driven by the surge in digital transformation initiatives across MENA, which aim to increase AI adoption by 25 per cent annually through 2030.[147] As countries like Saudi Arabia and the UAE heavily invest in AI infrastructure and data capacity, the demand for Arabic-focused AI solutions is expected to expand rapidly, especially in customer service, healthcare, and financial services where language nuances are critical.

AMMAN, JORDAN

JALIL ALLABADI

Another incredible example of an AI use case is with Altibbi, who have partnered with CORE42 to harness a wealth of healthcare data gathered over the years to fine-tune their Arabic LLM, 'Jais', that is significantly improving how primary care is delivered. When we consider that the region has less than half the number of doctors per capita than Europe or the United States do, and that the ability to provide primary care remains a challenge, an Arabic LLM focused on primary health can change millions of lives. By enabling real-time responses to users' medical questions and offering guidance on a range of health concerns, the 'Jais' LLM provides a crucial lifeline to people in remote or underserved areas, where access to primary care remains a challenge.

Leveraging the trove of Altibbi data, Jalil and the team have refined the Jais model to handle millions of consultations, enabling it to understand diverse Arabic dialects and effectively translate conversations between doctors and patients into comprehensive medical terminology. This adaptation allows the platform to automatically capture vital information – like symptoms, patient demographics, and context of the consultation – directly from conversations, updating patient profiles with details such as age, smoking habits, and gender.

The platform not only supports immediate health inquiries, symptom-checking, and on-demand consultations but also introduces proactive tools that improve care quality. For example, during doctor-patient interactions, the model suggests pertinent questions for the doctor to ask, ensuring thoroughness and accuracy. Additionally, it flags potential issues within conversations, like prescription errors or missing context on symptoms. In the upcoming phase, Altibbi aims to launch a quality module that will score doctors' consultations across eight global standards, continuously enhancing healthcare delivery through AI.

* * * * *

THE RELEVANCE OF AI

The emergence of new technologies often sparks fear of disruption. Each new technology brings with it the threat of being made increasingly redundant as humans, and fear of the end of the world as we know it. Artificial intelligence is no different. Yet, far from being an end to the world as we know it, AI is proving to be a transformative force that redefines every industry and everyday life.

AI's application across industries makes it incredibly important and relevant to most people, if not everyone. The AI-powered global economy is expected to drive a $15.7 trillion economic boost by 2030, a significant portion of which will come from productivity gains in key sectors.[148]

"We are building tools to help us advance our knowledge," says Mehdi Ghissassi, head of product management at Google's DeepMind. "The previous phase was about automating repetitive tasks. With the latest advances in AI, we can start to equip humans with superpowers in the cognitive space. For example, it takes decades and billions of dollars to develop and bring a new drug to market. With our greatly expanded understanding of biology and the detailed structure of proteins, researchers can use AI to accelerate their efforts and explore new areas for solving complex problems."

In supply chain management, AI and machine learning are advancing capabilities including forecasting, inventory optimisation, and real-time order management, laying the groundwork for resilient, intelligent global ecosystems. These AI-driven supply chains are not only data-powered but also highly adaptive, enabling rapid responses to shifting market conditions, optimising efficiency, and proactively minimising disruptions. By transforming traditional logistics into dynamic, interconnected networks, AI is driving the supply chains of the future – ones that are smarter, more efficient, and better equipped to meet the demands of a globalised economy. The global AI-powered supply chain market size is expected to reach $40.5 billion by 2027, growing at a CAGR of 24.8 per cent from 2020.[149]

With AI implementation, the future of financial services is set to become more interactive, immersive, and personalised, driven by the transformative power of generative AI. By enabling dynamic, real-time interactions, generative AI is helping financial institutions meet the growing demand for seamless, high-quality customer experiences. From personalised financial advice to automated, conversational customer support, this technology is enhancing every touchpoint, making financial services not only more efficient but also more engaging and attuned to individual customer needs. AI has already driven advancements in algorithmic trading, fraud detection, risk assessment, and personalised customer service, helping institutions better anticipate market shifts and personalise interactions. Yet, issues around transparency, ethics, and potential biases in AI decision-making present challenges, highlighting the need for explainable AI solutions.

In agriculture, AI is transforming how we grow and manage food by enabling precise crop monitoring, automating irrigation, enhancing land use efficiency, and managing plant requirements at a granular level. AI-powered farm management systems integrate data from soil sensors, weather forecasts, and crop health diagnostics to help farmers make informed decisions that maximise yield while conserving resources. These advances not only help address the challenges of climate change, resource scarcity, and a growing global population but also set the stage for more resilient food systems.

In healthcare, AI is transforming diagnostics, predictive analytics, drug discovery, and personalised medicine, with the potential to reduce healthcare costs drastically everywhere, and quantified at $150 billion annually by 2026, through improved diagnostics and tailored treatments.[150] This impact is expected to be just as significant in the MENA region, where AI is advancing telemedicine and remote diagnostics to address gaps in basic healthcare access in addition to prevention. However, healthcare AI faces strict regulatory and clinical challenges, from data privacy to accuracy standards in sensitive medical applications.

"Think of all these areas, or individual sectors, as a list of workflows," says Mehdi. "With these technologies you can automate a number of tasks. You can also augment the abilities of humans in a number of cognitive roles and uncover insights from huge data sets that humans wouldn't be able to make sense of on their own. Many energy companies will significantly enhance their operations by leveraging data analytics to gain valuable insights and automate various workflows. They will also be able to identify operational improvements across various areas and discover new strategies for product commercialisation."

AI will leave no industry undisrupted. It will not only change industries – it will become essential for them to function effectively.

This future will see the blurring of boundaries between human and machine, challenging what it means to have agency and consciousness in the modern world. As intelligent systems become increasingly autonomous and sophisticated, they will compel us to rethink ethical frameworks, social structures, and our understanding of what it means to be human in a world where intelligence and innovation are no longer exclusively our own.

MENA AND AI

In 2017, the UAE made a bold and visionary move to appoint the world's first Minister of Artificial Intelligence, signalling its commitment to leading in AI long before it became a global phenomenon. This proactive decision reflected the UAE's belief in the transformative potential of AI – not just as a futuristic concept but as a tool for shaping society and the economy. While the global wave of AI hype surged in late 2022, with the launch of OpenAI's ChatGPT drawing a record-breaking 1 million users in just five days and 100 million in two months, the UAE had already laid the groundwork, investing in AI-driven strategies to support its development goals and position itself as a technology hub.

Artificial intelligence, though not new – it has roots stretching back to the 1950s – remained largely experimental until recent advancements in data processing and model sophistication.

The UAE recognised these possibilities early on, anticipating the technology's far-reaching implications well before the world took notice. This foresight has positioned the UAE as a leader in the AI landscape, illustrating how a forward-looking national strategy can drive innovation, attract global talent, and shape the future of technology on a global scale.

As far as MENA is concerned, this is a fundamental technology of paramount importance to the future of the region – for the population, the governments, and the entrepreneurs. All elements of the ecosystem are supporting its development, taking a position on the world stage as pioneers and leaders in this domain.

The UAE has taken a strategic, multi-pronged approach to position itself as a global leader in artificial intelligence by 2031. This vision began with the launch of the National Strategy for Artificial Intelligence, BRAIN, in 2017, setting ambitious goals to integrate AI across sectors, advance AI research, and fuel the nation's technological leadership. A critical component of this strategy is the world's first graduate-level AI university, the Mohamed Bin Zayed University of Artificial Intelligence, which is producing a robust pipeline of AI talent. This institution aims to train specialists capable of leading advancements in AI and contributing to the UAE's ambitious goals.

Beyond vertical applications of AI, the UAE recognised the critical importance of physical infrastructure for positioning the nation on a global scale. To this end, it has made substantial investments in data centres and cloud capabilities, understanding the necessity for high-performance computing and advanced data processing. Abu Dhabi's Khazna Data Centres recently inaugurated the UAE's largest data centre, marking a significant milestone in the country's digital infrastructure expansion. Located in Abu Dhabi, this facility is part of Khazna's broader vision to reach a data centre capacity of 850 megawatts (MW) by 2029, a substantial increase aimed at supporting the UAE's growing demand for data processing, AI applications, and cloud computing solutions. Additionally, Amazon Web Services (AWS) has expanded its footprint with new data centre regions, ensuring that organisations in the UAE can store and process data locally, meeting regulatory and security standards. Microsoft Azure and Oracle have also established dedicated cloud regions in the UAE, further enhancing cloud-based AI solutions tailored to the region's privacy and security requirements.

To support scalable AI innovation, G42 developed its own AI-focused cloud platform, combining high-performance computing (HPC) with AI optimisation. The G42 Cloud provides on-demand computing power tailored for machine learning and big data analytics, enabling rapid deployment of AI applications for both government and businesses.

At the policy level, the Artificial Intelligence and Advanced Technology Council (AIATC) in Abu Dhabi is responsible for guiding AI-related research, policy, and investments. This council ensures that AI advancements align with national priorities and industry needs, driving forward-thinking regulations and frameworks to support sustainable AI growth.

Aligned with its UAE Centennial 2071 plan, the government has committed to integrating AI across all federal ministries to improve efficiency, customer experience, and decision-making. This comprehensive approach is especially focused on transforming key sectors such as healthcare, education, and infrastructure, with AI serving as a tool for modernisation and enhanced public service delivery.

In 2023, the Technology Innovation Institute (TII) in Abu Dhabi released Falcon 40B, the UAE's first large-scale open-source AI model. Falcon 40B represents a milestone in the country's AI journey, marking its commitment to open innovation and enhancing the UAE's research capabilities on a global scale.

On the hardware front, the UAE has made significant investments in semiconductor technology, particularly through Dubai Silicon Oasis (DSO), a government-owned technology park focused on driving innovation in AI, IoT, and semiconductor manufacturing. DSO provides a collaborative environment for high-tech companies, supporting advanced R&D and the entire semiconductor supply chain, from research and development to production. This initiative is pivotal in reducing dependency on global suppliers and establishing the UAE as a regional leader in AI-enabling hardware.

Complementing DSO's initiatives, the Mubadala Investment Company joined forces with G42 to establish MGX, a technology investment firm dedicated to three key domains: AI infrastructure, semiconductors, and core AI technologies and applications. Mubadala also owns a significant stake in GlobalFoundries, one of the world's largest semiconductor foundries, which focuses on developing AI-optimised chips designed for high-performance applications in sectors such as healthcare, automotive, and finance. Through this investment, the UAE is supporting the development of next-generation semiconductor technology that can efficiently handle complex AI workloads, strengthening the nation's AI infrastructure and positioning it as a leader in the region's semiconductor ecosystem.

Together, DSO's local innovation ecosystem, Mubadala's strategic international investments and G42's core AI focus, create a robust framework for advancing semiconductor capabilities in the UAE, reinforcing the country's commitment to building a comprehensive AI infrastructure from hardware to applications.

In Saudi Arabia, the Vision 2030 plan is driving the Kingdom's transformation into a global technology and AI innovation hub, with a multibillion-dollar focus on AI, advanced technology, and infrastructure. A central pillar of this vision is NEOM, a $500 billion smart city project that will be powered by AI and autonomous technologies, setting new standards for urban sustainability and smart infrastructure. NEOM integrates AI across city management functions, including transportation, healthcare, energy, and urban planning, creating a real-world laboratory for AI-driven solutions on an unprecedented scale.

Saudi Aramco is also deploying significant resources to expand its AI capabilities, leveraging its position as one of the world's largest energy producers. Recently, Aramco launched a groundbreaking large language model, Aramco MetaBrain, with 250 billion parameters trained on 7 trillion data tokens from both public and internal sources.

This advanced generative AI model is expected to transform the company's internal operations, enhancing productivity and enabling data-driven decision-making in critical areas like exploration, production optimisation, and sustainable energy management.

In parallel, Saudi Arabia is building a robust AI talent pipeline through institutions like King Abdullah University of Science and Technology (KAUST). KAUST collaborates with leading global universities and research centres to advance AI research, develop specialised training programmes, and establish a sustainable base of AI experts within the Kingdom. Supporting this effort, the Saudi Data and Artificial Intelligence Authority (SDAIA) guides national AI policy, governance, and regulatory frameworks, ensuring that AI development aligns with ethical standards and national priorities.

To further solidify its position as a global AI hub, Saudi Arabia's Public Investment Fund (PIF) is spearheading an ambitious $100 billion investment in AI and related technologies. Part of this initiative is a partnership with Google to establish an advanced AI hub expected to contribute up to $71 billion to the local economy. This hub will focus on developing AI applications across key sectors – healthcare, retail, and finance – emphasising Arabic-language tools to create solutions tailored to regional needs. Additionally, Google's AI hub aims to upskill local talent, building a workforce prepared to drive long-term growth in AI innovation.

Saudi Arabia has also invested heavily in data infrastructure, launching its largest data centre in Riyadh in 2021 through a collaboration with Saudi Telecom Company (STC) and Alibaba Cloud. Representing part of Alibaba's $500 million commitment to cloud infrastructure in the region, this data centre enables secure, low-latency data processing essential for AI, big data analytics, and cloud solutions across sectors like healthcare, finance, and energy. In the cloud sector, the Kingdom has further strengthened its AI capabilities by establishing Oracle Cloud and Microsoft Azure regions within Saudi Arabia, offering scalable, compliant solutions specifically tailored for large-scale AI and machine learning workloads, with data processing in-country to comply with local regulations.

In the semiconductor sector, Saudi Arabia is working with Foxconn, one of the world's leading electronics and semiconductor manufacturers, to establish a joint venture focused on producing AI-optimised chips domestically. This $9 billion investment will support NEOM's smart city ambitions by providing advanced processors for autonomous systems, robotics, and IoT applications, reducing the country's dependency on imported technology. Additionally, the Advanced Electronics Company (AEC), a subsidiary of Saudi Arabian Military Industries (SAMI), is collaborating with global semiconductor firms to develop custom chips for defence and civilian AI applications. AEC's expertise in secure, high-performance chips is crucial for sectors with unique requirements, such as energy and national security, ensuring data integrity through advanced encryption and processing technology.

Through these comprehensive initiatives in AI infrastructure, talent development, partnerships, and sector-specific innovations, Saudi Arabia is positioned to challenge regional leadership and establish itself as a powerhouse in the global AI landscape.

As the UAE and Saudi Arabia become global players in the AI arena, fostering innovation within the GCC, the onus is on building robust AI infrastructure and talent pipelines to support continuous learning and development. As a whole, the region is seeing massive AI-driven growth, with the MENA AI market expected to reach $5.2 billion by 2026.[151]

THE FUTURE OF AI

The emphasis on AI, and the support from the GCC's leadership is trickling down to the founders and ecosystem. From the perspective of highly-adaptable MENA entrepreneurs, the world of AI is just beginning; and the opportunities in the region are tremendous.

The influx of talent, combined with governmental support and sufficient capital, is proving to be a significant accelerator for the MENA ecosystem, particularly in AI. With many global contenders vying for a position as AI leaders, the MENA region stands out by offering incredible talent and infrastructure to both founders and corporates, positioning itself to lead the way in the development of this transformative technology.

As AI integrates into each industry, and every part of our lives, there is little that can be done to slow down the acceleration of the adoption of this technology. Accordingly, working closely as an ecosystem of funders, regulators, entrepreneurs and technologists provides the highest opportunity for success in harnessing the abilities of AI to improve industries and humanity at large.

As the founders in the MENA region look to build AI companies in their respective ecosystems, the government initiatives and support have put MENA on the map as a potential global AI hub. The stark contrast with where this ecosystem was just a decade ago could not be more apparent. The technology ecosystem across MENA has not only caught up, but is now paving the way for future generations around the world.

CHAPTER 12

DEMOCRATISATION OF MONEY

خبي قرشك الابيض ليومك الاسود

Save your white penny for a black day.

- ARABIC PROVERB

OLA DOUDIN, BITOASIS

From an early age, Ola Doudin was encouraged to explore her own path. Growing up in Jordan with five sisters, her curiosity was constantly fed by parents who valued open dialogue, creativity, and learning. Science clubs, tech camps, and books filled her summers, fostering an early passion for hands-on experimentation and technology. "My parents always encouraged my curiosity," she recalls, "and that gave me the freedom to push boundaries without fear." That passion for discovery would later lead Ola to become a pioneer for an entirely new industry in the region.

Her interest in crypto began in 2015 with a Reddit post about Bitcoin. For Ola, the idea of a decentralised currency independent of traditional banks and governments was both bold and practical. She quickly became fascinated with blockchain technology, pouring over Satoshi Nakamoto's whitepaper and immersing herself in the possibilities and promises of the technology. What was then considered niche and experimental was, for Ola, a glimpse of the future. "Crypto seemed like it had the potential to reshape how we store and exchange value," she says. "It was about building a new financial system, and that really excited me."

In 2016, after finding that there was no reliable, secure way for people in the Middle East and North Africa to access digital assets, Ola co-founded BitOasis. The mission was clear: to create a secure, localised platform for buying, selling, and holding digital assets. With her co-founders, she set out to tackle the technical and logistical challenges of launching a crypto business in a region with limited regulatory frameworks and a nascent market. "We saw a clear problem and an equally clear opportunity in the region," she says.

The journey came with steep challenges. In a market that was both young and cautious, BitOasis had to carve out trust and credibility from scratch, without the benefit of established industry standards or the backing of venture capital early on. Ola and her team relied on determination and adaptability to navigate the growing pains of a fledgling industry.

Their efforts paid off. BitOasis quickly evolved from a Bitcoin wallet service into a full-scale crypto brokerage platform that transacted over $6.6 billion since its launch and secured $40 million in funding from leading global and regional investors, including Wamda Capital, Jump Capital, Pantera Capital, and Global Founders Capital.

In 2016, they became the first regional platform to offer users a seamless option to withdraw assets to local bank accounts. BitOasis was also the first in the region to register as a Virtual Asset Service Provider with the UAE's Financial Intelligence Unit. When Dubai established the world's first dedicated crypto regular, the Virtual Assets Regulatory Authority, BitOasis was one of the first platforms to secure a provisional operating permit, marking it as a leader in compliance and safety. "These weren't just milestones for us," Ola notes. "They were crucial steps forward for the industry as a whole."

BitOasis continued innovating, introducing instant deposits and new product features to make trading more seamless for users. In

2023, they became the first regional crypto broker-dealer to secure an Operational MVP license from VARA, cementing BitOasis as a regional leader in a fast-growing market.

The turning point came in 2024, with BitOasis's acquisition by CoinDCX, India's largest and highest-valued crypto exchange. The deal was unprecedented in the region, underscoring the maturity of MENA's crypto market and opening new growth avenues for BitOasis. "This partnership with CoinDCX was a big step for us," Ola says, "It wasn't just about scaling, but about the broader impact on the region."

Ola's journey with BitOasis reflects both the opportunities and the risks of launching a new business in uncharted territory. Today, BitOasis stands as a testament to what's possible in the region, proving that the Middle East is ready to embrace new financial technologies and lead the way in regulatory innovation. "Crypto's potential is still unfolding," Ola shares. "But our goal remains the same – to create a fairer, more accessible financial system, where anyone can trade and invest with confidence."

HENRI ARSLANIAN, DUBAI, UAE

Born in Montreal, Canada, to Armenian parents, Henri Arslanian excelled academically, initially charting a stable path in law. But his calling was elsewhere. After watching a documentary called *The Rise of a Chinese Dragon*, he turned to his father and declared, "Dad, I'm going to China." He immersed himself in Chinese culture, learning the language quickly and earning a master's in Chinese law from Tsinghua University in Beijing, setting the stage for a career that would defy conventional expectations.

In Hong Kong, Henri worked as a hedge fund lawyer and then at Swiss investment bank UBS, but soon grew disillusioned with the traditional finance system. "Why do we need so many humans to do finance?" he questioned. His curiosity led him to ask the UBS CEO about the potential threat of tech giants like Alibaba and Tencent in the future of finance, a question that was met with laughter and disdain. Unfazed, Henri saw the writing on the wall and turned his attention to crypto, where he believed a financial revolution was unfolding.

Henri's belief in crypto was unwavering, even when it made him stand out in a world dominated by tech enthusiasts. Nicknamed "Suit Henry" for his banker attire in the midst of crypto's early days of casual culture, he was undeterred by scepticism. In 2014, he organised one of Hong Kong's first Bitcoin events, positioning himself as a pioneer in the space. "Bitcoin's ability to send money from one person to another without intermediaries was a game-changer," he says, convinced that crypto was not just an investment but the future of global transactions.

Henri's ventures, including the founding of Nine Blocks, a market-neutral crypto hedge fund, and ACX International, the world's largest crypto compliance services firm, put him at the forefront of the industry. His work was instrumental in securing the first crypto licenses in Dubai, a key milestone in the Middle East's growing crypto landscape. But for Henri, the impact of crypto goes beyond business; it's about providing financial autonomy to those in need. "Bitcoin gives people an option," he explains, especially in regions with unstable currencies. He's seen how it empowers people in Africa, Latin America, and Turkey, where traditional systems fail to provide stability.

Today, Henri sees crypto as a response to a global need for financial sovereignty. He believes Bitcoin is a better version of gold: "People have a choice," he says. "If they don't trust their policymakers, they can protect their wealth." Henri remains optimistic about crypto's future, confident that it will drive a broader financial revolution. As he looks to the next stage, he insists that for crypto to mature, it needs regulatory frameworks. "You have a duty to understand it," he says, emphasising that everyone in finance or tech must engage with crypto's potential, whether they believe in it or not. Henri's journey is driven not just by business ambition but by a deeper mission to democratise finance globally.

MENA AND CRYPTO

Similar to the incorporation of the Ministry of AI, Dubai established VARA, the Virtual Asset Regulatory Authority, in 2022. Ahead of its time, and while the rest of the world was still grappling with whether to allow digital currencies, the UAE leadership began a detailed understanding and regulation of what is one of this century's most disruptive inventions yet.

Abu Dhabi and Dubai are leading efforts to establish strong regulations for digital assets, aiming to attract significant institutional investment. Accordingly, there is a two-phased approach: first, adapting existing regulatory frameworks for traditional finance to encompass digital assets, and second, creating innovative regulations specifically for digital asset exchanges. These include the UAE cabinet introducing the first federal-level regulation for virtual assets, a supervisory framework designed to oversee the industry and protect investors, the DIFC enacted its Digital Assets Law, along with a new Law of Security and amendments to current legislation, providing greater clarity for investors and ensuring the zone keeps pace with technological advances, and in November 2023, the ADGM introducing the Distributed Ledger Technology (DLT) Foundations Regulations 2023, establishing a comprehensive framework for DLT foundations and decentralised autonomous organisations (DAOs) to operate and issue tokens. This framework has encouraged the development of major Web3 protocols and projects in the region.

These frameworks have attracted both regional players like Rain, a virtual assets brokerage, and international ones including Binance, OKX, and Bybit. Additional frameworks are in place for virtual assets within free zones such as DIFC and DMCC. According to Coindesk, Dubai and Abu Dhabi ranked fifth and sixth, respectively, on the 2023 Crypto Hubs list, a testament to the UAE's favourable regulatory environment, which has drawn global players like Binance, the first virtual asset exchange to secure an operational MVP license in Dubai.

Whereas crypto is often perceived as a technology with questionable utility, its main purpose is to enable the creation of decentralised financial services, or DeFi, that allow people, businesses, or other entities to transact directly with each other. The key principle behind DeFi is to remove intermediaries like banks from the financial system, thereby reducing costs and transaction times. This enables not only traditional financial transactions, but also the development of exchanges, cross-border transfers, and the tokenisation of all assets.

This is where crypto and blockchain technology are currently being used the most, hidden in plain sight. The core technology enables big banks to increase efficiency in their transactions, as well as transparency, all while reducing costs.

Ultimately, cryptocurrencies enable the democratisation of financial services, where decentralised finance (DeFi) puts the user in charge of their own finances and cryptocurrencies eliminate the need for intermediaries. By removing the need for banks, exchanges or brokerages, crypto and DeFi have significantly disrupted traditional financial systems, leading to increased efficiency and transparency, and empowering individuals to maintain direct control over their assets. The removal of bureaucratic layers and manual processes has enabled near-instantaneous transactions, meaning individuals and businesses can transfer money globally without the need for currency conversions or intermediary banks, greatly reducing the cost of cross-border transactions. This self-custody model allows users to maintain ownership of their private keys and data, eliminating the need for intermediaries.

DeFi in the MENA region, particularly in the UAE and Saudi Arabia, is primarily being used for its ability to facilitate peer-to-peer transactions without intermediaries, potentially reducing costs and increasing accessibility for payments, lending, and trading activities. Additionally, decentralised exchanges (DEXs) are drawing attention as they allow users to trade cryptocurrencies directly without the need for centralised operators, thereby eliminating the risks associated with centralised exchange hacks and high fees.

The GCC countries have proactively issued regulatory frameworks for crypto service providers and have signalled a positive approach to DeFi. For instance, the UAE's new stored-value facilities regulation covers crypto assets and the Central Bank recently announced in-principle approval for the first AED-pegged stablecoin, while Bahrain has allowed cryptocurrencies as an official payment method (though not legal tender) and enabled banks to work with crypto exchanges for easy withdrawals and deposits. This regulatory support could help build consumer confidence and attract investment while mitigating risks associated with DeFi, such as cybersecurity and compliance with anti-money laundering and KYC requirements.

"The real innovation is the ability to send money from one person to another without any intermediaries," says Henri. "If we think about the core element of Bitcoin, it is a decentralised cryptocurrency. It provides people with an option and a choice."

Cryptocurrencies hold the promise of creating a more inclusive financial system by offering services to unbanked and underbanked populations. In regions where access to traditional banking infrastructure is limited or non-existent, cryptocurrencies allow individuals to engage in the financial system. People can store value, make transactions, and access financial products directly through their mobile devices, without needing a bank account or going through lengthy verification processes. This accessibility empowers people in underserved areas to save, invest, and participate in the economy, ultimately contributing to economic growth and stability in these communities.

Beyond local impact, cryptocurrencies enable borderless transactions and global accessibility, allowing users to transact with anyone, anywhere, at any time. Cryptocurrencies make cross-border transactions faster and more affordable by eliminating barriers like currency exchange fees and international banking delays. This opens up new opportunities for small businesses in emerging markets to reach global customers and suppliers, expanding their market reach and economic potential. As the cryptocurrency ecosystem grows and matures, it has the potential to democratise access to financial services on a global scale, helping to build a more inclusive and resilient financial system.

"The countries where we're seeing the most activity on digital assets are Vietnam, Nigeria, and many parts of Latin America," explains Henri. "In the US, if somebody's buying Bitcoin it's mainly speculation. In many other parts of the world, they're using digital assets in their day-to-day activities – to be able to actually pay and make payments and as a store of value. So I think Bitcoin has a very strong chance of becoming a reserve currency or an asset that people hold that they are actually able to use." This is particularly true in countries that suffer annual currency depreciation or devaluation. For example, Egypt has experienced over a 100 per cent devaluation in its currency over the past year, making some cryptocurrencies a way to store value, and Turkey has experienced severe inflation and devaluation, which have also driven the adoption of stablecoins.[152]

Cross-border payments are crucial for international trade, remittances, and global financial flows and can also be enabled through crypto. Traditionally, cross-border payments are facilitated through banks and international financial systems like SWIFT, which can be costly, slow, and complex due to the multiple intermediaries involved, currency exchange processes, and regulatory requirements. Cryptocurrency transactions are often peer-to-peer, reducing or eliminating the need for intermediaries, which can significantly lower transaction costs, and they are also much faster and more efficient. Finally, since they operate on blockchain technology, they provide a higher level of trust and transparency.

Tokenisation in financial services refers to the process of converting assets, rights, or real-world items into digital tokens on a blockchain. These tokens represent ownership or rights to the underlying asset and can be easily traded or transferred on a blockchain, enhancing liquidity, accessibility, and security in asset transactions. By tokenising assets, financial institutions can facilitate fractional ownership, reduce transaction costs, and enable broader participation in financial markets. Different assets can be tokenised for different reasons, with the UAE recently allowing the tokenisation of real estate, commodities, intellectual property and art, and Qatar launching its regulatory framework for RWA tokenisation.[153]

Tokenisation has the potential to significantly transform financial markets by improving liquidity, accessibility, and efficiency. It enables fractional ownership, which lowers entry barriers and allows more individuals to invest in high-value assets like real estate or private equity. Tokenised assets can also be traded 24/7 on blockchain-based exchanges, enhancing liquidity and market efficiency.

Hamilton Lane, a leading private equity firm, has collaborated with Securitise to tokenise one of its private equity secondary funds, broadening investor access to private equity assets. Through this initiative, accredited investors can purchase digital tokens representing shares in the fund, significantly reducing the usual high minimum investment requirements in private equity. Facilitated by Securitise on a blockchain platform, tokenisation allows for fractional ownership, creating a more accessible entry point for investors. This approach enabled the firm to lower the minimum investment threshold to $20,000, compared to the traditional $5 million.

For younger generations that have grown up digitally native, spending as much time online as they do in the physical world, digital assets hold greater value than those in the physical realm. These assets include everything from gaming skins and collectibles to NFT art and real estate, or anything else digitally recorded on the blockchain. Although the promise of a universe of interconnected virtual worlds (the original premise of the metaverse) has yet to materialise, within this universe people will be able to move freely between worlds, carrying with them any digital assets they own and engaging in everyday acts of commerce.

Such virtual worlds already exist in the likes of Fortnite, Roblox, and World of Warcraft, but interoperability and transferability are absent. This will change as those who have grown up in the digital world expect and demand seamless connectivity and accessibility of their virtual possessions and identities across platforms. The demographic tipping point.

"Consider your driver's license, your university diploma, and every time you need a certified copy of your passport," says Henri. "I am convinced that all these documents will eventually be issued as NFTs. This transformation will eliminate the need for intermediaries that currently verify the authenticity of such documents, like your diploma or driver's license. Now, imagine bringing this concept into a gaming ecosystem. The true potential of digital assets becomes evident. For instance, if I own a specific piece of clothing for my avatar in a video game, and I can use, sell, and trade it freely, it truly becomes a valuable asset."

In such a reality, digital assets are inherently valuable. They are no longer speculative investments but integral parts of a person's digital life, meaning the role of crypto and blockchain technology will expand significantly as these younger generations demand more interconnectedness and accessibility. As the digital ecosystem evolves, the ability to seamlessly transfer and use cryptocurrencies across different platforms and virtual environments will become increasingly important.

THE FUTURE OF CRYPTO

The MENA region may have the sixth largest crypto economy in the world, with an estimated $389.8 billion in on-chain value received between July 2022 and June 2023.[154] Furthermore, between July 2023 and June 2024, the MENA region received an estimated total value of $338.7 billion in virtual assets, representing 7.5 per cent of the world's total transaction volume.[155] However, the average number of daily crypto traders stood at just 500,000 in February 2024.[156] The region is still in the nascent phases of crypto adoption, accounting for a modest seven per cent of the transactional value of crypto currencies globally, although anticipated advances in blockchain technologies are expected to contribute to the scalability of DeFi.

In an effort to embrace the latest technologies after the success of regulating them, the UAE has allowed the payment of its residence visa transactions to occur in USDC, bringing crypto into the ecosystem even further.

As the world becomes increasingly multi-polar, and as an increasing number of corporations become larger than country GDPs, the question is if crypto and technology will become the currency of the future, representing the increase in power of technology for the world rather than the power of government?

CHAPTER 13

FUEL FOR TOMORROW

دق الحديد و هو حامي

Strike the metal while its hot.

– ARABIC PROVERB

MUSCAT, OMAN

TALAL HASAN, KARAN KHIMJI AND EHAB TASFAI

"The challenge was no longer capturing CO_2. It was what a company would do with it once it was captured." Forests and natural carbon sinks absorb 2 billion tonnes of CO_2 yearly,[157] but novel carbon removal projects account for only 0.1 per cent (1.3 million tonnes)[158] – far less than the 36.6 billion tonnes of CO_2 released annually. Limiting global warming to 1.5°C or 2°C, as per the Paris Agreement, will require 7–9 billion tonnes of CO_2 to be sustainably removed every year.[159]

However, even those 1.3 million tonnes that were captured had almost nowhere to go. Talal was stunned. Working in 2020 at IDO Investments, the venture capital arm of the Oman Investment Authority, with a mandate to invest in climate technologies to support the country's transition to net zero, Talal was exploring direct air capture and other carbon capture technologies. While there, he discovered many of the companies involved in these technologies faced a common challenge: finding a viable solution for their captured CO_2.

Meanwhile, serendipity was key: scientists working on the Oman Drilling Project identified that peridotite rocks could be used to sequester CO_2 as stable carbonate minerals, potentially offering a robust solution for long-term carbon storage.

Two of the project scientists were Peter Kelemen, a geologist at the Lamont-Doherty Earth Observatory at Columbia University, and Juerg Matter, a professor of geoengineering and carbon management at the University of Southampton in the UK. Kelemen estimated the worldwide storage capacity of peridotite rocks to be between 60 and 600 trillion tonnes of CO_2 – an astounding figure equal to an estimated 25 to 250 times the amount of CO_2 added to the atmosphere by humans since 1850. He and his fellow researchers also noted that, regardless of the approach taken to sequester CO_2, it will be essential to permanently sequester about 10 billion tonnes of CO_2 a year by 2050, and roughly twice that each year by 2100.[160]

Drilling took place in Wadi Lawayni, a scenic valley deep within the Hajar Mountains. A rugged and dramatic mountain range stretching for 350 kilometres from north-eastern Oman into the eastern part of the UAE, the Hajar Mountains contain the largest and best subaerial exposure of ancient fast spread ocean crust and upper mantle. It is these geological features that scientists hypothesised could be used to permanently remove CO_2 by injecting and mineralising it deep in the mantle rock.

Between 2016 and 2018, they dug 400 meters into the wadi, extracting rock core to study the chemical reactions happening far below the surface. Their preliminary research, published in 2019, revealed promising insights into the natural processes that can convert CO_2 into stable carbonate minerals, effectively locking away the carbon dioxide and preventing it from re-entering the atmosphere.[161]

Recognising the significance of the scientists' research, Talal quit IDO Investments with the idea of marrying carbon capture and carbon sequestration. He reached out to Karan, an old friend who had recently returned to Oman from Paris (where he had been consulting on the transition from fossil fuels to renewable energy), and partnered with Juerg, whose scientific expertise would be essential, as the company's head of subsurface.

Together, with Ehab, an engineer with expertise in water management, they founded 44.01 with the mission to make a meaningful impact on the climate crisis. Between March and June 2020, they focused on ideation and experimentation before formally incorporating the company at the end of June. "It was one idea after another," says Karan. "How do we use this rock? Do we mine it and try to expose it to CO_2? Do we bring the CO_2 to the rock? We were trying to figure it out. Eventually we decided on one idea, which was to bring the CO_2 to the rock itself."

Peridotite naturally reacts with CO_2 via carbon mineralisation, converting the $CO2$ into carbonate minerals (rocks) and providing a permanent and environmentally safe method of storing CO_2 underground. By combining captured CO_2 with water and injecting it into seams of peridotite rock deep underground, the increased pressure, elevated temperatures, and the high concentration of CO_2 speed up the mineralisation process. "Natural catalysts cause the reaction to happen faster. Instead of taking decades, or thousands of years, it takes months underground," explains Karan. "So we can put more CO_2 into the ground, have more CO_2 react and turn into rock, and be gone forever".

To achieve this, they needed a piece of land to trial their technology, which was obtained from Oman's Ministry of Energy and Minerals. The founders conducted their first pilot injection in early 2021 – and continued with small pilot tests between 2021 and 2023 aided by $5 million in seed funding, which effectively proved the accelerated mineralisation process worked underground. "It proved that it was safe," says Karan. "Our pilot ensured that there was no CO_2 leakage or damage to the subsurface – no negative environmental consequences – and we proved that the reaction was fast."

The success of the pilot injections led to the Omani government awarding a concession for the world's first commercial-scale peridotite mineralisation project in Al Qabil, a small village on the northern edge of Oman. The pilots also created considerable buzz. The company won the 2022 Earthshot Prize – an annual highly prestigious environmental award – which boosted its visibility and finances (the prize money was $1.25 million). It also accelerated expansion into the UAE, where a mineralisation demonstration project commenced in the emirate of Fujairah in late 2023. Conducted in partnership with ADNOC, Masdar, and the Fujairah Natural Resources Corporation, the initial injection of ten tonnes of CO_2 was the first peridotite mineralisation project to utilise seawater, marking a significant advancement in the company's ability to deploy its technology sustainably around the world. The project successfully demonstrated mineralisation could be achieved with saltwater rather than freshwater, significantly enhancing the potential to scale, especially in arid regions where fresh water is scarce.

"We have scaled our technology up to a point where we've de-risked the science significantly," says Karan. "We're driving down our unit economics to make this commercially feasible. We're on the precipice of commercial viability and are expanding into commercial projects in the next two years in both Oman and the UAE, as well as entering our first non-Middle Eastern location. It's a really exciting time because we get to take a regional technology outside the region."

The results are potentially staggering, for the region and the world at large. For the company's pilot projects, the founders set a target of mineralising 1,000 tonnes of locally captured CO_2 a year, but their long-term goal is to help countries around the world to decarbonise. "The rock itself is not the constraint – we have enough of this rock in Oman and the UAE to eliminate all the emissions that both countries have ever emitted since the pre-industrial age," shares Karan. "Massive, massive capacity. In other parts of the world, this rock can help other countries decarbonise cost effectively, particularly to facilitate the decarbonisation of industries alongside incentives or taxes or compliance mechanisms to force them to do so."

Carbon storage commonly involves injecting CO_2 into geological formations, such as depleted oil and gas reservoirs or deep saline aquifers, which have historically contained hydrocarbons for millions of years. These formations are chosen for their ability to securely trap CO_2, however, monitoring is crucial to ensure the integrity of these storage sites and to detect any potential leaks.

Regulations typically require storage operators to monitor the CO_2 for twenty to fifty years after injection. After this, monitoring responsibility may be transferred to a governmental authority, a process known as 'transfer of liability'. 44.01 provides a complementary solution to this method.

"We provide a solution that eliminates the CO_2 from existence," says Karan. "We believe we can deliver a permanent, safe and affordable form of carbon storage to the planet. Of course, it will take time and resources, but we believe our solution can significantly contribute to mitigating the impacts of climate change."

In June 2024, the Company raised a Series A funding round of $37 million to expand commercial-scale projects. In November 2024, 44.01 announced it would be scaling up activities in the UAE, beginning with a 300-tonne injection which will compete for the international XPRIZE. This project has been named one of XPRIZE's top twenty world finalists, reflecting the excitement around the potential of this technology.

Bumps in the road ahead are a given. Geologically, peridotite's limited porosity could restrict fluid circulation, and pore spaces may clog with carbonate minerals, though there are examples in nature of rocks that have undergone full carbonation. More pressing is the reliance on hardware. In the energy industry, the transition to clean, affordable, and reliable energy is chiefly contingent on the development and deployment of expensive equipment. Ensuring that 44.01's hardware is economically viable will be crucial for global expansion. Global innovation in energy hardware over the last decade has led to early commercialisation of critical technologies, and their widespread deployment globally. Once the initial investment is made, value optimisation can take place similar to what was seen in the development of solar, and wind energy hardware.

"I think the main challenge is that we are building stuff," says Karan. "We're moving atoms, not bytes, so it's a much harder problem – drilling wells, working with suppliers. The lead times for equipment are months, so your cycle times, your feedback loops, are much longer than you would find in software. We also repurpose talent and resources from the oil and gas industry, which is very strong. There is a challenge in building hardware that is very expensive, and we have to raise a lot more capital to deploy our type of solution. We need to be smart about how we grow. We have to choose which partners we want to work with to ensure that they continue to be long-term partners, because these things will take time to develop and really make an impact at scale. But when they do, the growth trajectory can be exponential, even though the initial period takes more time to develop. It's a patience game."

This ambitious vision highlights the scale of 44.01's commitment. It also sets a precedent for how large-scale carbon capture can be integrated into broader sustainability strategies. As the GCC continues to lead in innovative energy solutions and sustainability practices, other regions of the world are increasingly looking to regional models for guidance on how to address the global energy crisis.

MENA AND ENERGY

As we face the existential and systemic challenges of climate change and resource depletion, the ways we produce, consume, and manage energy will significantly impact our future. So, too, will our efforts to capture and sequester CO_2 – the invisible burden of industrial legacy. Burning coal, oil, and natural gas has fuelled economic growth and technological advancement, but at a huge cost to our environment.

Nowhere is this clearer than in the MENA region.

Between 1980 and 2022, temperatures in the MENA region surged by 0.46°C, significantly surpassing the global average increase of

0.18°C over the same period. Climate change is driving changes in precipitation patterns, leading to severe droughts in Morocco in 2022 and Tunisia in 2023, [162] and significant flooding in the UAE, KSA, Qatar and Oman. Bahrain is one of the most water-stressed countries on Earth.[163] Without scientific progress, Kuwait is predicted to become unlivable by 2050,[164] and rising sea levels threaten to overwhelm low-lying coastal areas of the Arabian Gulf. Beyond the GCC, climate change effects are arguably worse.

Iraq is extremely vulnerable to climate breakdown and faces a perfect storm of soaring temperatures, diminishing rainfall, intensified droughts, frequent dust storms, and flooding.[165] Like many nations in the wider MENA region, it also lacks the financial resources to face these issues alone, unlike the nations of the GCC, whose high income levels and soaring temperatures correlate strongly with energy demand and economic growth. Within these markets, entrepreneurs are emerging as key enablers of solutions to mitigate the rising temperatures on the region's ecosystems and industries. Aquaporo, based in Jordan, has built proprietary hardware to convert air into potable water, while Manhat, in the UAE, has built solutions to sustainably harvest freshwater from open water surfaces.

Bahrain recorded its highest-ever electricity consumption rate in August 2023, and the nation continues to be one of the highest per capita consumers of electricity in the world.[166] It also had the world's second-highest CO_2 emissions per capita in 2021, behind only Qatar.[167] Kuwait, meanwhile, remains entirely dependent on fossil fuels for its energy needs and will see demand triple by 2030.[168] Across the border, Saudi Arabia has the highest per capita greenhouse gas emissions among the G20 nations,[169] with the research consortium Climate Action Tracker noting the country's commitments to net zero greenhouse gas emissions "do not resolve concerns about its role as one of the world's leading fossil fuel exporters".[170]

In response, GCC nations are seeking to contribute and leapfrog into the sustainable energy sector. At the heart of this focus lies solar power. The UAE has the highest solar energy capacity in the GCC, an estimated 4.5 gigawatts, and is home to three of the world's largest solar sites. These include the Mohammed bin Rashid Al Maktoum Solar Park in Dubai and the Noor Abu Dhabi Solar Power Plant in Sweihan. The former has a planned capacity of five gigawatts by 2030, while the latter currently generates 1.2 gigawatts of power. In Saudi Arabia, renewable energy projects with a capacity of 11.4 gigawatts are under development, including the world's largest single-site solar power plant in Al Shuaibah, which is expected to begin operations in 2025 – with a generation capacity of 2.6 gigawatts.

Globally, solar and wind energy adoption is expected to grow significantly in the next three decades, with renewable generation projected to reach 80 to 90 per cent of the global energy mix by 2050.[171] Solar power is abundant, cheap, and the fastest-growing energy source in the world. As such, it will play a key role in combatting climate change, with between 20 and 50 per cent of the world's energy expected to be produced by solar farms by 2050.[172] To illustrate recent growth – in 2023, the world deployed 447 gigawatts of new solar PV (photovoltaic) capacity, an increase of 87 per cent on 2022,[173] although solar's share of global electricity generation stood at just 5.5 per cent in 2023.[174]

Electricity Access
Number of People Without Access to Electricity

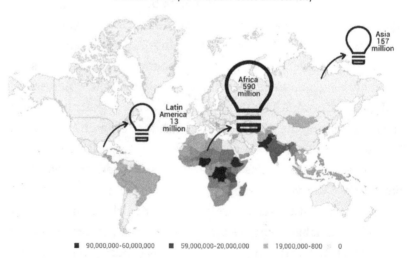

Latin America 13 million

Africa 590 million

Asia 157 million

■ 90,000,000-60,000,000   ■ 59,000,000-20,000,000   ▩ 19,000,000-800   □ 0

Source: Our World in Data (2019)

What is clear is the GCC is utilising its resources to spearhead green technologies. Researchers at the KAUST Photovoltaics Laboratory in Saudi Arabia, for example, are at the forefront of research into perovskites, a relatively new family of semiconductor materials that, when combined with traditional solar cells, consistently break world records for the efficiency of solar panels. The GCC is on a path to becoming a key player in the global renewable energy landscape, driven by ambitious targets, significant investments, and strategic initiatives, as well as by the regional entrepreneurship ecosystem.

Entrepreneurs continue to be a central part of innovation in the regional renewable energy narrative. Yellow Door Energy, a UAE-based energy tech platform that raised $400 million from Actis and the IFC in 2022, has been a key enabler in the increased adoption of solar power across the region, with operations in the UAE, Saudi Arabia, Bahrain and Jordan. The company provides a variety of financing solutions, both to project suppliers and the end client, enabling suppliers to scale and build more renewable energy projects, while also providing flexible payment structures to clients to help increase the adoption of renewable energy. Through its platform, the company has helped generate 787k MWh of clean energy, resulting in the avoidance of 307 metric tonnes of carbon emissions.

Additionally, there have also been new solutions developed to enable the improved management of renewable energy sites and installations. FalconViz, through its platform and fleet of UAVs, provides a range of services to renewable energy provides, including solar panel and wind turbine inspection solutions and pre-installation site analysis and simulations. Regional entrepreneurs are partnering with regional energy incumbents to drive more efficiency, and transparency across the energy value chain.

Oman, meanwhile, is looking to become one of the world's most competitive producers of green hydrogen. The country has identified hydrogen production as a core component of its transition to net zero, and in 2022 established Hydrogen Oman

(Hydrom) to lead and manage its green hydrogen strategy. That strategy hopes to see Oman produce at least a million tonnes of renewable hydrogen a year by 2030, rising to 8.5 million tonnes by 2050. The majority will be produced in the governorates of Al Wusta and Dhofar, where various projects have already been allocated land. For its part, the UAE has the regulation and political commitment to drive substantial change as it seeks to triple its renewable energy capacity to 14.2 gigawatts by 2030. The country accounts for over 60 per cent of the region's total renewables capacity and close to 70 per cent of renewable energy investments.[175]

THE FUTURE OF ENERGY

By harnessing the power of the Tiber river, the Romans were able to generate energy and power, leading to the development of aqueducts that provided water and generated power, which was used to power machinery, enabling the most advanced technology of the time, including the famous Cenatio Rotunda, a perpetually rotating dining room that moved day and night ensuring that Emperor Nero always had the best views of Rome; the ability to build the largest colosseum in the world in only eight years (a building housing 70,000 spectators and forty-eight metres high – or three times as wide as an American football field and almost twice as long); and ultimately the ability have the largest city in the world, Rome, reach 1 million inhabitants. The abundance of water as an energy source was fundamental to the growth and development of the economy and empire.

In more recent history, the harnessing of coal – leading to the method by which we powered the steam engine (invented in 1778) – spurred the Industrial Revolution. This enabled the UK, where coal was abundant and therefore cheaper to harness, to grow its empire and economy between 1750 and 1919, with British coal production increasing from 5.2 million tonnes per year to 62.5 million tonnes per year. Most recently, in the 1940s, the discovery of oil and natural gas started replacing coal as a dominant energy source, and most cheaply available in the US; this has allowed the US economy to outpace global growth and become a world-dominant power over the last eighty years in the same manner as other empires before it.

Across time, it becomes evident that a direct, causal, and reciprocal relationship exists between energy consumption and economic growth. Longitudinal studies reveal that a 0.6 per cent increase in energy consumption correlated with a 1 per cent increase in real GDP per capita. In OECD countries, a 0.9 per cent increase in electricity usage between 1981 and 2007 corresponded to a 1.7 per cent GDP growth.[176] This effect is even more pronounced in emerging markets, where a 2 per cent annual increase in electricity consumption in non-OECD countries resulted in an impressive 3.7 per cent GDP growth.

The development of solar panels has been properly following Moore's Law: doubling in efficiency and halving in costs each year for the last five years. As the ability to capture the sun's power becomes scalable and affordable, will the availability of this resource, the sun, become an indicator of economic growth? Will the countries with the most 'sun' see a competitive advantage in their ability to build their economies, just as those that could have the cheapest access to oil or coal did before them?

The potential of crypto and AI cannot be discussed without paying attention to the role of energy, as each of these technologies is highly energy-consumptive, there needs to be an accelerated solution to energy as a whole if we expect these technologies to be embraced and adopted.

In January 2024, International Energy Agency (IEA) released its predictions for energy consumption till 2026, which for the first time considered the consumption requirements for AI, crypto and data centres.[177] The IEA's estimates project that the consumption of energy for these use cases will be equivalent to that of the entire country of Japan.

The question of how the crypto and AI revolution will be powered is becoming more relevant in the global energy and environmental landscape. The ability to meet the energy demand for the data centres required to run, develop and train AI models will become a global differentiator in the race to deploy advanced AI tools. Global players such as the US, China and Russia are all proactively working on upgrading antiquated grids and energy sources to participate in the global AI race.

Could the ability to harness the sun as a cheap power source enable the region to harness the power of AI in an even better way, propelling it even faster into the future? The MENA region's focus on the transition story and its ability to leapfrog to modernised grids, powered by efficient and clean energy, position the region well to lead a sustainable AI future.

CHAPTER 14

OUR FUTURE

رحلة الألف ميل تبدأ بخطوة

The journey of a thousand miles

begins with a single step.

– ARABIC PROVERB

146. 147. 148. Stepping out onto the Top Sky of Burj Khalifa, I could see the city in its entirety, along with seemingly endless desert surrounding it. I thought back to my early days in Dubai in 1995, when almost everything now visible to me was not yet built and how, as I had grown up, so had this city, this country, and this region. Could the part of the world I visited as a child with power rationing now be leading the future of power generation and creating enough power to light up other countries?

I could only imagine the coming-of-age stories of the generation now leading the incredible companies, industries and ministries. Where had all these people come from? The 'return' of a third-culture generation, and the embrace of all third-culture people had created one of the most cosmopolitan, open-minded and forward-thinking parts of the world. In recent years, the influx of global talent has also translated into many second- and third-time global founders coming to the region, calling it home and building their new companies and the world's best technology from a place in the midst of the global south.

The region's youth, its greatest asset, lies at the heart of this transformation – and as this youth bulge 'rose', with the average age increasing from the twenties to the thirties, so did the population's aspirations, productivity, and desire and ability to build. Just a decade ago, when the Originals began their journey, MENA was a blank canvas for innovation and entrepreneurship. With limited visibility of opportunity and leadership at home, and a struggle to find regional talent, the Originals were 'lonely'; whereas today, creative isolation feels like a distant memory. The influx of talent into the region, with second and third-time founders choosing the region as their base to build from, is testament to the changing face of MENA and is reflective of my own journey – from a time just thirty years ago when the term 'third culture' was barely defined to a future where the region is home to the next generation of innovators. Today, under the leadership of governments with clearly defined agendas for economic growth, the region's young leadership is looking to define and build the future alongside the population.

The region's first decacorn, Talabat, brings together the ultimate narrative of MENA. Originally formed in Egypt in 2004, acquired by a Kuwaiti investor-entrepreneur a few years later, and ultimately scaled through investment by Delivery Hero, Talabat, now based in Dubai, is not only run by an Italian, but employs ninety different nationalities, attracting talent from Silicon Valley, Asia and Europe, as well as the local tech talent, which, Tomaso says, gets stronger by the day.

With its recent public listing on the Dubai Financial Market, Talabat's market capitalisation was multifold larger than its original parent company, Delivery Hero, illustrating the potential of the region to create substantial, profitable, high-growth companies that serve the local demographic. "Today, Talabat is the leading on-demand online food ordering, delivery, takeaway, grocery and retail platform in the MENA region, with operations in the UAE, Kuwait, Qatar, Bahrain, Egypt, Oman, Jordan, and Iraq," shares

Tomaso. "We are the leading MENA partner of choice for over 65,000 active restaurant and grocery partners, with 119,000 active riders meeting the food, grocery, and retail needs of over 6 million active customers across our eight regional markets."

Talabat's IPO was a stepping stone for the region. As MENA's largest technology company, the oversubscribed listing underscored a true coming of age of the regional opportunity for expansive and long-term value creation across its markets. Tomaso continues, "In fact, my favourite part of this IPO journey has been to share the Talabat story with global and regional investors." The opportunity to convey the potential of the region when considered as a single market excites him.

Despite the potential to scale now proven beyond doubt, the region still has a long way to go in terms of venture funding. In 2023, it reached a total of $2.7 billion, compared to the global figure of $285 billion. However, this is still a significant increase from the $38 million in 2010 when the Originals first started their journeys. With capital starting to flow into MENA at an unprecedented rate, and the UAE and Saudi Arabia becoming hubs for venture capital, attracting global investors and nurturing home-grown start-ups that are poised to make their mark on the world, the region is well-positioned to continue its strong growth trajectory.

As governments continue to foster an environment conducive to innovation, there is a new breed of entrepreneurs emerging, ones that are armed not only with ideas but with the financial backing needed to bring them to life. Alongside these changes in entrepreneurship, the shift in the region's sovereign wealth funds from their historical world-leading position as Limited Partners and late-stage investors to also beginning to participate in the regional ecosystem has seeded the possibility of regional funding for founders. Additionally, founders in the region are attracting growing interest from international investors, drawn to the focus on profitability and capital efficiency that is ingrained in the companies being built across MENA. These investors accounted for half of regional venture funding in 2023. As the influx of capital increases and the ecosystem continues to grow, the shift in focus from the

West to the Global South as a global leader in innovation continues to become ever more apparent.

Today, MENA cities are no longer just regional hubs – they are global innovation centres. From cutting-edge fintech solutions to new blockchain regulations, the region is laying the groundwork for an ecosystem where technology can thrive. As I reflect on my early childhood when power cuts were a regular occurrence and the rationing of power was a very evident reality, it is almost inconceivable to think that today, the region is home to one of the world's largest single-site solar power plants, Noor Abu Dhabi, and is taking leaps and bounds towards building the future of energy. Not only has the region identified the fundamental drivers of true technology across future-looking sectors of Artificial Intelligence, Crypto and Energy, but advancements in these sectors from a regulatory perspective to increasing investment initiatives are setting the region apart on a global scale.

A decade ago, early founders struggled with the fragmented market in the region, grappling with challenges of cross-border scale and nuances of markets across the region. The region has moved from a time when entrepreneurship was considered too risky and failure was culturally unacceptable, to Dubai taking the top spot as the world's fastest-growing VC ecosystem from 2018 to 2023.[178] Today, regional entrepreneurs remain committed to solving the most pressing challenges from financial inclusion to food security to access to healthcare, and are fortunate to operate in an environment in which regulatory authorities are enabling growth and proactively nurturing the innovation economy. As we look to the future, it is clear that certain industries and technologies will evolve dramatically compared with the previous half-decade. MENA's growing market is no longer just a consumer base – it is a launchpad for ideas that will change the world.

* * * * *

As we look ahead, it is impossible not to feel the contagious energy exuding across the MENA region. For years, the world has watched as our dynamic, evolving region has transformed from an emerging market to a global powerhouse of innovation and entrepreneurship. As we have moved from copycat to emulation to innovation, we find the MENA region at the forefront of new technologies, be it the introduction of the world's first Ministry of AI, the adoption and regulation of crypto and blockchain, or the embrace of new energy sources and building the world's largest solar farms.

With a rapidly growing middle class, a young, eager population ready to participate in the digital revolution, and one of the highest mobile penetration rates in the world, the MENA region truly has the perfect combination with which to catalyse growth and truly leapfrog in sectors that will shape future economies.

The Originals who have paved the way for today's entrepreneurs have set the stage, and the next generation is ready to build on their legacy. The entrepreneurs shaping this future will hail from diverse corners of the globe, driving us towards a more advanced and connected world. In this context, the region will emerge as a key player, *inshallah*, harnessing its vibrant youth, cutting-edge technology, and progressive regulators to establish itself as a leading hub of entrepreneurship and innovation.

Our ability to maintain our traditions and culture, embracing the fluidity of time and strength of community and relationships while leaning into the future, inventing technologies and building companies, is allowing us to redefine the future and the way by which it is created.

Combined with the influx of talent and the advancement of technology, as the region's geographic position where 'East Meets West' repositions MENA as a global talent and innovation hub, it is poised to lead the next phase of global growth – the place where East meets West: the Middle East.

As I stood at the top of the world looking out at the endless desert, I could only be hopeful – the endless desert representing the endless opportunities for this generation. As we come of age, our future is ours to imagine, create and build.

ACKNOWLEDGEMENTS

THIS BOOK WOULD not have been possible without the contributions, hard work and patience of so many incredible people around me. First and foremost, my deepest gratitude goes to every founder who generously shared their time, experiences and insights for this project. Each interview was a testament to your resilience, vision and the remarkable journeys you've undertaken. I want to especially thank in order of appearance, Samih Toukan, Ronaldo Mouchawar, Mudassir Sheikha, Magnus Olsson, Rabea Ataya, Mona Ataya, Michael Lahyani, Hosam Arab, Islam Shawky, Omair Ansari, Naif Abu Saida, Nadine Hachach-Haram, Jalil Allabadi, Nadin Karadag, Sundeep Sahni, Karim Khashaba, Hamdi Tabbaa, Fatima Rizwan, Fadl Al Tarzi, Edward Hamod, Fahim Al Qasimi, Ryan Lefers, Fahmi Al Shawwa, Charif Mzayek, Azam Pasha, Constantin Robertz, May Habib, Dina Alsamhan, Nour Taher, Omar Mansour, Ola Doudin, Henri Arslanian, Talal Hasan, Karan Khimji, Ehab Tasfai and Tomaso

Rodriguez. Thank you for your time, candour and for trusting me to share your stories with the world.

The founders featured in this book represent only a slice of our incredible ecosystem. To all the other founders whose stories are equally inspiring and impactful – your tireless progress and innovative solutions continue to propel our region forward.

I am also deeply grateful to the ecosystem players and investors who enriched this narrative by sharing their thoughts and experiences. A special thank you to Reid Hoffman, Bill Ford, Christopher Schroeder, Oliver Rippel, Alexander Lazarow, Fadi Ghandour, Tony Fadell, Deepak Chopra, Hala Gorani, Maha Ibrahim, Anne Glover, Brent Hoberman, Hermann Hauser, Randy Komisar, Ian Fairservice, Mona Kattan, Steve Drobny, Tim Draper, Steve Ciesinski, Luisa Alemany, Henadi Al Saleh, Sophie Schmidt, David Fialkow, Dr. Samer Haj-Yehia, GV Ravishankar, Amal Dokhan, Abdallah Yafi, Ghaith Yafi and Mamoon Hamid for your contributions, wisdom and guidance.

This book would not have been realised without the dedication and support of my exceptional team. My heartfelt thanks to Diya Kumar, Lana Azhari, Maria Najjar, Victoria Geoghegan, Nick Lambert, Omar Al Khawaja and the entire Global Ventures family. Your belief in this project and your unwavering commitment, made all the difference.

To every founder and co-investor in our ecosystem: I continue to learn and grow from each of our interactions. Thank you for allowing me to be a part of your journeys and for inspiring me daily.

On a personal note, this book would not even have been conceivable had I not been fortunate to deeply understand and live what it means to be Middle Eastern and Arab at my roots. My infinite gratitude goes to my father and mother, who instilled in me a profound love for our culture, language and heritage. The Arabic expressions, traditions and values you taught me are woven into every page of this book.

To my fellow VCs in the region: thank you for your partnership and for being instrumental in building our ecosystem together.

To each of my partners and investors: your faith and support have been the backbone of this journey. I am endlessly grateful to you.

To the leadership of the 'Rising Falcons': your vision and support have created fertile ground for innovation and entrepreneurship to thrive and I am proud to be a part of this incredible story.

Lastly, to the countless others who have supported me along the way – there are not enough pages to name you all, but you know who you are. Your encouragement and belief in me have meant everything.

REFERENCES

1 World Bank
2 World Bank
3 Office of the United States Trade Representative
4 UNICEF
5 Ethnologue
6 Ethnologue
7 World Population Review
8 Pew Research Center
9 Winkel, Carmen; Strachan, Laura; Aamir, Siddiqua: 'From east to west and back again: the effects of reverse culture shock on female Saudi Arabian university students studying abroad' in Journal for Multicultural Education
10 British Council: 'MENA and Gulf countries: UK study updates'
11 Ibid
12 Population Council: 'Survey of Young People in Egypt'
13 UNICEF
14 OECD
15 Mo Ibrahim Foundation
16 Pew Research Center
17 Pan American Health Organisation
18 GSMA
19 World Bank
20 Ibid
21 Ipsos
22 OECD
23 MAGNiTT classification
24 The National
25 According to Abu Dhabi Police, the number of vehicles in the Emirate of Abu Dhabi in 2016 amounted to 1,016,740
26 According to the General Authority for Statistics, a total of 1,833,164 pilgrims performed the Hajj in 2024
27 Time Magazine
28 Ibid
29 UAE Cabinet
30 TechCrunch
31 Albawaba
32 Helios Investment Partners
33 Startup Scene
34 General Authority for Statistics
35 World Bank
36 McKee, Musa; Keulertz, Martin; Habibi, Negar; Mulligan, Mark; Woertz, Eckart: 'Demographic and Economic Material Factors in the MENA region'
37 Statista
38 Eurostat
39 MIT REAP
40 World Bank
41 Arabian Business
42 MAGNiTT
43 Etihad
44 Sovereign Wealth Fund Institute
45 Network.ae
46 World Bank
47 IFC
48 Mordor Intelligence
49 WHO
50 United Nations Population Division
51 World Economic Forum
52 Food and Agricultural Organisation
53 Mordor Intelligence
54 Invest Emirates
55 Mordor Intelligence
56 Global Findex Database
57 Global Findex Database
58 PwC
59 FX Empire
60 The Global Economy
61 Saudi Central Bank
62 PwC
63 Merchant Machine
64 World Bank
65 World Economic Forum
66 World Economic Forum
67 Mastercard
68 OECD
69 Global Findex Database
70 We are Social/Meltwater
71 World Bank
72 Ibid
73 Ibid
74 World Bank
75 Ibid
76 World Bank
77 UNICEF
78 Kharazmi, E; Bordbar, S; Bordbar, N; Tavakolian A: 'Are Doctors Equally Distributed Throughout the World?' Iranian Journal of Public Health
79 Ibid
80 Wamda Research Lab and GE
81 Ibid
82 Middle East Economic Digest
83 World Bank
84 Ibid
85 Ibid
86 GSMA
87 GSMA

88 World Bank
89 National Library of Medicine
90 World Bank
91 PwC
92 McKinsey
93 El Jardali F, Jabbour M, Bou-Karroum L, Bou-Karroum K, Aoun A, et al: 'Digital health in fragile states in the Middle East and North Africa (MENA) region: A scoping review of the literature'; PLOS ONE
94 World Bank
95 Ibid
96 United Nations Population Fund
97 OECD
98 Ibid
99 Department of Statistics
100 World Bank
101 UNHCR
102 Department of Statistics
103 World Bank
104 Ibid
105 Egyptian Ministry of Education
106 Ibid
107 Oxford Business Group
108 European Commission
109 World Bank
110 UNICEF
111 OECD
112 Statista
113 UNESCO
114 UNICEF
115 UNESCO
116 UNICEF
117 UNESCO
118 UNICEF
119 UNICEF
120 Education Data Initiative
121 Arab Youth Survey
122 World Food Programme
123 Insecurity Insight
124 Food and Agriculture Organisation
125 Strategy&
126 Abu Dhabi Global Environmental Data Initiative
127 Ibid
128 According to the United Nations Food Waste Programme, Saudi Arabia accounts for 50 per cent of global food waste. In the UAE, 38 per cent of the food prepared every day is wasted at a cost of $1.6 billion. Food waste is a major global concern. In the US, over a third of the food produced is not eaten. Wasted food is the single most common material landfilled and incinerated in the US, comprising 24 per cent and 22 per cent of landfilled and combusted municipal solid waste.
129 World Economic Forum
130 Food and Agricultural Organisation
131 Ibid
132 Coral Reef Alliance
133 World Wildlife Fund
134 World Economic Forum
135 Nature
136 World Wildlife Fund
137 Food and Agriculture Organisation
138 World Health Organisation
139 Food and Agriculture Organisation
140 World Resources Institute
141 United Nations
142 International Fund for Agricultural Development
143 World Bank
144 UAE Ministry of Industry & Advanced Technology
145 WorldAtlas
146 W3techs
147 PwC
148 PwC
149 MarketsandMarkets
150 Accenture
151 BofA Artificial Intelligence
152 Chainalysis
153 Thomson Reuters
154 Chainalysis
155 Chainalysis
156 Bitget
157 University of Oxford
158 Ibid
159 Ibid
160 Kelemen, P; Benson, S; Pilorge, H; Psarras, P; Wilcox, J: 'An Overview of the Status and Challenges of CO2 Storage in Minerals and Geological Formations'. Frontiers in Climate
161 Ibid
162 IEA
163 World Resources Institute
164 Bloomberg
165 United Nations
166 Electricity and Water Authority
167 World Bank
168 Ministry of Electricity & Water & Renewable Energy
169 Climate Change Performance Index
170 Climate Action Tracker
171 International Energy Agency
172 International Energy Agency
173 Solar Power Europe
174 International Energy Agency
175 International Renewable Energy Agency
176 Energy Economics
177 Vox
178 FDI Intelligence, MAGNiTT, Dealroom, Crunchbase News

www.ingramcontent.com/pod-product-compliance
Lightning Source LLC
La Vergne TN
LVHW042307210425
809248LV00017B/46/J